Archaeological Excavations
at
Glebe South and Darcystown,
Balrothery, Co. Dublin

Archaeological Excavations
at
Glebe South and Darcystown, Balrothery, Co. Dublin

Judith Carroll, Frank Ryan and Kenneth Wiggins

Typesetting, layout and design, including cover design:
Environmental Publications

ISBN No: 978-0-9559584-1-0

Ordnance Survey Ireland Licence No. EN 0062608
© Ordnance Survey Ireland / Governmment of Ireland

This publication has received funding from the Heritage Council under the
Unpublished Excavations Scheme 2007.

TABLE OF CONTENTS

LIST OF FIGURES

Chapter 4

Chapter 5

LIST OF PLATES

Chapter 4

ACKNOWLEDGEMENTS

The authors would like to express our sincere thanks to Mulllen Developments Ltd and Fingal County Council for funding the excavations and giving us the opportunity to carry out the excavations at Glebe South and Darcystown in advance of developments there, and to the Heritage Council for funding towards the costs of this publication.

We would also like to thank the archaeological staff at every level who participated in the Glebe South and Darcystown excavations from initial testing and monitoring to final report preparation. The individuals are too many to name here but the project managers and supervisors were Alistair Clarke, Geraldine Dunne, Eoghan Kieran, Stuart Halliday, Jane Hamill, David Swift and Yvonne Whitty. The specialists who carried out work on human, animal, wood, charcoal and plant remains were Catherine Bonner, Jennie Coughlan, Patricia Lynch, Meriel McClatchie and Ellen O'Carroll, while the prehistoric pottery was analysed by Eoin Grogan and Helen Roche. Rose Cleary, University College Cork, also very kindly commented on some prehistoric pottery from the site. We are very grateful to Dr. Elizabeth O'Brien who visited the site at Glebe South, giving us invaluable information from her wealth of knowledge on burials of the prehistoric and medieval periods.

For the preparation of the publication, we would like to acknowledge with thanks the work of Claire Phelan, who prepared the drawings and other images for the publication as well as assisting with the editing and index, and also Emily Prunty for her assistance in the preparation of the text. Thanks also to Katrina Bouchier of Environmental Publications for bringing this work to its final publication and to Ian Doyle of the Heritage Council.

CHAPTER 1

Introduction and archaeological/historical background

INTRODUCTION

The townlands of Glebe South and Darcystown are located to the east and south-east of the village of Balrothery. A series of archaeological sites were found here during monitoring for housing developments between 2002 and 2005.

The town of Balrothery is listed in the Record of Monuments and Places as DU005-057. The excavations described in this volume are just outside and to the south of the constraint zone of DU005-57, which include the townlands of Balrothery and Rosepark. To the north of the excavations described here are the enclosure site, DU005-05708, and a 'Holy Well', DU005-05707, both in Rosepark. There is a standing stone, DU005-05702, directly to the north of the enclosure (in Balrothery townland) on a low hill.

In 2002, Judith Carroll and Company carried out test trenching at Glebe South and Darcystown townlands proposed for development by Mullen Developments Ltd (licence no. 02E0043). In 2003, testing by this company was carried out for Fingal County Council on a site in Darcystown adjacent to Mullen Developments site. This was excavated under licence no. 03E0067. In 2004, full excavation took place on Mullen Developments site under licence no. 02E0043 and two new licences, 04E0680 and 04E0741. Full excavation took place between 2004-5 on Fingal County Council's site (licence no. 03E0067).

The subject of this publication is three burial site excavations that resulted from this work. Each chapter deals with a separate excavation by each of the three authors examining the main burial findings from each of the excavations. Other features such as corn drying kilns, structures and burnt mounds are also included within each report. The excavations reveal Balrothery to be a major centre from prehistory to the medieval period with occupation extending from the Middle Neolithic. Burials dating from the Bronze Age to the Late Iron Age/early medieval period show that there was continuity of burial which was likely to be contemporary with the main period of habitation at Rosepark during the Late Iron Age.

The sites described in this volume are treated in rough chronological order of their main findings, though each report includes later/earlier features found during the investigation under the particular licence number.

The first excavation is described is Darcystown 1 by Kenneth Wiggins (licence no. 03E0067). During testing in 2003 and resolution in 2004-5, in advance of the housing development by Fingal County Council, a number of urns containing cremation burials of Mid to Late Bronze Age date were found. These did not appear to relate to any structure or enclosing feature. A pit containing Neolithic pottery and two burnt mounds of Late Bronze Age date were also found in Darcystown 1.

The site at Darcystown 2, excavated under licence 04E0741 by Judith Carroll, describes a ring ditch containing two phases of Late Bronze Age burial and four cut features, including a cereal drying kiln dated to the early centuries AD.

The site at Glebe South, excavated by Frank Ryan under licence no. 04E0680, revealed two Iron Age ring ditch burial sites with long stone cist inhumation burials cut into, and clearly related to, these. The excavation also showed that a Bronze Age cremation burial site had predated the Iron Age/early medieval burials. It also revealed a Middle Bronze Age hut site as well as cereal drying kilns and a ditch of medieval date.

THE PREHISTORIC AND EARLY MEDIEVAL ENVIRONMENT

The town of Balrothery is situated in the gently rolling, but hilly, area of north Fingal and is part of the rich, arable farming lands of north Dublin and east Meath. Austin Cooper visited the town in June 1783 and described it as 'a small village about 14 miles from Dublin on the Great North road which circumstances is the only thing that preserves it. It has always been reckoned famous for one extraordinary perfection-making Cakes' (Cooper 1942). This observation may well be rooted in the particular suitability for cereal production of the

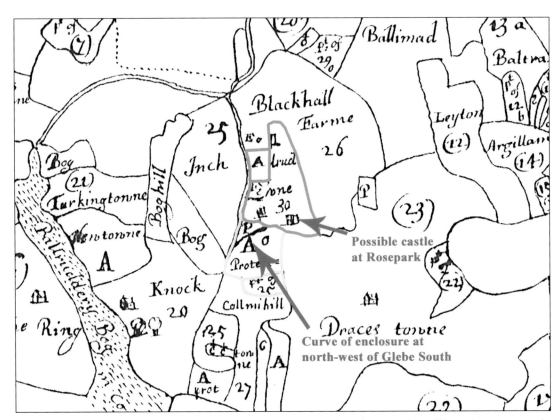

Figure 1: Petty's map (circa 1655) showing Balrothery and Rosepark with curve of possible enclosure on north-west side of Glebe South, present on Petty's map but not present on the later first edition Ordnance Survey map (below). Petty's map also shows the development of the townlands and can be compared with Figure 2.

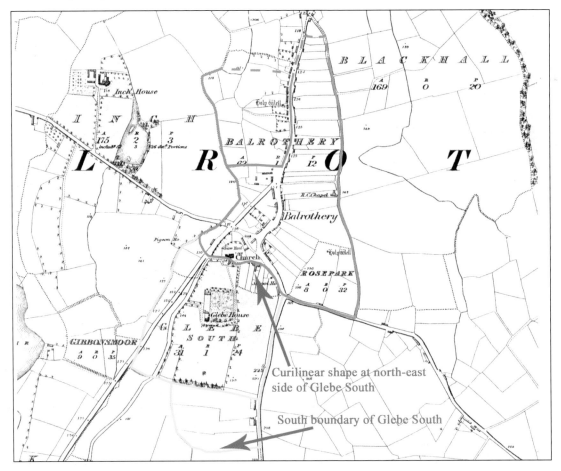

Figure 2: First edition Ordnance Survey map of 1837 - 1841 showing the townland divisions compared to Figure 1

area throughout the ages, as it seems that the townland attracted constant settlement of land. The town is only two miles from the coast, where fishing and trading was undoubtedly an amenity. The steep hilltops of Balrothery were natural defensive sites, affording views of the surrounding countryside.

Some of the most important sites in the area include Passage tombs. The Passage tomb site of Hampton Demesne (RMP DU005-056) is situated only 2.3 km east of Balrothery on the coast. On the promontory of Bremore, about 5km north-east of Balrothery, is the Passage tomb cemetery of Bremore (RMP DU002-001-001-5). Less than 2km north of Bremore is the Passage tomb cemetery of Gormanstown (ME028-020-21). The coastal siting of the Bremore, Gormanstown and Hampton Demesne Passage tombs suggests that they may be early in the sequence of such tombs and have the potential to inform us about the beginning of the Neolithic around 4000 to 3800 BC (Condit and Cooney 2007).

Significant evidence of prehistoric activity in the area, in particular throughout the Bronze Age, has been brought to light by the Bord Gáis Éireann Pipeline to the West (Grogan, O'Donnell and Johnson 2007, 133-5). The publication gives details of excavations of Bronze Age habitation sites, a possible ritual site and burnt mounds in the vicinity of Balrothery. Just to the south of Balrothery, at Knock, two burnt mounds, roughly 1km west of the sites of Darcystown 1, were excavated during the Bord Gáis excavations (ibid., 225-6).

Potential Bronze Age or Iron Age burial sites listed in the RMP include DU005-015, a ring ditch at Hampton Demesne, just over 1km north-east of Balrothery; DU005-005, a ring ditch at Stephenstown, just over 1km north-west; DU005-014, a ring ditch at Gibbonsmoor, around 650m south-west of the sites discussed here.

Directly north of the three sites of this report was the hilltop enclosure site of Rosepark (DU005-057-08) where a burial site of Iron Age to early medieval date is proposed to have been located at the highest point (Carroll 2008). The Rosepark enclosure itself is suggested to have dated from circa the 3rd century AD and continued in use till the early Anglo-Norman period. There was a standing stone, DU005-05702, directly to the north of the enclosure on a low hill in the townland of Balrothery.

The first edition six inch Ordnance Survey map of the area, dated between 1837 and 1841, shows a distinct curve of the townland boundary line around the north end of Glebe South, south of St. Peter's Church (Fig. 2). This line is further accentuated on William Petty's map of circa 1655 (Fig. 1). Both maps suggest a curvilinear enclosure south of the St. Peter's Church. St. Peter's Church dates to at least the 13th/14th century but, from the various archaeological testing and monitoring operations at the site, there is no evidence that it predates the Anglo-Norman period. It is suggested that an enclosure, which may have been the site of the earliest church in Balrothery, was located in Glebe South in the early medieval period.

HISTORICAL BACKGROUND

The modern village of Balrothery is situated in north county Dublin on the western edge of the barony of Balrothery East. Before the division of Balrothery into East and West in the nineteenth century, the barony of Balrothery comprised an area extending to Naul on the west, Garristown and Balscaddan to the north and the Irish Sea to the east. It roughly comprised the modern county of Fingal and the area referred to in the Annals as 'Saithne' in the pre-Norman period.

Between the 7th and the 10th century AD, this area formed the eastern part of the Bréga territory of the Síl nÁedo Sláine branch of the southern Uí Néill, which took in most of Meath, Louth and parts of north Dublin (Byrne 1968, 397). The Ui Neill kings of Bréga, whose royal seats were the sites of Lagore, seat of the kings of southern Bréga (from the 7th century), and Knowth, centre of the kings of northern Bréga (from at least the 9th) exerted control over the lands of Bréga and contended for its kingship. Though the Uí Néill were all-powerful between the 7th and the 10th centuries, the area was occupied and controlled on a local level by indigenous tribal groups who were likely to have paid tribute to the Uí Néill during their period of hegamony.

The tribal groups associated with the Fingal area around the 7th century probably included the Árd Ciannachta whom Michael Byrnes has recently placed between Dublin and the River Delvin up to end of the 7th century, from the records of Adonmnán, disciple of St. Columba (Byrnes 2000, 131-36), and the Gailenga.

The Gailenga were an important group in the area throughout the early and high medieval period and are referred to several times in historical records.

From at least the beginning of the 11th century, the Uí Cathasaig were dominant in this region. and contended with other major groups, including the Uí Neill, for the kingship of Bréga.

By the 12th century, the Uí Cathasaig could be referred to as rulers of the lands of Saithne, the area

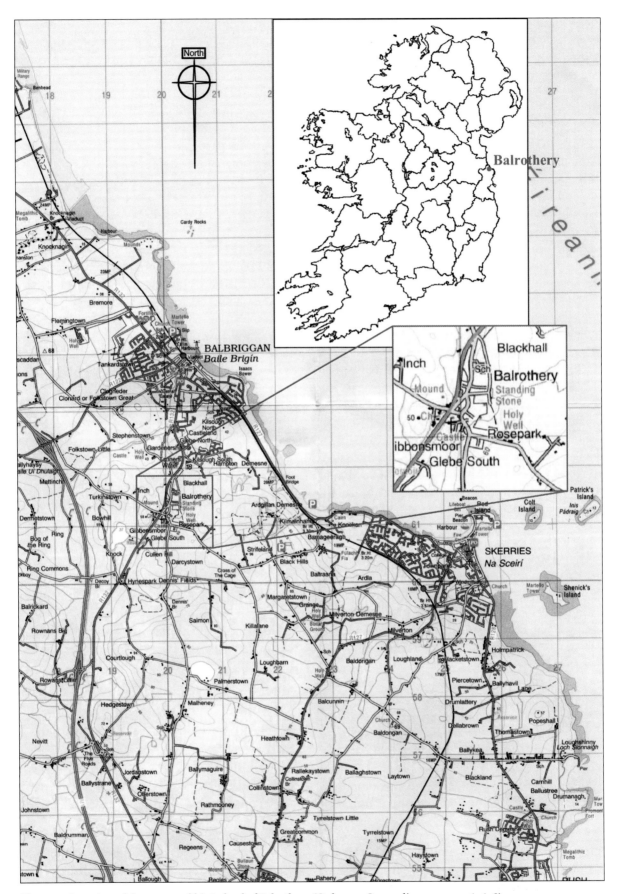

Figure 3: Location of the town and hinterland of Balrothery (Ordnance Survey licence no. 0062608)

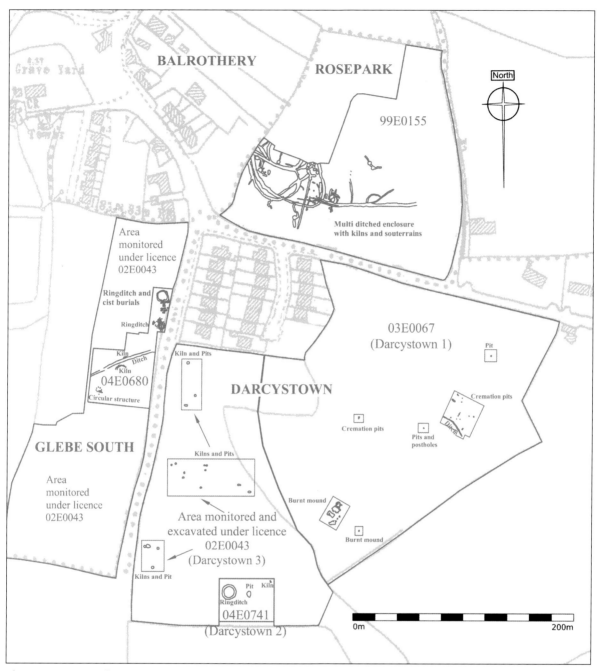

Figure 4: Location of areas excavated under licence by Judith Carroll and Company Ltd. during 2000-5

of their rule equating to the pre-19th century barony of Balrothery. Indeed, in late 12th century Anglo-Norman charters, it is called the 'land that was once Ukadesi' or 'the lands of Occadesi' as noted by Flanagan in her discussion of medieval landholdings in Balrothery (Flanagan 1994, 75).

The name Balrothery is proposed in the Ordnance Survey Name Book, Co. Dublin, by John O Donovan (O'Donovan 1840, 60) to have derived from the Irish word *ritire*, meaning 'knight' and relating to the Anglo-Norman knights and their meetings in Balrothery. It has, however, been convincingly argued by Marie Therese Flanagan (1994, 71-94) that

this name is more likely to evolve from that of 'Richerid' or 'Rytherid', a landowner of the immediate pre-Norman period in the area.

In her paper entitled *Historia Gruffud vab Kenan and the origins of Balrothery, Co. Dublin*, O'Flanagan proposes that the name may refer to Richerid/ Rytherid/Ryheri Machanan/ Makanam, a descendant of the Gywnedd royal dynasty. This connection was documented in a minor land dispute, as set out by Flanagan.

Some time after the Anglo-Norman invasion, Geoffrey de Costedin, a major owner of land in Balrothery, granted the church of Balrothery '...with

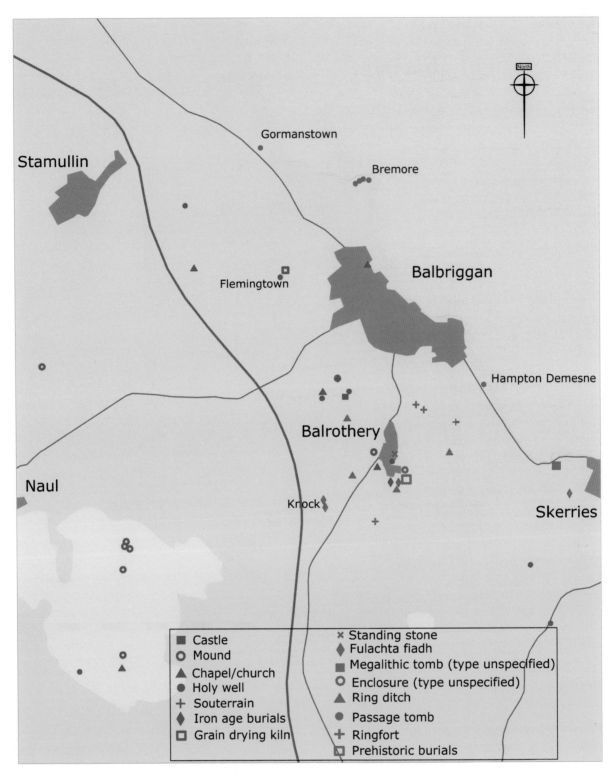

Figure 5: Map showing location of archaeological sites in the area surrounding Balrothery

the assent of Patrick de Rosel, parson of the church of Balrothery' (McNeill 1950, 33), to the Priory of the Blessed Virgin Mary at Tristernagh, Kilbixi, Co. Westmeath. Charters of settlement were issued by Geoffrey, prior of Llanthony (on behalf of Tristernagh), and Archbishop John Cumin of Dublin.

In these charters, areas around Balrothery are listed along with the tithes and offerings of the land of Richerid Machanan, which are referred to in a complementary charter as 'the tithes and offerings of Rytherid'. This Rytherid is identified by Flanagan (1994, 86) as being very likely to be of the family of Gruffyd ap Cynan, king of Gywnedd (c. 1075-1137). A link between the descendants of Gruffyd ap Cynan and landholdings in north county Dublin can be shown to have existed in the early second millennium AD as a result of intermarriage between the father of Gruffyd ap Cynan and the daughter of Olaf, king of Dublin. The lands held by the ap Cynan family as a result are proposed to be lands in the Barony of Balrothery, including the lands of the modern village of Balrothery.

The lands, or some lands, in the modern village of Balrothery appear to have been granted in the early years following the Anglo-Norman invasion to a Robert de Rosel (members of whose family also signed themselves de Russel or Rosel) by Richard de Clare, Earl of Pembroke, or 'Strongbow' (Wiffen 1833, 90). The family of de Russel seems to have retained interest in land in Balrothery into the early 13th century (Carroll 2008, where the later history is treated in more detail), though the family of Geoffrey de Costedin was the major landowner there during the 13th century and well into the 14th (Clarke 1941, x-xi). The lands of Balrothery donated by the Anglo-Norman de Costedin remained in the hands of Tristernagh until the dissolution of the monasteries in the early 16th century. They were granted in 1562 to the Piers family of Tristernagh.

PREVIOUS EXCAVATIONS IN BALROTHERY

The record of archaeological excavations in Balrothery dates back to 1994, including trial testing assessments and full scale excavation in advance of development.

Several investigations have taken place in recent years around the area of the site. Trial trenching was carried out by Hilary Opie in 1994 (Opie 1995) in land adjacent to the church and tower house. No archaeological features or finds were revealed. In 1996, Claire Walsh carried out trial trenching,

directly to the west of Rosepark, at 20-21, Main St., Balrothery (Walsh 1998). Again, no features of archaeological interest were discovered.

To the west of Rosepark, at St. Peter's Church, assessment, monitoring and limited excavation took place by Donald Murphy in 1999. Burials of 13th-14th century date were revealed (Murphy 2000).

Trial trenching took place on land adjacent to St. Peter's Church and graveyard, in 2000, in Glebe South, by Christine Baker. This revealed curving ditches dated by pottery finds to the 13th-14th centuries (Baker 2001). A curved field ditch was found by Paul Stevens during monitoring under licence 04E0671 at St. Peter's Church. No finds were recovered from the ditch. A bullaun stone was found in the topsoil (Stevens 2005).

Christine Baker carried out the test trenching and the initial soil stripping of the site under licence 99E0155 at Rosepark in 1999 (Baker 2005, 319-331). The site was fully excavated under the same licence by Judith Carroll between 2000 and 2001.

The Rosepark site (99E0E155) is probably the most relevant to the series of excavations which form the subject of this publication. The site is directly north of the excavations at Glebe South and Darcystown (see *Archaeological Excavations at Rosepark, Balrothery, Co. Dublin*, Carroll 2008).

At Rosepark, a hilltop enclosure was revealed by aerial photography. It comprised a large number of ditches, burnt features, cereal-drying kilns, souterrains and structures. The finds, along with radiocarbon dates, suggest that the site was occupied from about the 3rd/4th century AD to circa the 8th/9th century AD. The hilltop enclosure was defended by ditched fortifications from perhaps the late 3rd century to the 7th/8thcentury. An open settlement may have evolved from the ditched defences in the 8th or 9th century and it is likely that the large number of souterrains found on the site may relate to the latest phase of settlement.

In 2001, Teresa Bolger carried out trial trenching in the field to the north of Rosepark, in Balrothery townland, under licence no. 01E0646. Archaeological layers and features, including material consistent with cereal drying as well as a cobbled surface were found. These features were dated to the medieval and early modern periods by pottery association (Bolger 2001).

The construction of a single dwelling in the village was monitored in 2002, but no archaeological material was discovered (O'Carroll 2004). Trial testing of a site at the Green, Balrothery, was carried out by Judith Carroll in 2005, under licence 05E1040, but no finds or features came to light during the testing (Carroll 2005).

References

Baker, C. 2001. Glebe South Balrothery. In I. Bennett (ed.), *Excavations: summary acccounts of archaeological excavations in Ireland 2000.* Wordwell, Bray, Wicklow.

Baker, C. 2005. Balrothery Co. Dublin. In T. Condit and C. Corlett (eds.), *Above and Beyond — essays in memory of Leo Swan,* 319-331. Wordwell, Bray, Wicklow.

Bolger, T. 2001. Archaeological testing at Old Coach Road, Balrothery, Co. Dublin. Excavation licence no. 01E0646. Unpublished. National Monuments Service, Dept. of the Environment, Heritage and Local Government.

Byrne, F.J. 1968. Historical note on Cnoba (Knowth). In G. Eogan 'Excavations at Knowth, Co. Meath 1962-5'. *Proceedings of the Royal Irish Academy* 66C, 383-400.

Byrnes, M. 2000. The Ard Ciannachta in Adomnans Vitae Columbae: a reflection of Iona's attitude to the Síl nÁedo Sláine in the late 7th century. In A. P. Smith, (ed.), *Seanchas-studies in early and medieval Irish archaeology, history and literature in honour of Francis J. Byrne,* 127-136. Dublin.

Carroll, J. 2005. Archaeological trial trenching and architectural survey at the Green, Balrothery, Co. Dublin. Licence no. 05E1040. Unpublished report by Judith Carroll and Co. Ltd. National Monuments Service, Dept. of the Environment, Heritage and Local Government.

Carroll, J. 2008. *Archaeological Excavations at Rosepark, Balrothery, Co. Dublin.* Dublin.

Clarke, M.V. 1941. *Register of the priory of the Blessed Virgin Mary at Tristernagh.* Transcribed and edited from the manuscript in the Cathedral Library, Armagh. Dublin.

Condit, T. and Cooney, G. (eds.) 2007. The Bremore promontory – a prominent and persistent headland in Fingal. Heritage Guide no. 39. *Archaeology Ireland.* Wordwell Ltd. Bray, Co. Wicklow. Wicklow.

Cooper, A. 1942. *An eighteenth century antiquary: the sketches, notes and diaries of Austin Cooper,* Dublin. Files in the RMP (Record of Monuments and Places) office in the Department of the Environment, Heritage and Local Government.

Flanagan, M.T. 1994. Historia Gruffad vab kenan and the origins of Balrothery, *Cambrian Medieval Celtic Studies,* no. 28, 71-94.

Grogan, E., O'Donnell, L. and Johnston, P. 2007. *The Bronze Age landscapes of the pipeline to the west – an integrated archaeological and environmental assessment.* Wordwell, Bray, Wicklow.

McNeill, C. (ed.) 1950. *Calender of Archbishop Alen's Register.* Dublin.

Murphy, D. 2000. St. Peter's Church, Balrothery. In I. Bennett (ed.), *Excavations: summary acccounts of archaeological excavations in Ireland 1999.* Wordwell, Bray, Wicklow.

O'Carroll, E. 2004. Balrothery. In I. Bennett (ed.), *Excavations: summary acccounts of archaeological excavations in Ireland 2002.* Wordwell, Bray, Wicklow.

O'Donovan, J. 1840. Ordnance Survey Name Books, Co. Dublin, no. 47. Unpublished. National Library of Ireland. Dublin.

Opie, H. 1995. Balrothery, Co. Dublin. In I. Bennett (ed.), *Excavations: summary acccounts of archaeological excavations in Ireland 1994.* Wordwell, Bray, Wicklow.

Rocque's map of the county of Dublin, 1760.

Simmington, R.C 1945. *The Civil Survey 1654-56.* Vol. 2. Dublin.

Stevens, P. 2005. St. Peter's Church, Balrothery. In I. Bennett (ed.), *Excavations: summary acccounts of archaeological excavations in Ireland 2004.* Wordwell, Bray, Wicklow.

Walsh, C. 1998. Main Street Balrothery. In I. Bennett (ed.), *Excavations: summary acccounts of archaeological excavations in Ireland 1997.* Wordwell, Bray, Wicklow.

Wiffen, J. H. 1833. *Historical memoirs of the House of Russell from the time of the Norman conquest,* vol. 1. London.

William Petty's Down Survey map of the Barony of Balrothery (1655).

CHAPTER 2

Excavation of prehistoric burials and burnt mounds at Darcystown 1

Kenneth Wiggins

Six areas containing material of archaeological significance were identified in the course of monitoring of groundworks prior to development by Fingal County Council, under archaeological excavation licence no. 03E0067, in the townland of Darcystown. The findings comprised a Late Bronze cemetery site, a ditch and two burnt mounds. These areas were excavated between 29 November 2004 and 28 January 2005. The site is referred to as Darcystown 1.

BACKGROUND

The site, trial-tested in November 2003 for Fingal County Council, was a field of 4.58 hectares on the southern side of the Skerries road in Balrothery (Fig. 1). The trial testing revealed a cremation pit of prehistoric date, but did not reveal any other archaeological features. Prior to development of the site for housing in November 2004, it was recommended by the National Monuments Service, DOEHLG, that archaeological monitoring should take place with the understanding that, should archaeological features come to light, these should be resolved. The construction contractor, Quinn Construction Ltd, commenced topsoil stripping, under archaeological supervision, on 15 November 2004. Six areas (Areas 1–6) containing material of archaeological significance were identified in the course of the topsoil stripping. The features appeared quite small and scattered, though the combined evidence was to prove to be of significance. All were resolved under the monitoring licence. The areas

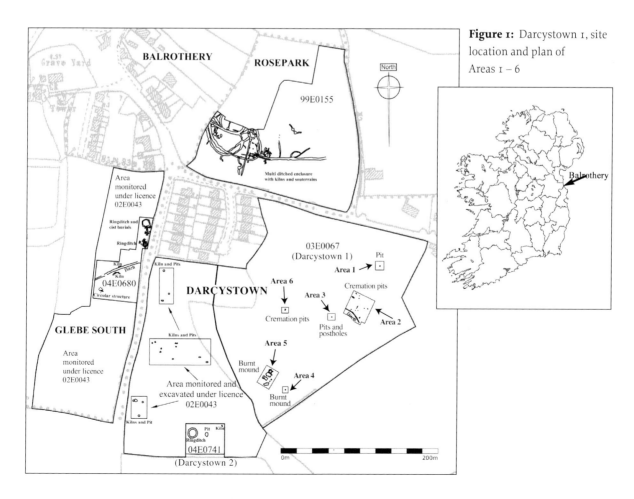

Figure 1: Darcystown 1, site location and plan of Areas 1 – 6

were excavated between 29 November 2004 and 28 January 2005 by Kenneth Wiggins for Judith Carroll and Company.

The pottery from the site was examined by Eoin Grogan and Helen Roche (Appendix III), the wood and charcoal analysis was carried out by Ellen O'Carroll (Appendix II) and the cremations were examined by Jennie Coughlan (Appendix IV). C14 dating was carried out by Beta Analytic Inc. (Appendix 1).

THE SITE

The development was situated in the townland of Darcystown, on the southern side of the village of Balrothery. The area comprised a single large pasture field south of the Skerries road running south-east of Balrothery village. The field is undulating pasture, with its highest point at the north-east corner, sloping to the south and west. The topography of the locality consists of a fertile, low-lying landscape dotted with occasional small hillocks

THE EXCAVATION

As well as the six areas of archaeological features, numerous other features, including field drains and agricultural furrows were identified. A number of levelled field boundaries were also exposed and investigated. The levelled boundary ditches identified on site all corresponded with the field system represented on the first edition six-inch Ordnance Survey Map of 1841.

The topsoil consisted of friable, mid-brown, medium silty sand. The average topsoil depth was 0.31m. Areas 1, 2 and 3 were located on high, well-drained ground in the eastern half of the field.

Area 1 contained only one feature of archaeological significance, a pit of Late Iron Age date. Area 2, yielding the remains of a Late Bronze Age cemetery with a Neolithic pit also found, was by far the largest of the six areas. Area 3 consisted of two small pits or post-holes located close to the south-west corner of Area 2.

In contrast, Areas 4 and 5 were located on low-lying ground near the south-west corner of the field, where accumulations of peat bog were stratified on the subsoil, and a large volume of surface water was

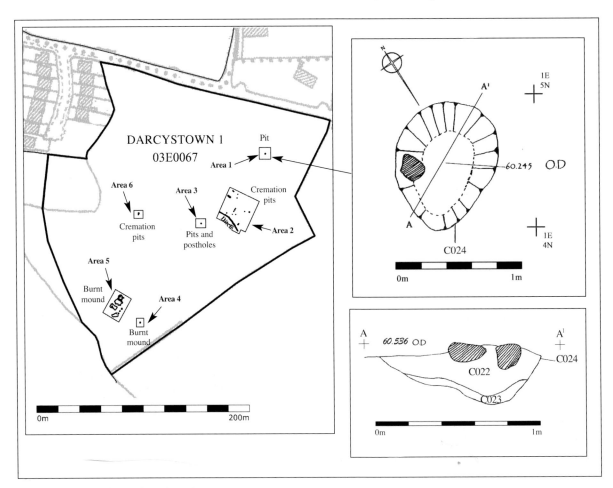

Figure 2: Area 1 plan and section of C024

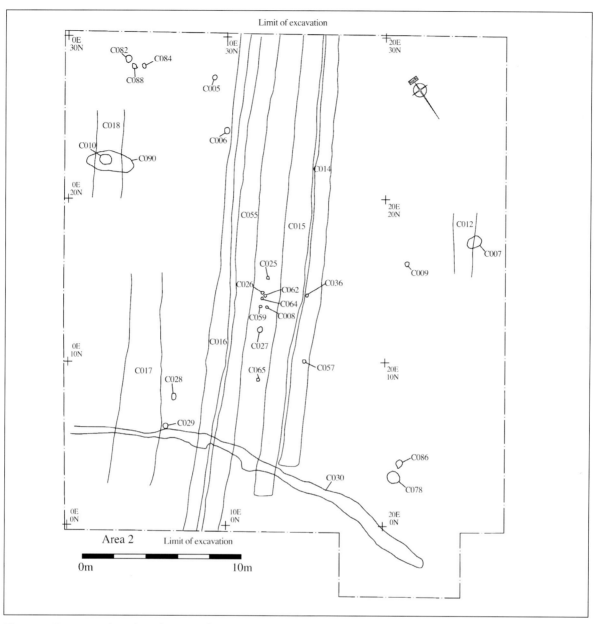

Figure 3: Pre-excavation plan of Area 2 where a number of features containing pottery and cremated bone were found

present. Machine-cut drainage channels facilitated excavation of Area 4, a single thin burnt spread located on the bog itself. Area 5, which consisted of a number of thin burnt spreads, was located just above the rim of the wet, boggy ground.

Area 6, located further south-west, consisted of just two archaeological features, both containing pottery, one containing cremated bone.

Area 1

The area, 10m north/south by 8m east/west, contained a single bowl-shaped pit, C024 (Fig. 2). The pit, which was sub-circular in plan, was 0.96m north/south by 0.77m east/west and had a maximum depth of 0.35m.

The break of slope at the top was sharp and it had sheer, straight sides with a slightly concave base. C023 was the primary fill and consisted of loose, black, silty sand and charcoal. The maximum extent of C023 was 0.68m (north/south) by 0.67m (east/west) and 0.07m in depth. Directly overlying C023 was the top fill, C022, which consisted of medium, compact, mid brown silty clay and contained 15–20% inclusions of angular to sub-rounded pebbles. C023 produced a C14 date of 1670±40 BP calibrated at 2 sigma range to AD 260 to 280 and AD 450 to 460 (Beta 232225).

Pit C024 (Plate 1) was cut by C034, a north-west/south-east orientated cultivation furrow of relatively recent origin. Parallel to C034 were a stone-lined drain, C033, and another cultivation furrow. Both features

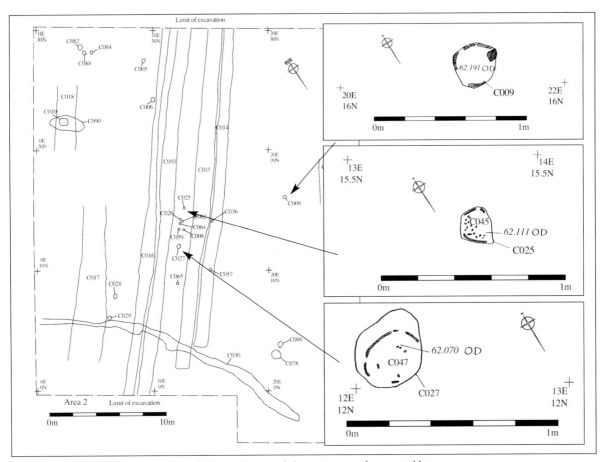

Figure 4: Area 2, plans of C009, C025 & C027, pits containing pottery and cremated bone

were modern and bore no stratigraphical relation to any feature of archaeological significance.

Area 2

Area 2 (Fig. 3) was located circa 45m south of Area 1. It was approximately 30-34m north/south by 28m east/west and was the largest of the six areas investigated at Darcystown. Area 2 comprised 23 pits containing cremated bone and/or fragments of pottery vessels, eight substantially intact. Descriptions and dimensions of the vessels can be found in the pottery report (Appendix III).

Pits containing pottery and cremated remains
There were seven pits, C009, C025, C027, C036, C082, C084 and C088, containing both cremated remains and substantially preserved vessels. Seven vessels in all were found. All were coarse ware vessels of Late Bronze Age date (Appendix III). They were lifted from the ground by the conservators, Arch Con Ltd, and material from the vessels was partly removed in their laboratories. In 2003, a Late Bronze Age pottery vessel was found during texting of Area 2 (Halliday et al. 2003) and was conserved by Arch Con Ltd. Its context is referred to as F4 in Appendix III.

C009 was the most easterly of the cremation pits and contained fill C041 and a cremation vessel, 03E0067:41:1. The cut of pit C009 was sub-circular in plan and was 0.28m north/south by 0.29m (Fig. 4). The pit yielded a C14 date of 2770±40 BP, calibrated to 1010-820 BC (Beta 244076).

Pit C025, containing cremation fill C045 and a cremation vessel, 03E0067:45:1, was sub-circular in plan and was 0.19m (north/south) by 0.17m (east/west). C045 was composed of loose dark brown clayey silt containing cremated bone (Fig. 4).

Pit C027 (Plate 2) was located 2.85m south of the position of C025. C027 contained fill C047 and cremation vessel 03E0067:47:3. C027 was sub-circular in plan and was 0.33m in diameter (Fig. 4). C047 consisted of loose, dark, brownish-black, clayey silt with cremated bone.

Pit C036 came to light during the excavation of cultivation furrow C014. It contained fill C052 and the remains of cremation vessel 03E0067:52:4 (Plate 22). The cut of pit C036 was circular in plan and was 0.21m north/south by 0.16m (Fig. 5).

Pits C082, C084 and C088 were placed close together in a tight cluster (Plate 3, Fig. 6). The centre pit of these three, C088, was located 0.26m south of C082 and 0.29m west-north-west of C084.

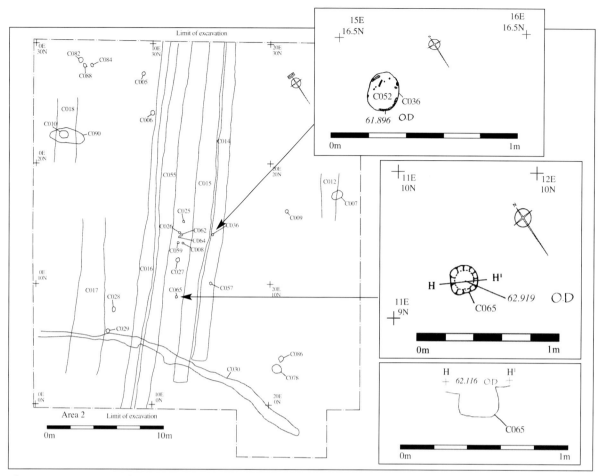

Figure 5: Area 2, plans of C036 and C065

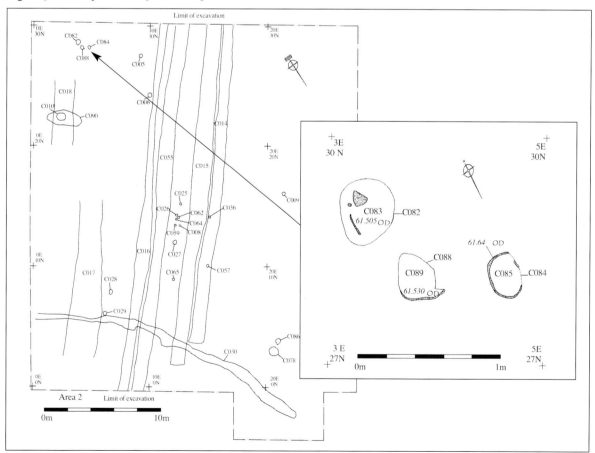

Figure 6: Area 2, plans of pits C082, C084 and C088

Pit C082 contained fill C083. C082 was sub-oval in plan with maximum dimensions of 0.43m north/south by 0.3m east/west. C083 consisted of loose dark brownish-black, silty, fine sand containing cremated bone. Cremation vessel 03E0067:83: 1, found within, was badly damaged by ploughing (Fig. 6).

Pit C084 was sub-oval in plan with maximum dimensions of 0.31m north/south by 0.23m east/west. It was approximately 0.03m in depth (Fig. 6). The fill, C085, consisted of loose, dark brownish-black, silty, fine to medium sand containing cremated bone. Only the base of cremation vessel 03E0067:85:1 (found within) survived (Plate 20).

Pit C088 contained fill C089 and vessel 03E0067:89:1. C088 was sub-oval in shape with maximum dimensions of 0.38m north/south by 0.27m east/west by 0.29m in depth (Fig. 6). C089 consisted of loose, dark, brownish-black, silty fine sand with cremated bone.

Pit C057 was located 3.84m south of C036, under cultivation furrow C014. Due to truncation by C014, only a very shallow portion of the pit survived. C057 was sub-circular in plan and was 0.26m north/south by 0.22m east/west by 0.04m in depth. It had an imperceptible break of slope at both the top and the

base. The sides were very slightly concave and the base was flat. C057 contained C056 which was composed of loose, mid brown, coarse, silty sand with small sub-angular pebbles and a small amount of cremated bone. Two sherds of prehistoric pottery came to light (03E0067:56:1–2).

Pits containing cremated bone but no pottery

There were three pits in Area 2, which contained cremated bone but no pottery

C005, on the northern side of Area 2, was sub-circular in plan, 0.3m north/south by 0.27m east/west by 0.07m in depth (Fig. 7). The break of slope at top on the western edge was sharp, gradual to the north and imperceptible to the southern and eastern sides. The sides were slightly concave and the base was flat with an imperceptible break of slope. C005 was filled with C037 which consisted of loose, mid brown, medium, silty sand and small burnt bone pieces.

Pit C006, located 2.93 south of C005, was sub-circular in plan, 0.2m north/south by 0.26m east/west by 0.05m in depth. The break of slope at the top was gradual to imperceptible. The sides were slightly convex on the southern edge but were otherwise straight. The base was flat with an

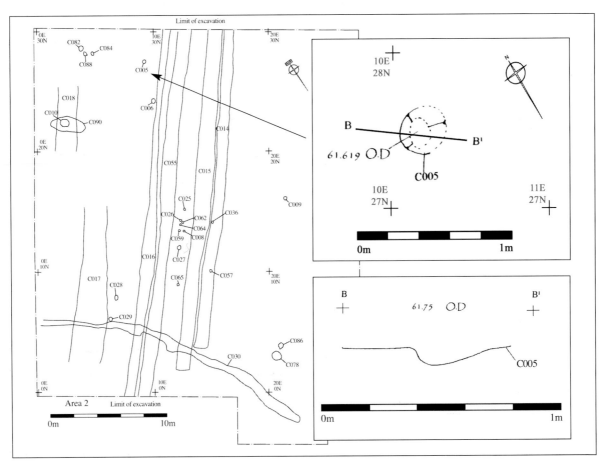

Figure 7: Area 2, plan and profile of pit C005

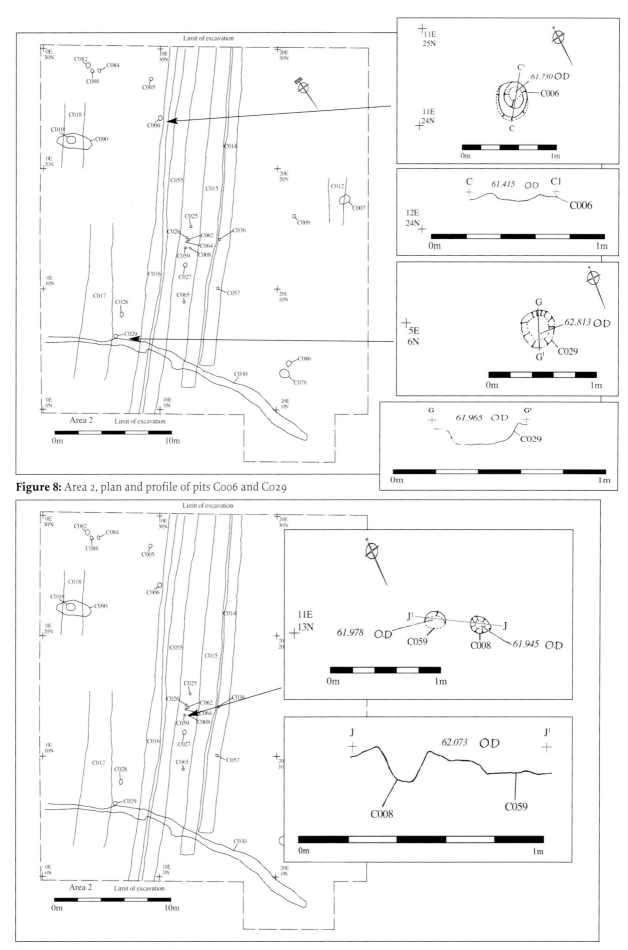

Figure 8: Area 2, plan and profile of pits C006 and C029

Figure 9: Area 2, plans and profiles of pits C008 and C059

imperceptible break of slope. C006 contained fill C038, which consisted of loose, mid to dark brown, fine, silty sand and cremated bone (Fig. 8).

C029 was on the southern side of Area 2. Its western and southern edges were disturbed by cultivation furrow C017 and linear feature C035 respectively. The undisturbed parts of C029 indicate that the pit was sub-circular in plan, 0.6m in diameter and 0.22m in depth (Fig. 8). The sides were vertical and the base was flat. C029 contained fill C049 and was lined with stones C031. C049 consisted of black, silty clay with small burnt bone pieces, charcoal and 5% small stones of angular to sub-rounded shape. Stones, C031, lay on the natural subsoil at the base of C029 and it appeared that they may have collapsed inwards from the sides of the pit. The stones were cobble-sized, flat and sub-angular.

There were three pits which contained only faint traces of burnt bone, cuts C008, C026 and C062. A fourth pit located to the eastern side of the site, C007, contained a single piece of cremated bone.

C008 (Fig. 9) was sub-circular and was located 1.08m north from cremation C027. The cut was 0.18m north/south by 0.13m east/west by 0.13m in depth. The base sloped downwards to the west. C008 contained fill C040, which was composed of loose,

mid dark brown, clayey silt with small sub-rounded pebbles and a very tiny amount of burnt bone.

C026 was sub-circular in plan and was located 0.77m south of cremation pit C025. The cut of C026 was 0.19m north/south by 0.22m east/west by 0.16m in depth (Fig. 10). The break of slope at the top was sharp and the sides were concave. The base was concave. C026 contained fill C046, composed of loose, mid dark brown, fine, silty sand with a very tiny amount of burnt bone.

C062 was circular in plan (Fig. 10). The cut was 0.21m north/south by 0.20m east/west by 0.11m in depth. In profile, the base was flat. C062 contained fill C061, which was composed of loose, dark brown, clayey silt with small sub-rounded pebbles and burnt bone.

C007 was a sub-circular-shaped cut, 0.7m north/south by 0.9m east/west by 0.28m in depth. The western side was almost vertical where the cut was also at its deepest, while the profile of the other sides sloped evenly to a sharp break of slope at the base (Fig. 11). The base was very irregular and uneven. C007 contained fill C039, which was composed of loose, dark bluish-black, fine, silty sand with 15% inclusions of red sandstone and other sub-angular stones. A single piece of cremated bone was

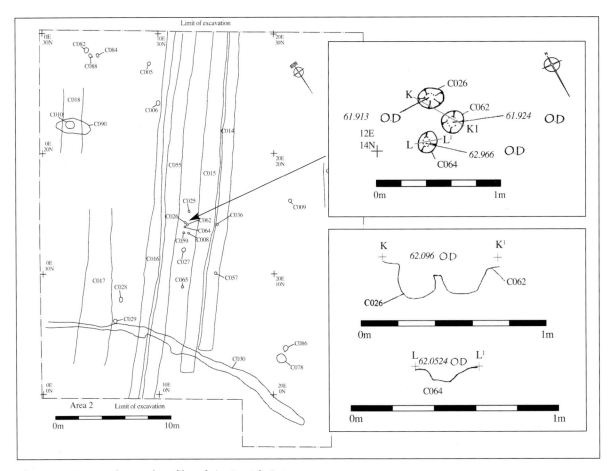

Figure 10: Area 2, plans and profiles of pits C026 & C062

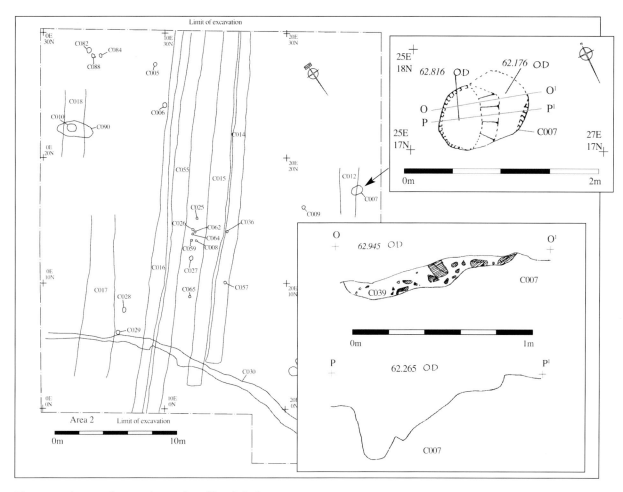

Figure 11: Area 2, plan, section and profile of pit C007

retrieved from C039, and a small rounded stone. C007 was cut by north-north-east/south-south-west cultivation furrow C012.

Pits containing prehistoric pottery but no cremated bone
On the western side of Area 2 there were two pits, C010 and C090, with the latter cutting/ superimposing the former. Both of these features contained a large quantity of prehistoric pottery sherds, rim sherds of which were decorated with horizontal grooves (Plates 16-18). This assemblage was identified as Neolithic in type (Appendix III). C090 was cut by north-north-east/south-south-west orientated cultivation furrow C018.

Pit C010 (Plate 4) was sub-oval in plan and was orientated north-north-west/south-south-east. It was 0.76m long by 0.65m wide by 0.22m in depth. The break of slope at the top was imperceptible and the sides were steep and slightly concave (Fig. 12). C010 contained two fill contexts, C076 and C042, which were respectively its primary and secondary fills. C076 was composed of relatively firm, mid grey, silty sand with 5% inclusions of small sub-rounded and sub-angular pebbles. There were also 2% inclusions

of charcoal flecking present. The extent of the fill was 0.6m north/south 0.73m east/west by 0.11m in depth. Lying directly above C076 was C042, which consisted of medium, compact, black, fine sandy silt with 15% inclusions of charcoal chunks and 15% inclusions of angular sandstone. Its maximum extent was 0.76m east/west by 0.65m north/south by 0.15m in depth. The fill contained sixteen fragments of Neolithic pottery (03E0067: 42:1–4, 7 and 9–19) and three worked flints (03E0067: 42:5, 6 and 8). Pottery fragment, 03E0067:42:4, was decorated with horizontal grooves and appeared to be part of a rim. C042 yielded a date of 4840±40 BP, calibrated to 3700 to 3630 BC.

Pit C090 was an elongated oval in plan and was 3.37m (north-north-west/south-south-east) by 1.4m (west-south-west/east-north-east) by 0.18m in depth. The break of slope at the top was obscured by the truncation caused by cultivation furrow C018, except to its eastern end where the break of slope was gradual (Fig. 12). The base was uneven, but generally flat.

C090 contained a single fill, C071, which was very mixed due to disturbance by cultivation furrow

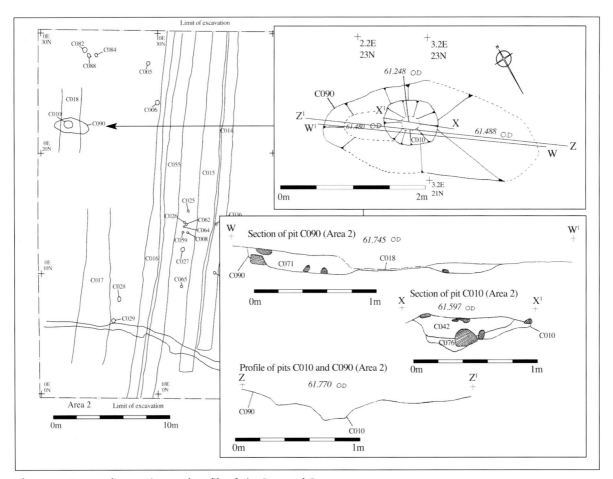

Figure 12: Area 2, plan, sections and profile of pits C010 and C090

C018. C071 was composed of medium, compact, dark brown, sandy silt mixed with light to mid brown cultivation furrow fill containing angular sandstone and charcoal flecking. C071 contained 24 sherds of Neolithic pottery (03E0067:71:1–9, 11–16, 18–20 and 22–27) and three pieces of flint (03E0067:10, 17 and 21). Pottery sherds 03E0067:71:1, 4 and 5, were rim sherds decorated with horizontal grooving similar in style to 03E0067:42:4. Pottery from both contexts, C071 and C042, may belong to the same vessel. It is likely that both pits were filled simultaneously with the same material, as the vessel was deposited. Cultivation furrow C018 subsequently disturbed cut C090 and fill C071, damaging the vessel.

Pits containing neither cremated bone nor pottery
Six other pits, which contained neither prehistoric pottery nor cremated remains, were present in Area 2. These were cuts C028, C059, C064, C065, C078 and C086.

Located 1.02m north-north-east from cremation pit, C029, pit C028 was sub-circular in plan and was 0.33m north/south by 0.48m east/west by 0.04m in depth. It had a gradual break of slope at the top with straight sides tapering to a flat base. C028 contained

one fill, C048, which consisted of loose, mid to dark dark brown, fine, silty sand.

Located 0.2m south-east of pit C008, C059 was a shallow sub-circular pit, 0.16m in diameter by 0.14m in depth. It had a gradual break of slope at the top with straight sides tapering evenly to a flat base (Fig. 9). C059 contained fill C058, which consisted of loose, light to mid brown, fine, silty sand. The feature appeared to be much reduced through damage caused by later agricultural activity.

Pit C064 was located immediately adjacent to south edge of C062 and was sub-circular in plan. It was 0.17m north/south by 0.21m east/west by 0.06m in depth (Fig. 10). The break of slope at the top was gradual, with straight sides tapering to a flat base. C064 contained fill C063 which consisted of loose, mid brown, medium, silty sand with 15% inclusions of small sub-rounded pebbles.

Pit C065 was located 2.71m south of cremation pit C062 and was sub-circular in plan. It was 0.21m north/south by 0.24m east/west by 0.17m in depth. The break of slope at the top was sharp with concave sides, which, at the top, slightly overhung the base. The break of slope at the base was sharp with the base itself being relatively flat. C065 contained fill

C060, which consisted of loose, mid greyish-brown, fine, silty sand containing sub-rounded stones and pebbles. C065 may represent a post-hole (Fig. 5).

Pit C078 was located in the south-eastern part of Area 2. It was sub-circular in plan. It constituted a relatively substantial pit cut, 0.78m north/south by 0.18m east/west by 0.17m in depth. The break of slope at the top was sharp on all sides except to the south-east where it was more gradual (Fig. 13). The sides were slightly concave and the base was relatively flat. C078 contained fill C077, which consisted of loose, dark brown, sandy silt with charcoal and angular heat-shattered stones. C077 produced a C14 date from the charcoal of 2350±40 BP calibrated to 410-370 BC (Beta 232226).

Pit C086 was located adjacent to, and north-east of, pit C078 and was sub-circular in plan with an elongated south-west end (Fig. 13). It was 0.42m north/south by 0.58m east/west by 0.15m in depth. The break of slope at the top was sharp at the west but not at the east where it was gradual to imperceptible. The base was irregular and uneven. C086 contained C079, which consisted of loose, light to mid brown, fine, silty sand with 1% inclusions of charcoal and small sub-angular pebbles.

Cultivation furrows

Area 2 was subjected to intensive ploughing with eight north-north-east/south-south-west orientated cultivation furrows. From east to west, these were C012, C013, C014, C015, C055, C016, C017 and C018. The cultivation furrows all spanned the north/south axis of the site and were 1.4m, 0.62m, 1.26m, 1.73m, 1.29m, 1.25m, 3m and 1.65m in width respectively. All contained modern material and were of no archaeological significance.

Cultivation furrow, C014 yielded three flints (03E0067:14:1–3). These were most likely associated with the two cremations which the furrow overlay, C036 and C057.

Cultivation furrow, C015 also yielded three flints (03E0067:15:1–3). No cremations or other prehistoric features underlay C015, but cultivation furrow C014 was immediately adjacent to C015. Therefore, the flints may similarly be associated with cremation cuts C036 and C057.

Cultivation furrow C018 yielded two flints (03E0067:18:1 and 6), three sherds of prehistoric pottery (03E0067:18:2, 3 and 5) and one 13/14th century medieval strap-handle sherd.

03E0067:18:1–3, 5 and 6 are almost certainly

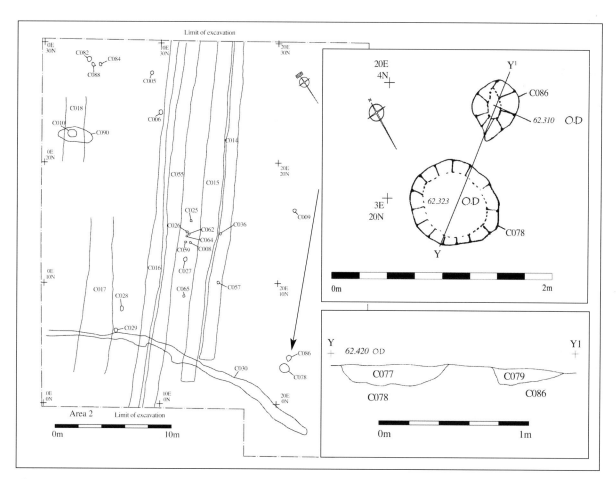

Figure 13: Area 2, plans of C078 and C086

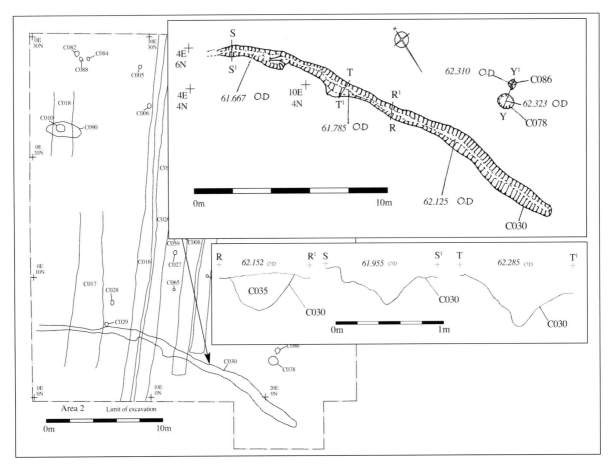

Figure 14: Area 2, plan of slightly curved linear feature C030

associated with pit cuts C010 and C090, as the three prehistoric sherds are of a similar fabric to the other Neolithic sherds discussed above.

The ditch

A slightly curved linear feature, C030, was located along the southern side of Area 2 (Fig. 14, Plate 5). C030 was orientated in a north-west/south-east direction, curving west on its north-west end. It was in total 20.6m long, 0.88m wide and 0.46m in depth. It had a sharp break of slope at the top and straight sides which gave the ditch a V shaped profile (Plate 5). The break of slope at the base was gradual and the base was concave. The ditch terminated at each end in a gradual rounded point. C030 contained fills C035, C021 and C044.

C035 was the primary fill of C30 and consisted of loose, mid brown, silty clay with tiny, sub-rounded pebbles. No finds came to light in C035. C021 superimposed C035 approximately 1.4m west of the south-eastern terminal of C030. C021 was a thin layer of poorly sorted sub-rounded cobble-sized stones mixed with loose, mid brown, silty clay containing sub-rounded pebbles and tiny stones. The maximum extent of C021 was 1.5m north-west/

south-east by 0.55m north-east/south-west by 0.04m in depth.

C044 was a roughly sub-oval lens, wholly enclosed within fill C035, located towards the north-western end of C030. Its maximum extent was 0.2m north/south by 0.4m east/west by 0.1m in depth. It was composed of moderately compact, dark brownish, black, silty clay mixed with redeposited boulder clay throughout, occasional charcoal flecks and frequent moderately sorted small stones. C044 probably represents the remains of a layer of organic origin. There were no finds from C030. It may have been a drain as there was a large number of drainage features in close proximity to the south-east of Area 2 which stretched down as far as Areas 4 and 5. Alternatively, it may have been a boundary or enclosure ditch of some form. The ditch cut cremation pit C029/C049, but was cut by the cultivation furrows.

Area 3

Area 3 consisted of two pits, cuts C066 and C067, which were located 15m south-west of Area 2 (Fig. 15, Plate 6).

Pit C066, the larger of the two, was roughly sub-oval in plan and was 0.7m north/south by 0.45m east/west by 0.58m at its deepest point. The break of slope at the top was sharp and the sides were vertical to the east and west, while they were more sloped to the north and south. The base was narrow and flat, 0.26m east/west by 0.1m north/south. C011, C050 and C019 were the fills of C066. C011, the primary fill, was composed of soft, grey, silty clay and charcoal flecks. C011 was 0.08m in maximum depth. The secondary fill, C050, was soft grey silty clay, heavily flecked with charcoal, while the uppermost fill, C019, a soft, greyish-brown, silty clay with charcoal flecks, was 0.12m in maximum depth.

Pit C067 was located 0.6m east of pit C066. C067 was sub-circular 0.34m north/south by 0.3m east/west by 0.26m in maximum depth. The break of slope at the top was sharp and the sides were almost vertical. The base was narrow and slightly concave, 0.16m east/west by 0.06m north/south. C051 and C043 were the fills of C067. The primary fill, C043, was soft, grey, fine, silty sand 0.075m in maximum depth. C051, the secondary fill, was composed of soft, dark grey, silty clay heavily flecked with charcoal.

The maximum extent of C051 was 0.4m north/south by 0.18m east/west by 0.3m in depth.

In shape, the features resembled post-holes, although there was no evidence for packing stones or related post-holes.

Area 4

Area 4 comprised a burnt spread (C123), a linear feature of post-medieval date (C124) and a pit (C128) with a piece of cut timber (C129) lying above it. The burnt spread, C123, comprised moderately compact, dark brown to black silty clay. It contained 40% inclusions of burnt angular stones, averaging 0.05–0.06m across. It was truncated on its southern edge by linear feature C124. The spread was 15.5m in length north-west/south-east by approximately 9.25m north-east/south-west (Fig. 16, Plates 7 & 8).

The pit, C128, was an irregularly shaped cut and had maximum dimensions of 1.2m north/south by 0.8m east/west with a depth of 0.85m. C128 was superimposed by the cut timber piece, C129, which was located under the burnt spread, C123 (Fig. 17, Plate 9). The break of slope at the top was gradual and the sides were slightly convex with a gentle slope to

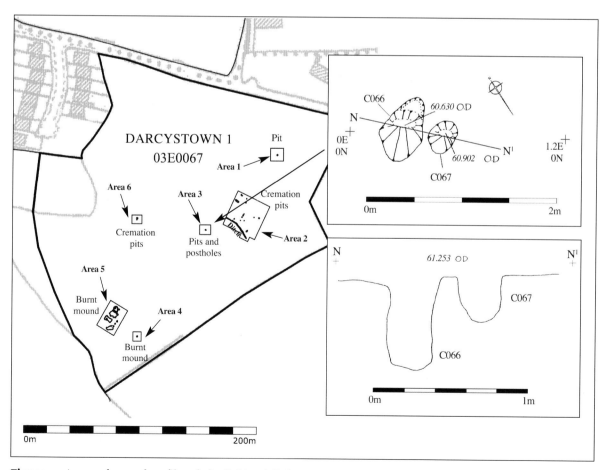

Figure 15: Area 3, plans and profiles of pits C066 and C067

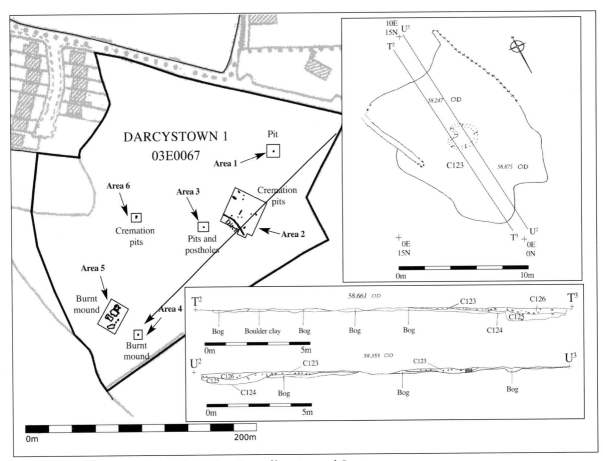

Figure 16: Area 4, pre-excavation plan and sections of burnt spread C123

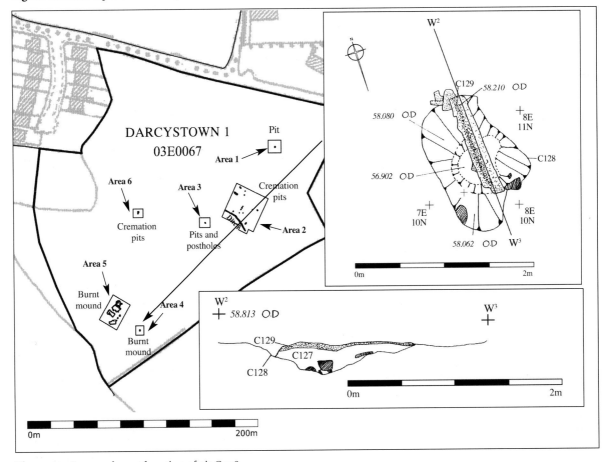

Figure 17: Area 4, plan and section of pit C128

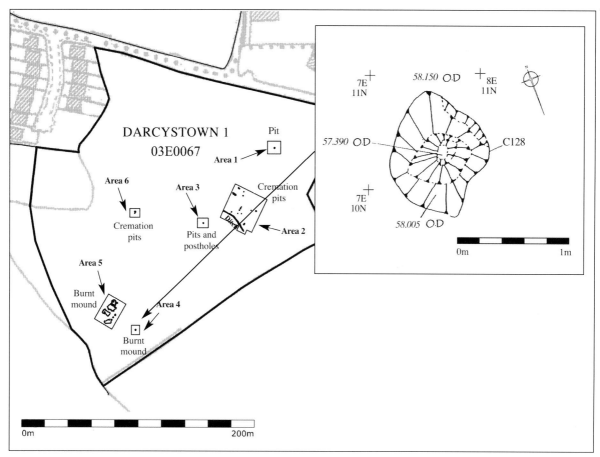

Figure 18: Area 4, post–excavation plan of pit C128

the north and west. The southern and eastern edges were more irregular and convex. The lower part of the cut was cylindrical and regular while the base was irregular.

The fill of pit C128 was C127, which was composed of moderately compact, black, silty clay containing wood pieces of various sizes and pieces of red, angular sandstone up to 0.15m across. No packing stones were present.

Timber C129 was a plank-like piece of wood, orientated north/south and located immediately above pit C128. The maximum dimensions of C129 were 1.3m in length, 0.19m wide and 0.05m in depth. The wood was very soft and was a similar dark, reddish-brown to the roundwood pieces (hazel and alder) found within C127, the fill of the underlying pit. It is uncertain whether the timber, C129, was deliberately placed across pit C128, or if its position above the pit was simply coincidental (Plate 9). A C14 determination for pieces of roundwood found in C127 yielded a date of 2900±60 BP calibrated to 1260–900 BC at 2 sigma range (Beta 239117).

Area 5

Area 5 was located near the south-western corner of the field, approximately 18m north-west of Area 4 (Fig. 19). Seven burnt spreads (C091, C092, C093, C095, C096, C097 and C098), five pits (C105, C109, C110, C115 and C119) one linear feature (C120), one curvilinear trench feature (C113), a silted-up deposit (C104), a stone-lined drain (C102) and a cultivation furrow (C100) were found in the area.

Burnt mound C091/C092 superimposing trough C105/C119/C120

Pit C105 was a sub-oval cut, 3.6m north/south by 1.6m east/west by 0.42m in depth (Fig. 19, Plates 11 & 12). The sides sloped gradually, except to the north and south-east corners which were more vertical. The base was slightly stepped at the northern end but was otherwise flat. C119 was a sub-circular pit, cut into the centre of the base of C105. It was 0.8m in diameter and 0.25m in depth.

C105 contained three fills: C118, C107, and C106. C118, which was the primary fill of C105, was also the single fill of pit C119, suggesting that cuts C105 and C119 were contemporary. C118 consisted of moderately compact, light grey, silty clay containing

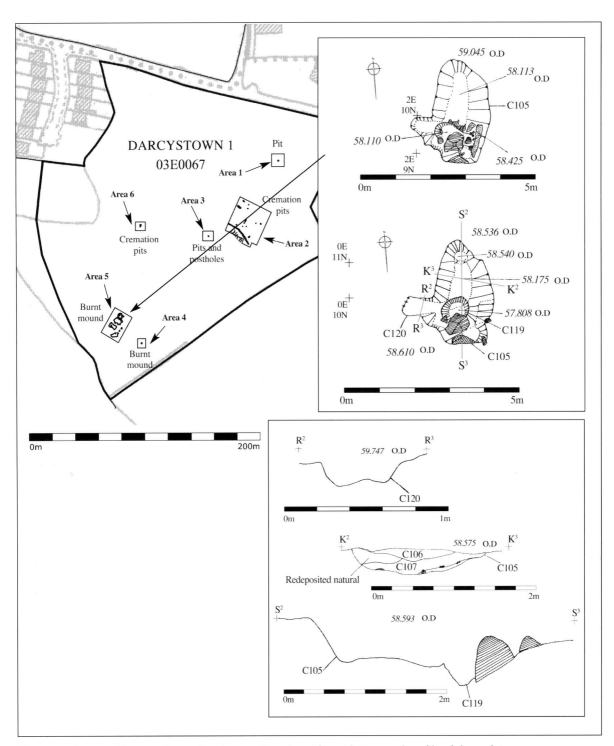

Figure 19: Area 5, mid-excavation and post-excavation plans of trough C105 and profile of channel C120

charcoal and preserved wood (Plate 11). The largest of the preserved wood pieces was 0.95m by 0.15m, but most of the remaining pieces were composed of tiny flecks. C107 was the secondary fill of pit C105 and had a maximum depth of 0.19m. It was composed of compact black, silty clay and contained both charcoal and decayed stone. There was no evidence for *in situ* burning. Overlying C107 was the upper fill of pit C105, C106. C106 consisted of compact, light greyish-brown, medium, silty sand. It is possible that pit C105 may represent the remains of a trough.

Associated with the trough, C105, was a sloping channel in the subsoil, C120, aligned east/west on the western side of the trough. C120 was 0.8m east/west by 0.5m north/south by 0.15m in depth (Fig. 19). The fill comprised a loose reddish-brown medium silty sand with sub-rounded pebbles. It is

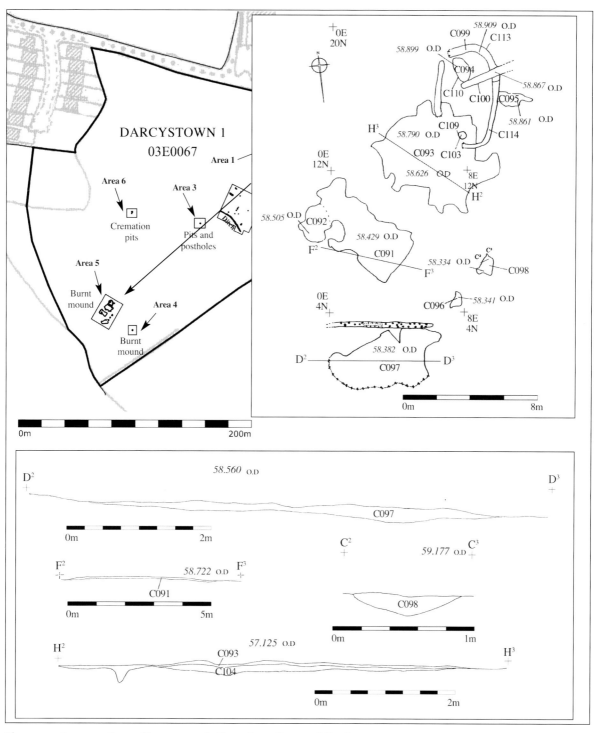

Figure 20: Area 5 sections of burnt spreads C097, C093, C091 and C098

possible that C120 was an earlier feature in the subsoil that was cut by the digging of trough C105. However, its distinct sloping base, aligned precisely with the deep C119 cut at the base of the trough, suggests that the feature may be related to the channelling of water into the trough from a point to the west or north-west

Superimposing C105/C119/C120 were C091 and C092 (Fig. 20, Plate 10). C091 was a roughly sub-

circular burnt spread located to the west of Area 5. It was composed of moderately compact, black, silty clay with 15–20% inclusions of shattered red, angular, sandstone. It was 6.5m north-west/south-east by 4.05m north-east/south-west by 0.1m in depth.

C092 was an irregularly shaped burnt spread located adjacent to the western side of C091. It consisted of loose, black, silty clay with 15–20% inclusions of shattered angular red sandstone.

Burnt spreads C096, C097 and C098

Burnt spread C096 was a small, irregular spread located in a natural hollow. C096 comprised moderately compact, black, silty clay with 20% inclusions of shattered sub-angular red sandstone and was 1.0m (north-west/south-east) by 0.9m (north-east/south-west) by 0.15m in depth.

C097 was an approximately sub-oval burnt spread (Fig. 20). It consisted of loose, dark brown-black, clayey silt with 30% inclusions of shattered/degraded sub-angular red sandstone and was 3m north/south by 6.6m east/west by 0.95m in depth.

Burnt spread C098 was a small, irregularly shaped deposit located in a natural depression (Fig. 20). It comprised moderately compact, black, silty clay with 15% inclusions of shattered sub-angular red sandstone and was 0.95m north/south by 1.4m east/west by 0.16m in depth.

Pits C109, C110 and C115, burnt spreads C093, C095 and curvilinear feature C113

Pit C109 was sub-oval in plan and was 1.13m north/south by 1.38m east/west by 0.2m in depth. It had a sharp break of slope at the top and a gradual break of slope at the base. The sides were straight and gradually sloped and the base was even and concave (Fig. 21). Pit C109 contained fills C108 and C103. The primary fill, C108, consisted of moderately compact, dark grey, silty clay with 1% inclusions of degraded sandstone. The maximum depth of C108 was 0.09m. C103 consisted of moderately compact, black, silty clay with 40% inclusions of angular sandstone, on average 0.09m in breadth, and charcoal chunks. The maximum depth of C103 was 0.11m. Pit C109 cut deposits C093 and C104.

Pit C110 was irregular in plan and was 1.55m north/south by 0.93m east/west by 0.23m in depth. The break of slope at the top was sharp and was imperceptible at the base (Fig. 21). The sides and base were concave and irregular except on the east side, which was even. C110 contained three fills: C111, C112 and C094. C112 was the primary fill and consisted of soft, dark brown silty clay containing charcoal. It was a maximum of 0.09m in depth (Plate 14). The secondary fill, C111, was composed of moderately compact, greyish-brown, silty clay containing charcoal. C094, the uppermost fill, was loosely compacted, brownish-black silty clay containing charcoal. C110 was cut by C100, a cultivation furrow of relatively recent origin.

Pit C115 was sub-circular in plan, 0.54m north/south by 0.58m east/west and 0.2m in depth, underlying burnt spread C093. The break of slope at the top was sharp, and the sides were straight. They tapered steeply to the base except to the east where the side was concave and the slope gentle (Fig. 21, Plate 13). The base was slightly concave. C115 contained fills C116 and C117. The primary fill, C116, was composed of moderately compact, greyish-brown, silty clay containing decayed stone and charcoal. C117, the uppermost fill, consisted of loose dark brown to black silty clay containing decayed and burnt stone and charcoal. The charcoal produced a date of 2990 ± 40 BP calibrated to 1310-1040 BC (Beta-232227).

Enclosing the pits was curvilinear feature C113 (Fig. 21). This feature, possibly a slot-trench, was a rounded sub-rectangular shape. On its west side, the trench was straight and to the east, it was slightly curved. It surrounded pits C109, C110 and C115, relating also to the superimposing burnt spreads. C113 was not continuous – there were two small gaps in the south corner, another gap in the north-west corner and a larger break in the south-west corner where pit C115 was located. The outside length of the feature was 5.84m (north-north-east/south-south-west) by 3.6m (north-west/south-east). On its west side, the slot-trench was 0.14m-0.18m in width. On its east side, it was 0.15m-0.2m in width with a maximum depth of 0.18m, at the north-eastern end, and 0.08m at the south-west part of the feature

In section, the south-western area of the slot-trench had gently sloping, straight sides, while the north-eastern part had generally vertical sides – some parts of which slightly under-cut the natural. The base was flat and straight in the north-eastern quadrant while to the south-west it was concave. C113 contained two fills, C099 and C114. C099 was the main fill of C113 and occupied the entire cut except for the south-eastern side, which was filled by C114. Both fills appear to have been contemporary with little to distinguish them in hue and inclusions. C099 was a moderately compact, mid grey, silty clay with 2% inclusions of charred wood. C114 was a moderately compact, dark brown to grey, sandy clay with 5% inclusions of sub-rounded pebbles. In plan the feature looked to be a structure or enclosure of sorts, although there was no evidence for any post-holes or stake-holes. C113 could possibly be interpreted as a slot-trench, even though the sides and base were very irregular in places.

C113 cut C095, a burnt spread, at its western end. C095 was a small, elongated and irregularly shaped deposit in a natural depression in the subsoil. The depression containing the burnt material was 1.5m east/west by 1.1m north/south by up to 0.16m in depth.

C113 was superimposed by burnt spread deposit, C093.

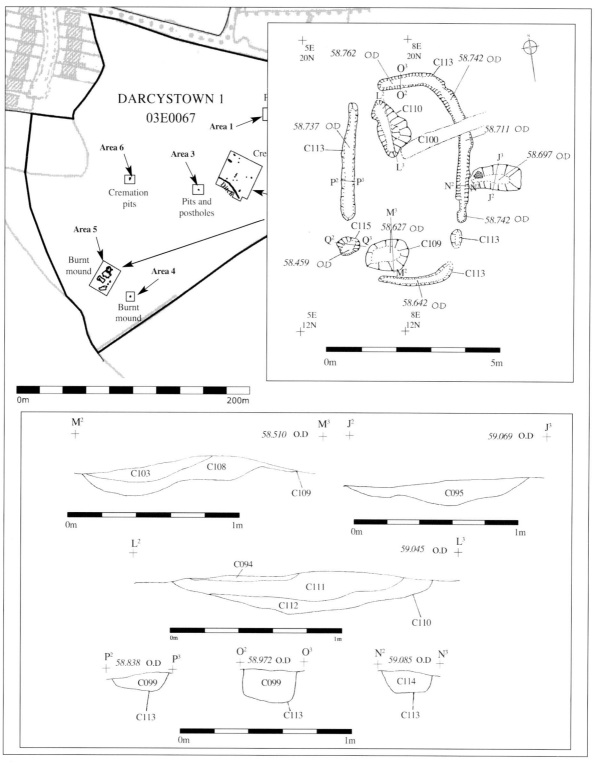

Figure 21: Area 5, post-excavation plans of structure C113 and pits C109, C110 and C115; sections of pits C109, C110 and C113

C093 was an irregularly shaped burnt spread and consisted of moderately compact, black, silty clay with 15–20% inclusions of shattered sub-angular red sandstone. It was 2.15m north/south by 2.6m east/west by 0.1m in depth.

Deposit C104 was an irregularly shaped silt layer immediately underlying burnt materia, C093. The maximum extent of C104 was 2m in diameter by 0.1m in depth. It was composed of moderately compact greyish-brown silty clay mixed with small sub-rounded pebbles.

Cultivation furrow C100, aligned east/west, cut the north-east quadrant of structure/enclosure C113. The fill of the furrow was composed of moderately compact, light brownish-grey, sandy clay with sub-rounded pebbles.

Stone-lined drain, C102, was an east/west orientated linear feature, 0.25m wide by 0.12m in depth. It was mainly composed of sub-rounded and rounded cobbles and contained a mid to dark brown sandy silt. The feature was interpreted as a 'French drain' of 18th or 19th century date.

Area 6

Area 6 was located 70m south-west of Area 2 and 60m north-north-east of Area 5. It yielded two small pits, C072 and C074, both of which contained prehistoric pottery (Fig. 22). C072 (fill C073) also yielded a very small quantity of cremated bone. Both pits were badly damaged by modern field drains and/or cultivation furrows.

Pit C072 (Plate 15) was an irregular shape, 0.42m (north-west/south-east) by 0.4m (north-east/south-west) by 0.07m in depth. The break of slope at the top was gradual and the sides sloped in a slightly concave shape. The base was concave. C073 was the fill of C072 and consisted of moderately compact, dark greyish-black, medium, clayey sand mottled with yellow clayey sand, containing pebbles and

small fragments of charcoal and cremated bone. C072 yielded fourteen sherds of prehistoric pottery (03E0067:73:1–14) which probably derive from a single vessel. The sherds were of Middle or Late Bronze Age date (Appendix III)

Located 1.28m west-north-west of pit C072, was pit C074. C074 was irregular in plan, 0.24m north/south by 0.32m east/west by 0.08m in depth. The break of slope at the top was gradual and the sides sloped in a slight concave shape. The top and the sides were concave. C074 contained fill C075 which consisted of moderately compact, dark greyish-black, medium clayey sand, mottled with yellow clayey sand containing occasional charcoal and pebbles. Though no cremated bone was recovered, C074 yielded 30 sherds of prehistoric pottery (03E0067:75:1–30), which probably originally derived from a single vessel. The sherds from C074 were too poorly preserved to be categorised. Those from C073 were Middle to Late Bronze Age in date (Appendix III). C080 was a north-east/south-west orientated cultivation furrow, 0.54m in width, which truncated pit C074 on its south-eastern side.

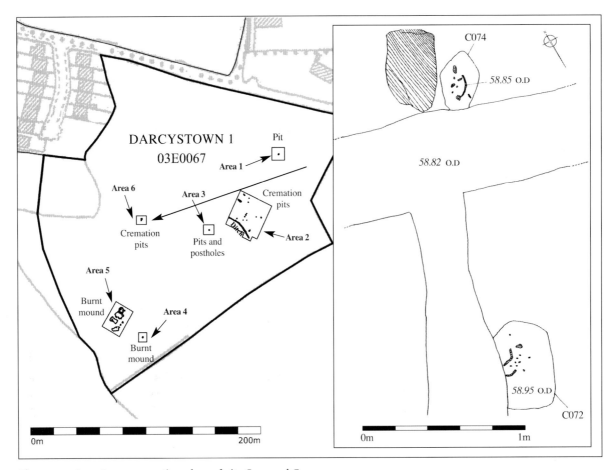

Figure 22: Area 6, pre-excavation plans of pits C072 and C074

The Finds

Unstratified finds recovered from the monitoring of site stripping or from the hand excavation of residual topsoil consisted mainly of mixed pottery sherds of 18th–20th century date, though a fine flint blade was recovered from the surface of burnt stone spread C123/bog spread at Area 4 (03E0067:130:1). The only other artefact from Area 4 was a post-medieval pot sherd from the fill of linear feature, C124, which cut the southern end of the burnt spread. No finds were recovered from the limited number of features comprising Areas 1 and 3. Finds from Area 5 consisted of a limited amount of lithic material. Several sherds from two prehistoric pots were recovered from two contexts in Area 6, the fill of cremation pits, C072 and C074. Area 2 was the largest of the six areas, and it is from here that most of the finds were recovered. The most significant finds include the remains of seven cremation vessels, each of which was removed from the ground by Arch Con Ltd for excavation and reconstruction in the laboratory. The vessels derived from cremation pits C009, C025, C027, C036, C082, C084 and C088. A pottery vessel was also recovered during trial testing in 2003 from Area 2 (F4). Several other sherds of prehistoric pottery were excavated in Area 2, including a number of decorated sherds associated with pits C010 and C090. Some possibly worked flint material was also recovered from Area 2, and the fill of cultivation furrow, C018, produced a strap-handle sherd of medieval date (03E0067:18:4).

DISCUSSION

The evidence from Darcystown 1 points to a significant phase of activity, principally in the Late Bronze Age. This is evidenced by cremation burial sites in Area 2 and Area 6; pits or post-holes in Area 1 and Area 3, and two levelled burnt mound sites in Area 4 and Area 5.

The first indication that a cremation cemetery was located in the field came with the discovery of a cremation deposit contained within the base of an upright ceramic vessel during testing in late 2003 (Area 2). Following the comprehensive excavation of the field between December 2004 and January 2005, it transpired that the ceramic pot marked the northern limit of a cremation cemetery in Area 2. The cemetery was established on the prominent dome of the field, and contained a number of burials. These were represented by the remains of seven other upright Late Bronze Age pottery vessels in addition to several pits containing cremations. A number of other pits containing cremations and fragmentary sherds were also found. Neolithic pottery was also found in association with a pit in Area 2, but no human remains were associated with it.

All the cremation burials, badly disturbed by ploughing, were concentrated in Area 2, apart from two detached cremation pits, C072 and C074. These were found in Area 6, in a lower part of the field, 70m south-west of Area 2. These produced a pottery type different to that found in Area 2 and may have a date earlier in the Bronze Age (Appendix III).

Neolithic pottery associated with an oblong pit

Thirty-six sherds of pottery representing at least two vessels, associated with oblong pit C010/C090, were well fired and highly decorated. They were identified as mid-Neolithic by Grogan and Roche (Appendix III). The vessels were deep hemispherical bowls of Dundrum type and were found in a variety of sites. The majority of this pottery type has come from domestic contexts. The pottery was associated with a great deal of charcoal and produced a date of 4860 ± 40 BP, calibrated to 3700 to 3630 BC (Beta 232328).

There were no human remains found in association with the pottery, but the fact that the pit containing pottery was found in Area 2l so close to the burials, suggests that it may possibly have been a burial in which the human remains had decayed. However, such pits have been found in several Neolithic domestic contexts. In the recently found Neolithic enclosure site at Magheraboy, Co. Sligo, 55 pits containing dark deposits and domestic rubbish, including pottery, constituted the only internal features found within the enclosure (Danaher 2007, 109-111). The position of the Neolithic pit in Area 2, on the highest part of the Darcystown 1 site would certainly be a most suitable place for a habitation site.

Late Bronze Age cremation burial pits

A pit containing a cremation in an upright coarse ware vessel was found in Area 2 during testing (Halliday and Hamill 2003). On excavation, a further 20 pits were found in Area 2, including seven further upright pots containing cremations. Other pits contained fragments of coarse ware, which were also found in disturbed contexts in the vicinity of the pits. Most of the pits contained cremated bone. In Area 3, coarse pottery was found in two pits, one containing a cremation. The pottery here differed from that found in Areas 1 and 2 and was coarse but poorly preserved. In one of the pits (C073) the pottery is described as Mid to Late Bronze Age. In the other (C075), it is described as 'probably' Bronze Age (Appendix III). Apart from the Neolithic sherds described above, all the pottery from Area 2 was identified as Late Bronze Age coarse ware (Appendix III).

Towards the end of the Middle Bronze Age, the use of special funerary vessels in burial contexts was replaced by domestic pots (Grogan 2004). The placement of vessels in upright positions in pits (rather than cists) becomes a feature of the record (Grogan and Roche 2004b, 2). Examples include burial pit no. 2 from Rathgall, Co. Wicklow, which included an upright pot containing the cremated remains of an adult and a child (Cooney and Grogan 1994, 145; Raftery 1973, 294) and the ceramic vessel 'buried in an upright position' (Hagen 2004) at Kilgobbin, Stepaside, Co. Dublin, where a small cremation burial complex was excavated in 2002.

At Darcystown 1, the site was extensively disturbed by ploughing and no enclosing or demarcating features such as ring ditches, barrows or cairns were found in relation to the burials. However, the possibility that these existed is suggested by the fact that the burial features were found in a number of small groups in Area 2 (Fig. 3).

Other sorts of structures less durable than ditches could have marked burial places. A possible 'mortuary house' was suggested by the excavation of an enclosure at Priestsnewtown, Kilcoole, Co. Wicklow, where very similar Mid to Late Bronze Age pottery (Grogan and Roche 2004a) to that found at Darcystown 1 came to light. At Priestsnewtown, a group of five upright vessels containing cremations and a number of cremation pits were excavated in 2004. Four of these were found in an area enclosed by a slot-trench with a flat to U shaped base and vertical edges. It had no entranceway. This feature was first identified as a ring ditch but, on excavation, was interpreted as a possible mortuary house (Tobin, Swift & Wiggins 2004, 21–23, 29). C14 dates for two of the Priestsnewtown burials suggest that plain, coarse ware vessels were in use by 1200-1300 BC (Grogan, Appendix III)

A 'mortuary house' may also be suggested by a structure at Caltragh, Co. Sligo, where a small group of Early/Middle Bronze Age cremation burials were associated with 20 stake-holes. These may have formed a structure marking the burial (Linnane 2007, 26).

The site at Darcystown 1 with its scattered, seemingly unenclosed burials and burnt mounds can be compared to a cemetery at Kilbane, Castletroy, Co.

Limerick (O'Callaghan 2006, 309), which contained a large number of Bronze Age cremation burials as well as burnt mounds. Here one area produced seven features containing cremated bone, three also producing pottery. A ring ditch, not directly related to the pits, was found in the same area. One of the pits was surrounded by stake-holes, supporting the suggestion of possible other less durable structure types enclosing burial monuments. Ninety further pits producing pottery and cremated bone were found in another area measuring 12m x 6m. The pottery was identified as Late Bronze Age (Grogan and Roche 2004b). Three burnt mounds were also found on the site at Kilbane.

At Carrig, Co. Wicklow, a burial cairn, a 'low circular pile of field stones and small boulders with no formal edging to the cairn' (Grogan 1990, 12) yielded burials dated from circa 2000 BC to the Late Bronze Age. Coarse Late Bronze Age pottery at Carrig has been compared to the Darcystown 1 burials (Grogan, Appendix III). This type of cairn may also possibly have covered the Darcystown 1 burials, particularly if the burial site originated earlier in the Bronze Age or during the Neolithic period.

Though Late Bronze Age coarse wares commonly range in date from circa 1100 to 800 BC (Grogan and Roche in Appendix III), the Priestsnewtown cremation urns (above) and a number of recent discoveries indicate that coarse wares of this type developed in the latter part of the Middle Bronze Age (pers comm. Dr. E. Grogan).

The possible enclosure ditch

Though no enclosing feature was found for the area of the burial, a linear/curvilinear feature, C030, was found the southern edge of Area 2 (Fig. 14). It, however, curved away from the area of the burial site and while the line of C030 pre-dated the furrows, the feature clearly cut one of the cremation pits, C029.

No finds were recovered from the fill of C030 and there is no evidence of its date. However, its curving line corresponds to the arc of the curved ditch in the nearby site of Glebe South (04E0680) to the west of Darcystown 1 (See Chapter 4, Fig. 1) and it may be suggested that these two arcs relate to form the same line, possibly a boundary. The fact that the ditch is found at the south end of the burial area may well reflect ancient divisions between burial and habitation areas.

Just to the north of this enclosure ditch in Area 2, two pit-like features, which did not produce any evidence of burial and may be post-holes, yielded a date of (C077) 410-370 BC (Beta 232226).

Burnt mounds

Darcystown 1 also revealed two burnt mound complexes in Areas 4 and 5, both approximately 120m south-west of Area 2. These areas were located towards the low south-west corner of the field, where the ground was marshy with an underlying marl subsoil.

Sites classified as 'burnt mounds' represent the most common field monument in the Irish archaeological record, a large majority of which are dated from *circa* 1800 to 800BC (Waddell 2000, 174, 177; Brindley and Lanting 1990).

Though the classic burnt mound complete with trough and hearth is also referred to as a *Fulacht Fiadh*, the exact meaning and translation of the Irish words is open to dispute (O'Neill 2003-4, 84) and the sites, complete or remaining only as spreads, are referred to here as 'burnt mounds'.

Despite the number of burnt mounds that have been uncovered and excavated in Ireland in recent years, these sites are by no means perfectly understood. It has been suggested that they were prehistoric cooking sites (O'Kelly 1954; ibid.1989, 223-7; Allen 1994) although other possibilities regarding function and purpose have been suggested (Ó Neill 2000 and 2003-4; O'Sullivan & Downey 2004). O Drisceoil (1988) refers to the early 17th century history of Ireland by Geoffrey Keating in which the author describes the tradition of the 'Fianna' using the troughs of the burnt mounds for both cooking and bathing. If burnt mounds had a 'bathing' function, would their use as 'steamrooms' not be suggested? If so, a structure or covering would surely be expected.

Burnt mounds were created by stones which were heated in a hearth and then immersed in a trough of water, making the water in the trough hot. Spreads of burnt stone fragments and charcoal around the trough were by-products of this process. Burnt mounds, therefore, have a number of features in common. These include fire-cracked stones which form a surrounding mound, troughs capable of holding water, hearths, and a local water source. Burnt mound material is highly distinctive, consisting of heat-shattered stones mixed with charcoal-enriched soil. Burnt mounds are classically horseshoe or *croissant*-shaped when found well preserved, as the natural method of discarding used burnt stones is to heap them up around the area of the trough, leaving room to access the trough. Burnt mounds are found up to 2m in height (Duffy and James 2000, 26).

Most burnt mounds are found after they have been levelled. Such levelled sites are only discovered when the topsoil cover is stripped, revealing evidence for the truncated burnt mound on the surface of the subsoil, and the outline of negative features, such as troughs and pits, cut into the surface of the subsoil.

The case for the presence of a burnt mound in Area 4 rests solely on thin burnt spread C123. The excavation of this material revealed just a single feature cut into the subsoil, pit C128. This feature would have filled with ground water as soon as it was dug and may be a truncated trough. It is possible that the trough was located at the southern limit of the burnt spread, and was subsequently destroyed by the digging of post-medieval linear feature C124. There was no evidence relating to a hearth in the area.

The roundwood fragments deposited in the fill of pit C128 in Area 4 suggest the possibility that the trough had a wattle lining such as that found in the trough of a burnt mound at Knock, Co. Dublin (Grogan, O'Donnell and Johnson 2007, 225) only about 1 km west of the site. Another recent example of a wattle basket-like trough comes from the burnt mound at Ballygawley found during the recent A4 Dungannon to Ballygawley, Co. Tyrone road corridor investigations (pers. comm. Paul Masser, Headland Archaeology, Ltd.). The burnt mound at Ballyvourny I, Co. Cork, had vertical stakes driven into the peat outside the edge of the trough (O'Kelly 1954, 109).

The large timber plank, C129, overlying the backfilled pit, is of interest given its broad association with the burnt spread, but it is difficult to guess what its original context and function might have been. The timber appears to have been randomly deposited on top of the pit, possibly as a result of field clearance work connected with the levelling of the mound.

Area 5 also revealed burnt mound activity. Like Area 4, the burnt spreads in Area 5 were very thinly stratified on the surface of the subsoil, indicating substantial levelling and erosion of the material through agricultural processes. However, the largest negative feature in the area, C105 (underlying spread C091) appears substantial enough to have functioned as a trough. The trough at the heart of a burnt mound can be stone-lined (O'Donovan 2002) or lined with timber planking (O'Kelly 1954, 109, 129-131) or wattle (Grogan, O'Donnell and Johnson 2007, 225) in order to increase its water-retaining capacity. Another technique utilised was to line the sides of the trough with clay to make it as watertight as possible (Duffy & James 2000, 14-5, 26-7). The trough in Area 5 is somewhat irregular in plan and depth, with some large natural boulders protruding from the sloping southern end. Some wood fragments were recorded at the southern end of the feature, but these appear associated with fill C118, and there is no suggestion that the trough was lined as such. The trough incorporates two other features of interest. One of these, C119, is a circular cut at the base of the trough. The other, C120, is a broad sloping channel adjacent to C119 in the western side of the trough. The deep C119 cut may have been dug as a sump to facilitate the supply of ground water into the base of the trough. The sloping C120 feature overhanging the sump was perhaps related to the channelling of additional water into the trough. There was no evidence for a hearth related to activity at the site. It is possible that the hearth was established at a higher level, on a ground surface subsequently removed by agricultural processes. The nearest water source was located along the field boundary at the south-west corner of the field, adjacent to Area 4 and circa 25m west of Area 5.

Radiocarbon dating has established that the burnt mounds in Areas 4 and 5 were broadly contemporary with the Late Bronze Age cremation cemetery in Areas 1 and 2. A charcoal sample from C117 of the burnt mound in Area 5, the fill of C115 (Fig. 21) produced a date of 2990±40 BP, calibrated to 1310 to 1040 BC (Beta 232227). Roundwood from the fill (C127) of the trough in Area 4 yielded a date of 2900±60 BP calibrated to 1260 to 900 BC (Beta 231997).

The other significant feature of the burnt mound in Area 5 was the evidence relating to structure/enclosure C113, the southern end of which cut burnt spread C093. The nature of this small enclosure, delimiting an area just over 5m in length north/south by just under 3m wide east/west, is strongly suggestive of a structure of some type. There is quite a wide break in the circuit to the south-west, where an entrance could have been located. If this interpretation is correct, the feature would have been a slot-trench into which panels of wattle would have been grounded to form the walls of the building. Though the curvilinear trench C113 revealed no post-holes or stake-holes, it was straight-sided and flat-based in places.

The other negative features recorded in this part of Area 5, pits C115 (from which the C14 date above was obtained), C109 and C110, all appear broadly contemporary with curvilinear trench C113.

Structures associated with burnt mounds are extremely rare. O'Neill (2003-4, 83) states that out of over 500 excavated burnt mounds, only 11 have produced structures of any kind (five timber and six stone-footed). Of these, the very well preserved burnt mound at Ballyvourney 1 (O'Kelly 1954, 126, Fig. 7) produced good evidence for a curvilinear structure

directly related to the burnt mound and associated features.

Since O'Neill's article, a burnt mound spread surrounded by stake-holes has been found in Rathpatrick, Co. Kilkenny, by Catríona Gleeson, Headland Archaeology Ltd. (Eogan 2007) and has been interpreted as a sweathouse, thus reinforcing the arguments for the use of the sites as what might be described today as steamrooms or saunas. Could this be what is meant by 'bathing' in the reference to the Fianna by Geoffrey Keating (O Drisceoil 1988) as discussed above?

Danaher in his publication on the archaeology of the N4 Sligo Inner Relief Road lists a number of Irish sites in which stake-holes (apart from stake-hole arrangements within troughs) occurred in association with burnt mounds. Examples are quoted from around the country (Danaher 2007, 39). Though these mainly do not seem to define any clear plan, they may have formed structures or windbreaks, as is suggested.

An isolated pit was found in Area 1 which yielded a date of 1670±40 BP, calibrated to AD 260-280 and AD 450-460 (Beta 232225). This date was very similar to the earliest occupation of the enclosure at Rosepark, just north of this area.

Conclusions
The site at Darcystown 1 has undoubtedly enhanced our knowledge of prehistoric activity in the area of Balrothery.

The relative proximity of burnt mounds to cremation burials is becoming more frequently noted, as indeed is the proximity of settlement to burial sites. The burnt mounds of Darcystown 1 were about 125-130m from the cremation cemetery to the north of the site. The burnt mounds and cremation burials from this site may be compared with the spatial relationship between the two burnt mounds at Priestsnewtown, Co. Wicklow, and the enclosed Late Bronze Age cremation burial group, 90m apart (Wiggins and Swift 2004).

At Kilbane, Co. Limerick, three burnt mounds were found in the vicinity of a large number of Bronze Age cremation burials (O'Callaghan 2006, 309). At Tonafortes, Co. Sligo, the Bronze Age ritual enclosure may be associated with the burnt mounds in close proximity to it (Danaher 2007, 41).

It should be noted that the proximity of burnt mounds to cremation burials may not necessarily point to a relationship. For example, a small group of Bronze Age cremation burials in Caltragh, Co. Sligo were associated with 20 stake-holes which may once have formed a structure. However, the fact that a burnt mound superimposed the stake-holes and the cremation burials suggests that their presence was forgotten by the time of the construction of the mound (Linnane 2007, 26).

The presence of possible post or wattle structures in relation to Bronze Age burial sites, in particular Late Bronze Age burial sites, has been noted above in relation to the cremation burials in this report. Such possible structures may account for the apparent lack of a barrow or ring ditch associated with the burials. Particularly in a field disturbed by cultivation, timber structures defined by post-holes or slot-trenches, would have less chance of surviving the plough or land improvements than ring ditches. Alternatively, the burial sites may have been marked by cairns.

It is interesting that two features which may be postholes have been found together north of the burial area and that one of these has produced a date of 410-370 BC (Beta 232225) which is only slightly earlier than the date from the Iron Age ring ditches from Glebe South.

The coastal Passage grave sites of Bremore, Gormanstown and Hampton Demesne only a few kilometres from Balrothery indicate the strong Early Neolithic associations of the area. In Area 2 we have seen that a large amount of Neolithic pottery and charcoal, producing a C14 date calibrated to 3700 to 3630 BC (Beta 232328), was found in an oblong pit close to a group of Late Bronze Age burials. It is not known if the oblong pit represented a burial as there was no evidence of bone, cremated or otherwise. It possible that the pit could have represented a Neolithic habitation site at the highest point of the field. In any case, the Neolithic material gives an early 4th century BC date, at least, for the earliest prehistoric settlement of Balrothery.

References

Allen, D. 1994. Hot water and plenty of it. *Archaeology Ireland*, 8 (1), 8-9.

Brindley, A. L. and Lanting J. N. 1990. The dating of fulachta fiadh. In V. Buckley (ed.), *Burnt offerings: international contributions to burnt mound archaeology*, 55-6. Dublin.

Buckley, V. (ed.) 1990. *Burnt offerings: international contributions to burnt mound archaeology*. Dublin.

Cooney, G. and Grogan, E. 1994. *Irish prehistory: a social perspective*. Wordwell, Bray, Wicklow.

Danaher, E. 2007. *Monumental beginnings: the archaeology of the N4 Sligo Inner Relief Road*. NRA Scheme Monographs 1. Dublin.

Duffy, P. and James, H.F. 2000. Flint scatters and burnt mounds: results from an archaeological watching brief on Island Magee, Count Antrim, in 1995 and 1996, Scotland to Northern Ireland Gas pipeline. *Ulster Journal of Archaeology* 59, 11-28.

Eogan, J. 2007. Cleansing body and soul? In *Seanda: the NRA archaeology magazine*, Issue 2, 38-9.

Grogan, E. 1990. Bronze Age cemetery at Carrig, Co. Wicklow. *Archaeology Ireland* 4 (4), 12-14.

Grogan, E. 2004. Middle Bronze Age burial traditions in Ireland. In H. Roche, E. Grogan, J. Bradley, J. Coles and B. Raftery (eds.), *From megaliths to metals. Essays in honour of George Eogan*, 61-71. Oxbow, Oxford.

Grogan, E., O'Donnell, L. and Johnston, P. 2007. *The Bronze Age landscapes of the pipeline to the west-an integrated archaeological and environmental assessment.* Wordwell, Bray, Wicklow.

Grogan, E. and Roche, H. 2004a. The prehistoric pottery from Site 6b, Priestsnewtown, Greystones, Co. Wicklow (04E0401). Unpublished report for Judith Carroll & Co. Ltd.

Grogan, E. and Roche, H. 2004b. The prehistoric pottery from Kilbane, Castletroy, Co. Limerick. Unpublished report for Eachtra Archaeology Ltd.

Hagen, I. 2004. 'Kilgobbin'. In I. Bennett (ed.), *Excavations: summary acccounts of archaeological excavations in Ireland 2002*. Wordwell, Bray, Wicklow.

Halliday, S. and Hamill, J. 2003. Skerries Road, Balrothery, Co. Dublin: results of an archaeological assessment. Licence no. 03E0067. Unpublished report by Judith Carroll & Co. Ltd. National Monuments Service, Department of the Environment, Heritage and Local Government.

Linnane, S.J. 2007. Area 1D excavation text March 2005. In E. Danaher, *Monumental beginnings: the archaeology of the N4 Sligo Inner Relief Road*. NRA Scheme Monographs 1, Dublin.

O' Callaghan, N. 2006. Kilbane, Castletroy (no. 1151). In I. Bennett (ed.), *Excavations: summary* acccounts of archaeological excavations in Ireland 2003. Wordwell, Bray, Wicklow.

O'Donovan, E. 2002. Shannakea Beg, Co. Clare. Gas pipeline to the West. Excavation report. Licence no. 02E0087. Unpublished report by Margaret Gowen and Co. Ltd. for Bord Gáis Éireann. National Monuments Service, Department of the Environment, Heritage and Local Government.

O'Drisceoil, D. 1998. Bunt mounds: cooking or bathing? *Antiquity* 62, 671-80.

O'Kelly, M.J. 1954. Excavations and experiments in ancient Irish cooking places. *Journal of the Royal Society of Antiquaries of Ireland* 84, 105-155.

O'Kelly, M.J. 1989. *Early Ireland; an introduction to Irish prehistory.* Cambridge University Press.

O' Neill, J. 2000. Just another fulachta fiadh story. *Archaeology Ireland* 18 (1), 35-7.

O' Neill, J 2003-4. Lapidibus in igne calefactis coquebatur: The historical burnt mound tradition. *Journal of Irish Archaeology* XII and XIII, 79-86.

O'Sullivan, M. and Downey, L. 2004. Fulachta fiadh. *Archaeology Ireland* 18, no.1 (issue no. 67), 35-7.

Raftery, B. 1973. A Late Bronze Age Burial in Ireland. *Antiquity* 47, 293-5.

Tobin, S., Swift., D., Wiggins, K., 2004. Greystones Southern Access Route (GSAR), Co. Wicklow. Sites 6/6a–g, Priestsnewtown. Excavation report. Licence no. 04E0401. Unpublished report by Judith Carroll & Co. Ltd. for Wicklow County Council. National Monuments Service, Department of the Environment, Heritage and Local Government.

Waddell, J. 2000. *The prehistoric archaeology of Ireland.* Wordwell, Bray, Wicklow.

Wiggins, K. 2003. Darcystown, Skerries road, Balrothery, Co. Dublin. Excavation report. Licence no. 03E0067 (ext). Unpublished report by Judith Carroll & Co. Ltd. for Fingal County Council. National Monuments Service, Department of the Environment, Heritage and Local Government.

Wiggins, K. and Swift, D. 2004. Greystones Southern Access Route (GSAR), Co. Wicklow. Kilpedder East, Priestsnewtown, Farrankelly. Monitoring report. Licence no. 04E0128. Unpublished report by Judith Carroll & Co. Ltd. for Wicklow County Council. National Monuments Service, Department of the Environment, Heritage and Local Government.

APPENDIX I

RADIOCARBON RESULTS FROM DARCYSTOWN 1, BALROTHERY, CO. DUBLIN (03E0067)

Beta analytic

Feature	Sample (site)	Description	Material	Sample (lab)	Results code	2 sigma calibration
C023	003	Fill of pit C024	Charcoal	232225	1670 ± 40 BP	260-280 & 450-460 cal. AD
C077	023	Fill of pit C078	Charcoal	232226	2350 ± 40 BP	410-370 cal. BC
C117	038	Fill of pit C115	Charcoal	232227	2990 ± 40 BP	1310-1040 cal. BC
C042	024	Fill of pit C010	Charcoal	232328	4860 ± 40 BP	3700-3630 cal. BC
C127	043	Fill of pit C128	Wood	239117	2900 ± 60 BP	1260-900 cal. BC
C041	001	Fill of pit C009	Charcoal	244076	2770 ± 40 BP	1010-820 cal. BC

APPENDIX II

ANALYSIS OF CHARCOAL FROM DARCYSTOWN 1, SKERRIES ROAD, BALROTHERY (03E0067)

Ellen O'Carroll

Introduction

Eight charcoal samples from archaeological investigations at Darcystown, Skerries Road, Balrothery were analysed in respect of suitability for dating and species selection in association with the excavated features. The sites consisted of a series of cremation pits, pits associated with prehistoric pottery sherds and vessels, undiagnostic pits and burnt mound spreads with associated pits. The charcoal assemblage, although as yet undated, is probably associated with the later prehistoric period (Bronze Age).

The charcoal was sent for species identification prior to 14C dating, and also to obtain an indication of the range of tree species which grew in the area, as well as the utilization of these species for various functions. Wood used for fuel at prehistoric sites would generally have been sourced at locations close to the site. Therefore charcoal identifications may, but do not necessarily, reflect the composition of the local woodlands. Larger pieces of charcoal, when identified, can provide information regarding the use of a species.

TABLE 1 WOOD SPECIES IDENTIFICATION AND ANALYSIS OF SAMPLES

Results

Area	Context no	Sample	Species	Comment	Weight	Site type
1	22	2	Pomoideae (1g) 3 fragments, Alder (6g) 10 fragments, Blackthorn (3.3g) 6 fragments.	Alder is quite rooty and was hard to id.	10.3g	Isolated pit (C024)
1	23	3	Blackthorn (7.7g) 10 fragments, Pomoideae (3.7g) 4 fragments. Alder (1g) and hazel (0.8g) present.	Blackthorn and Pomoideae, fine for conventional dating.	13.2g	Isolated pit (C024)
2	42	24	Oak (6g) 12 fragments, Alder (5g) 15 fragments, Pomoideae (0.6g) 3 fragments, Ash (0.7g) 4 fragments, Alder buckthorn (1 fragment- 0.2g).		12.5g	Fill of pit containing prehistoric pottery (C010)
2	49	10	Alder (0.2g) 2 fragments	Remaining sample is clay and stone. AMS dating..	0.2g	Fill of cremation pit (C029)
2	77	23	Hazel (3g) 12 fragments, Alder (4g) 10 fragments, Pomoideae (3g) 6 fragments.	Clay extracted from sample.	10g	Fill of pit (C078)
5	117	38	Ash (15 g) 12 fragments, Alder (5g) 8 fragments.	Partially crystallised. Insect channels in ash. Also iron staining.	20g	Fill of pit (C115)
6	73	29	No charcoal	Clay and stone	–	Fill of pit (C072)
6	75	33	Alder (0.1g) 3 fragments	Extracted from stone sample. AMS dating	0.1g	Fill of pit (C074)

Pomoideae (apple type) includes crab apple, wild pear, hawthorn and mountain ash.

Table 2 Species represented in the identified samples

Botanical name	Species	Weight
Alnus glutinisa	Alder	21.3g
Corylus avellana	Hazel	3.8g
Fraxinus excelsior	Ash	15.7g
Pomoideae	Apple, Mountain ash, Hawthorn	10.7g
Prunus spinosa	Blackthorn	11g
Quercus sp	Oak	6g
Frangula alnus	Alder Buckthorn	0.2g

Methodology

The process for identifying wood, whether it is charred, dried or waterlogged is carried out by comparing the anatomical structure of wood samples with known comparative material or keys (Schweingruber 1990). The identification of charcoal material involves breaking the charcoal piece so as a clean section of the wood can be obtained. This charcoal is then identified to species under an Olympus stereomicroscope with a magnification of 200. By close examination of the microanatomical features of the samples, the species were determined. The diagnostic features used for the identification of charcoal are micro-structural characteristics such as the vessels and their arrangement, the size and arrangement of rays, vessel pit arrangement and also the type of perforation plates.

Figure 1 Wood species identifications from all analysed samples

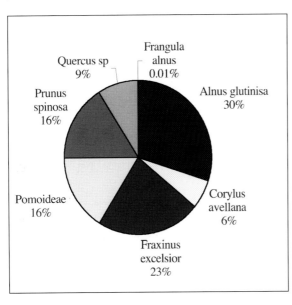

Quantification

The identifications were completed by weight and fragment count. The charcoal fragments from similar species were grouped together and then counted and weighed (Tables 1 and 2).

Discussion

There are seven taxa present in the charcoal remains. Species identified from the features analysed included large (oak, ash) and smaller (alder & hazel) trees and some hedgerow and shrubby trees (pomoideae, blackthorn & alder buckthorn). The charcoal was, for the most part, extracted from undiagnostic pits. Therefore, it was difficult to determine a function and use for the identified charcoal. The charcoal may simply represent kindling used for various functions at the site and does not appear to be associated with ant structural requirements.

Large quantities of alder were identified from all pits (**C022, C023, C042, C049, C075, C077 & C117**) analysed. Alder (*Alnus glutinosa*) is a widespread native tree and occurs in wet habitats along streams and riverbanks. Alder grows regularly on fen peat. It is an easily worked and split timber and does not tear when worked. Alder is commonly identified from wood remains associated with wet/boggy areas.

A small amount of hazel (*Corylus avellana*) was identified from the isolated pit **C024** and the fill of pit **C078**. Hazel was very common up to the end of the 17th century and was used for the manufacture of many wooden structures such as wattle walls, posts, trackways, and baskets. McCracken (1971, 19) points out that 'it was once widespread to a degree that is hard to imagine today'. With the introduction of brick, steel and slate the crafts associated with hazel became obsolete, and today the woods that supplied hazel have diminished rapidly. Hazel is normally only about 3-5m in height and is often found as an understory tree in deciduous woods dominated by oak. It also occurs as pure copses on shallow soils over limestone as in the Burren in Co. Clare and survives for 30 to 50 years. Its main advantage is seen in the production of long flexible straight rods through the process known as coppicing.

Ash (*Fraxinus excelsior*) was identified from the pit containing prehistoric pottery **C010** and the fill of pit **C115**. Ash timber is considered to be excellent fuel and its charcoal is held in high esteem. It is a native species preferring lime-rich freely draining soils. It is not very durable in waterlogged conditions but has a strong elastic nature. It is easily worked and lends itself well to a range of different requirements like the turning of wooden bowls.

Blackthorn was exclusively identified from the pit **C024**. Blackthorn (*Prunus spinosa*) is a thorny shrub or small tree of 1-4 metres height. It often has more than one main stem, due to the rapid spread of the roots and the growth of suckers from these roots. The Blackthorn is possibly one of the most common European shrubs and will grow on most soils, except for wet and acid peat-bogs. It thrives in hedges, in clearings, on the edges of woodlands, on the edges of neglected farmland, on dry slopes and waste land All parts of the tree are good firewood and make a hot, blazing fire.

Pomoideae, which was identified from the samples taken from pits **C024, C010** and **C078**, includes apple, pear, hawthorn and mountain ash. It is impossible to distinguish these wood species anatomically but, as wild pear is not native and crab apple is a rare native species to Ireland, it is likely that the species identified from Darcystown are hawthorn or mountain ash (rowan) (Nelson 194-200, 1993). Hawthorn (*Crataegus monogyna*) is a native species, and is found in many hedgerows throughout Ireland. Mountain ash (*Sorbus aucuparia*) is also a common tree to Ireland growing particularly well in rocky and hilly mountainous places.

Oak (*Quercus sp.*) was only prevalent in the fill of pit **C010** which contained Neolithic pottery. Oak is a dense wood and is very suitable for charcoal production. It also makes good firewood when dried and will grow in wetland areas when conditions are dry. Oak also has unique properties of great durability and strength. Sessile oak (*Quercus petraea*) and pedunculate oak (*Quercus robur*) are both native to and common in Ireland. The wood of these species cannot be differentiated based on its microstructure. Pendunculate oak is found on heavy clays and loams particularly where the soil is of alkaline pH. Sessile oak is found on acid soils often in pure stands and although it thrives on well-drained soils it is also tolerant of flooding (Beckett 1979, 40-41). Both species of oak grow to be very large trees (30-40m) and can live to an age of about 400 years.

The oak identified suggests that there was a supply of oak in the surrounding environment at the time of use of **C010**.

Alder buckthorn (*Frangula alnus*), which was identified from **C042**, is a small deciduous shrub up to 4-5 m in height, with wide-spreading branches. It is found on moist acid soils along riversides and on peat.

Comparative material

The absence of oak charcoal from the samples identified is surprising as oak charcoal has been identified from the majority of cremation pits identified by the author throughout the country. The absence of oak may be associated with the fact that these sites were cremation deposits associated with urns and vessels rather than simple pits. Charcoal identifications at Priestsnewtown, GSAR, Co. wicklow (04E0401), which yielded a similar assemblage of urns and vessels associated with cremation pits, produced largely ash charcoal from their identifications which is indicative of ash fuel being used in association with the ritual burnings rather than oak.

The author has carried out a large number of charcoal identifications from excavated *fulachta fiadh* or burnt mound sites similar to what was excavated in Area 5. A range of species is generally identified from these cooking places. Alder (*Alnus glutinosa*) is generally the most dominant species identified from excavated *fulachta fiadh* along with ash, hazel and oak which are represented among these assemblages.

Conclusions

Seven taxa were identified from the four areas investigated. The local environment of the sites included a variety of different habitats, although alder is more prevalent than any other species, which indicates access to wet marginal land. The ash, hazel and oak would have grown in drier conditions, preferring free-draining soils and nutrient rich clays. Alder indicates local wet condition along river banks or peat bogs.

The hawthorn/mountain ash and blackthorn identified at Darcystown 1 are indicative of those species, which may have grown locally in hedgerows or as scrub nearby to the sites.

It is surprising that oak was not identified from the cremation pits, as oak is normally associated with cremation burials throughout Ireland. The absence of large quantities of oak may be indicative of oak trees being rare from this area during the time of use of the site. This pattern is also reflected in pollen research conducted at various sites throughout Ireland where oak, along with elm woodlands, were prevalent in the earlier periods – to be replaced by ash in the woodland clearings created by the first farmers (Hall and Pilcher 2001, 35).

It is difficult to attribute a use to the remaining six species (alder, ash, blackthorn, pomoideae, alder buckthorn and hazel) identified above, but they may have simply been used for fuel and were collected from close to the site. Alder and ash are generally associated with *fulachta fiadh* sites as seen in Area 5, **C117**, Darcystown 1, Skerries Road, Balrothery.

References

Beckett, J.K. 1979. *Planting Native Trees and Shrubs*. Jarrold & Sons Ltd. Norwich.

Pilcher J.P. and Hall, V.H. 2001, *Flora Hibernica*. The Collins Press, Cork.

O Carroll, E. 2005. Analysis of charcoal remains from Priestnewtown, Greystones Southern Access Route (GSAR), for Judith Carroll and Co. Ltd.

O Carroll, E. 2003. Analysis of charcoal remains from Hardwood 1, Co. Meath, for ACS Ltd.

O Carroll, E. 2006. Analysis of charcoal remains from the Charlestown by-pass A022 for Mayo County Council.

McCraken, E. 1971. *The Irish woods since Tudor times, their distribution and exploitation*. Institute of Irish Studies, Belfast.

Nelson E.C. 1993. *Trees of Ireland*. The Lilliput Press, Dublin.

Warner, R.B. 1987. A proposed adjustment for the 'Old-Wood Effect'. In W. Mook and H. Waterbolk (eds.). *Proceedings 2nd Symposium of 14C & Archaeology, Groningen*, 29, 159-172.

Webb, D.A. 1977. *An Irish Flora*. Dundalgan Press Ltd, Dundalk.

Schweingruber, F.H. 1990. *Microscopic Wood Anatomy*. 3rd edition. Birmensdorf: Swiss Federal Institute for Forest, Snow and Landscape Research.

APPENDIX III

THE PREHISTORIC POTTERY ASSEMBLAGE FROM DARCYSTOWN 1, BALROTHERY, CO. DUBLIN (03E0067/03E0067 extension)

Eoin Grogan and Helen Roche

Summary
The site produced sherds from at least two Middle Neolithic vessels, a broad-rimmed bowl and a plain globular bowl (nos. 8–9), as well as the substantial remains of eight Late Bronze Age domestic vessels (nos. 1–7 and 10) from a cremation pit cemetery. The latter contained cremations and were placed upright in pits.

The Middle Neolithic
This assemblage consisted of 36 sherds (4 rim and 32 bodysherds, plus 11 fragments; total weight: 945g) representing the remains of at least two Middle Neolithic vessels (Nos 8–9). Both vessels are of fine, well-fired, red-buff fabric with inclusions of crushed coarse-grained quartzitic granite. Vessel 8 is a large broad-rimmed bowl. These are generally deep hemispherical bowls with broad flat, or gently curved, heavy 'club' rims and occasionally a short, frequently constricted (cavetto), neck (Case 1961: 'Dundrum bowls'; Herity 1982: 'Broad-Rimmed Vessels'); the rim top often has a pronounced outward expansion that projects over the wall. Decoration is common on the rim top but less so on the remainder of the pot. While they are found in a wide variety of sites the majority of this pottery type has come from domestic contexts.

Plate 1: Area 1: pit C024, half sectioned, facing north-west

Plate 2: Area 2: cremation pit C027, containing intact upright vessel, facing north-east

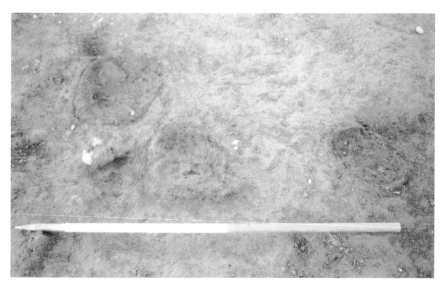

Plate 3: Area 2: cremation pit group C082, C084 and C088, each pit containing an upright cremation vessel, facing north-east

Plate 4: Area 2: pit C010, half-sectioned, facing south

Plate 5: Area 2: view of section of linear feature, C030, facing north-west

Plate 6: Area 3: post-excavation view of pits C066 and C067, facing east

Plate 7: Area 4: pre-excavation view of burnt spread, C123, facing north-east

Plate 8: Area 4: view of area following excavation of burnt spread, C123, facing south-east

Plate 9: Area 4: timber, C129, overlaying pit, C128, facing south-east

Plate 10: Area 5: pre-excavation view of burnt spreads, C091, C1092 and C093, facing north-north-east

Plate 11: Area 5: detail of timber fragments at the southern end of trough, C105, facing south

Plate 12: Area 5: post-excavation view of trough, C105, facing south

Plate 13: Area 5: pit C115, half-sectioned, facing north

Plate 14: Area 5: post-excavation view of ring-gully, C112

Plate 15: Area 6: pre-excavation view of cremation pit, C072. Part of the feature, along the right-hand edge of the picture, was destroyed by a plough furrow, facing south.

Plate 16: Neolithic pottery from Area 2, C071

Plate 17: Neolithic pottery from Area 2, C071

Plate 18: Neolithic pottery from Area 2, C071

Plate 19: Base of Late Bronze Age cremation urn, from cremation pit, Co45, Area 2

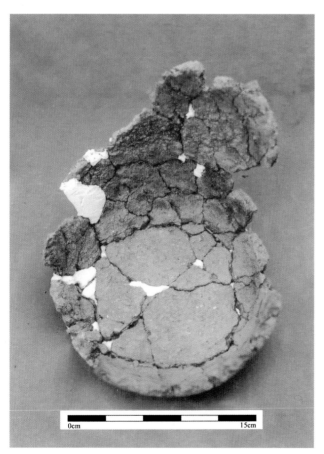

Plate 20: Late Bronze Age cremation urn from cremation
pit, Co84, Area 2

Plate 21: Late Bronze Age cremation urn from
cremation pit, Coo9, Area 2

Plate 22: Late Bronze Age cremation urn from cremation pit, C036, Area 2

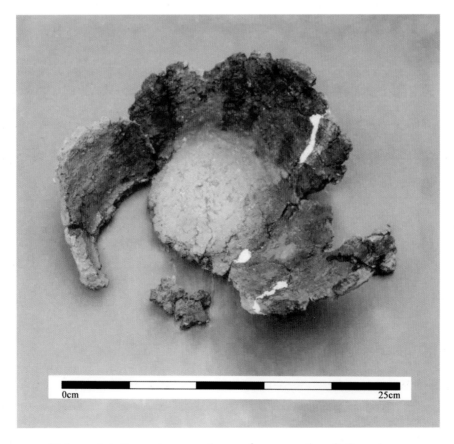

Plate 23: Late Bronze Age cremation urn from cremation pit, C027, Area 2

Close parallels occur on several sites in the region including Balregan and Townleyhall 2, Co. Louth (Ó Donnchadha 2003; Grogan and Roche 2005; Eogan 1963, 51–2, pot 3, Fig. 6), Murlough ('Dundrum Sandhills'1, see Herity 1982, Fig. 62.1–3; Case 1961, Fig. 16.1) and Ballyalton, Co. Down (Evans and Davies 1934, see Herity 1982, Fig. 43.2), Dalkey Island Site 5 and Newtown Little, Stepaside, Co. Dublin (Liversage 1968, 67–8, Pl. 2, p26, p27; Herity 1982, Fig. 66.2; Phelan 2005; Grogan and Roche 2006), and Knowth, Co. Meath (Eogan and Roche 1997, 75–7, Figs. 16.v 11, 17. v 17). Rim decoration consists of various motifs including circumferential, radial and oblique lines (incised or of cord), often in combination, as well as small circular dots and bird bone impressions. Outside the region a number of comparisons can be made with, for example, the vessel from the eponymous megalithic tomb at Linkardstown, Co. Carlow (Raftery 1944), and the rim forms and decoration of the modified carinated bowls from the Lough Gur area. Expanded rims, often of 'club' form, are a feature of the Lough Gur material (Ó Ríordáin 1954: 'Class 1a'; Case 1961: 'Limerick Style') although they occur on carinated vessels; there are both decorated and plain examples (Ó Ríordáin 1954, 326–33, Figs. 11–14, 33, Pls 29–30). The rim decoration, which is occasionally mirrored immediately beneath the shoulder, consists of largely incised lines (circumferential, radial, oblique) often combined to form lattice or herringbone patterns. Decorated carinated bowls with club, expanded or T-shaped rims also occur in the north-east at Ballyreagh, Co. Fermanagh (Davies 1942), Goodland, Co. Antrim (Case 1961, Fig. 15.1), and Tamnyrankin, Co. Derry (Herring 1941), and in less elaborate form amongst the modified carinated bowl tradition (Case 1961, Fig. 7: 'Lyles Hill style').

Current evidence indicates that broad-rimmed bowls were current c. 3500–3300 cal. BC. While this type of pottery, or closely related material, has come from widely distributed sites, there is a major concentration in the area of north Leinster/south-east Ulster and the Darcystown vessel is towards the southern edge of the main concentration (see Grogan and Roche 2005, Figs. 3–4). At a wider level there is a significant Irish Sea context with similar material occurring in western Scotland from the Hebrides and Skye down to the Clyde region, to the Isle of Man and further south into Wales (e.g. Gibson 1995). The importance of this context is the widespread emergence, before c. 3650 BC, of an Impressed Ware tradition in Ireland and Britain within which there were a number of important regional variations (Gibson 2002; Grogan and Roche 2005).

Vessel 9 is a smaller simple bowl of a general type (Case 1961: 'Sandhills Ware: Goodland bowls'; Herity 1982: 'Globular bowls') with a distribution concentrated in east Ulster and especially in counties Antrim, Tyrone and Derry but there are examples to the south of this area at Balregan, Ballyalton, Dundrum Sandhills and the court tomb at Clontygora, Co. Armagh (Davies and Patterson 1936–37), and they have a wide range of associations with other decorated pottery types. Decoration is frequently confined to the upper part of these vessels and plain examples are rare but occur at Kiltiernan, Co. Dublin, and Dundrum Sandhills, Co. Down (see Herity 1982, Figs. 36.14, 64.12).

The Late Bronze Age

This assemblage contains the remains of eight Late Bronze Age vessels (Nos 1–7 and 10); all of these are domestic flat bottomed coarse pots re-used in burial contexts. The Darcystown vessels all contained cremations and were placed upright in pits forming an apparently unmarked extended cemetery. It appears that later agricultural activity, probably ploughing, resulted in the removal of the upper portions of all seven. Only the base and lowermost part of Vessels 1, 2, 3 and 5 survived while substantial portions of the bodies of Nos 4 and 7 were preserved; only a small upper portion of No. 6 was removed while only a few sherds of No. 10 were recovered. Very few other sherds, and no rimsherds, were recovered although the lower parts of Nos 1 and 4–7 were only slightly damaged: this suggests a single episode of destruction that removed the upper parts of the pots but also caused the collapse of earth into the cremation pits, sealing, and offering further protection to, the pots. Vessel 3 suffered collapse, apparently after the initial damage, which resulted in the pot walls being forced outwards into the pit cavity. All of the pots were further affected by extensive root and water action causing splitting of the walls and erosion to the pot surfaces.

While there is some variation in the form, quality and size, the assemblage is reasonably homogenous and, from a ceramic perspective, the material appears to be contemporary. Despite the damage and environmental attrition, the pottery is, in general, in good condition. The Darcystown assemblage is made up of domestic pottery derived ultimately from settlement contexts. The fabric is similar in all of the pots. Local clays were combined with inclusions of crushed dolerite and occasionally quartzite and small, water-rolled, sandstone pebbles; generally these were ≤ 5mm in maximum dimensions although occasionally larger pieces up to 14mm in length are present. The pottery is well-fired and compact with a generally hard smooth finish. The outer surfaces of nos. 1–5 were smoothed over with a fine paste or slurry prior to drying and subsequent firing while the surfaces of nos. 6–7 were wetted and smoothed. Generally the Darcystown pottery is of medium to good quality within the overall Late Bronze Age range. Vessels 1, 3, 6 and 7 have unusually thin walls (8.8–11mm) and nos. 6 and 7 are of very fine quality. Apart from nos. 4 (which has no surviving internal surface), 5 and 10, which may have been unused prior to deposition, the pots display clear evidence, in the form of internal sooting or blackening, for prolonged domestic use. Coil breaks survive along the surviving top of Vessel 6 and it is probable that all of the pots were coil built. An interesting, and unusual, feature of the construction of the Darcystown 1 pots is the use of a narrow base plate around which the lowermost portion of the body was positioned. The attachment of the body to the base has resulted in a distinctive broad, irregular channel around the internal circumference of the bases of Vessels 2–4 where the clay was pressed in to form a firm connection. The bases are generally simple angular junctions but Vessels 1, 2 and 7 have a low vertical foot.

In the absence of rims, or the upper part of any vessel, it is difficult to determine the exact form of any of the Darcystown pots. However, some estimation is possible for nos. 5–7 as more

substantial portions of these survive. No. 6, the most complete example, appears to have been a relatively short pot (c. 25cm high) with a biconical profile similar to, but larger than, vessels from Priestsnewtown and Carrig, Co. Wicklow, and Kilbane, Co. Limerick (Fig. 1.B, C, E and F; Tobin et al. 2004; Grogan 1990; O'Callaghan 2006; Grogan and Roche 2004a; 2004b).

Vessels 5 and 7 are similar: the lower body is straight and expands gently from the base but above this it swells out into a more rounded profile. These are similar to vessels from Lough Gur Site C (Ó Ríordáin 1954, Fig. 16.2) and Kilbane, Co. Limerick (Grogan and Roche 2004b) (Fig. 1.A and D); Darcystown No. 7, with a base diameter of 16.8cm, is probably about the same size (30cm in height and 28cm in diameter at the rim). Vessel 5, 19.5cm in diameter at the base, was probably larger. Although only the lower 12cm of nos. 1 and 3 survived they may also be very similar vessels with base diameters of 19cm and 13.8cm respectively.

At a more general level the Darcystown 1 pots compare closely with the assemblage of five upright vessels in pits associated with a ringditch at Priestsnewtown (Tobin et al. 2004; Grogan and Roche 2004a). The fabric, firing and finish of these vessels is very similar to that at Darcystown 1 which, despite the particular damage to the upper portions of the pots, may also have had similar forms. At Kilbane both upright and inverted domestic vessels occurred in unenclosed cremation pits in close proximity to a contemporary ring ditch (O'Callaghan 2006; Grogan and Roche 2004b).

The regional context

During the Middle Bronze Age coarse domestic vessels, both inverted and upright, enter the burial record and by c. 1500–1200 BC had completely replaced cinerary urns (Grogan 2004). During the Late Bronze Age these burials occur in flat cemeteries, cairns and ringditches such as Kilbane, Carrig, Tankardstown South and Circle P, Lough Gur, Co. Limerick (Gowen and Tarbett 1988; Grogan and Eogan 1987), Knockaholet, Co. Antrim (Henry 1934), and Priestsnewtown. There are also a large number of apparently isolated burials of this type including Athgarret, Co. Kildare, and Kilgobbin, Co. Dublin (Sleeman and Cleary 1987; Hagen 2004). The Darcystown cemetery forms part of an important funerary landscape that includes ringditches at Darcystown Site 2 (04E0741), and Glebe South (ring ditches 1 and 2, 04E0680) (Carroll 2004; Ryan 2005). This forms part of a growing distribution of Late Bronze Age settlement, funerary and ritual sites in the

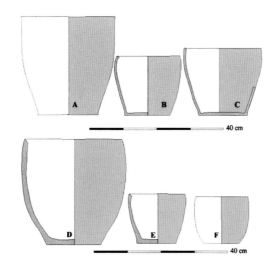

Figure 1: Comparative vessels for the Darcystown 1 assemblage. **A** and **F**: Kilbane, Co. Limerick (Grogan and Roche 2004b); **B** and **C**: Priestsnewtown, Co. Wicklow (Grogan and Roche 2004a); **D**: Lough Gur Site C (Ó Ríordáin 1954, Fig. 16.2); **E**: Carrig, Co. Wicklow (Grogan 1990).

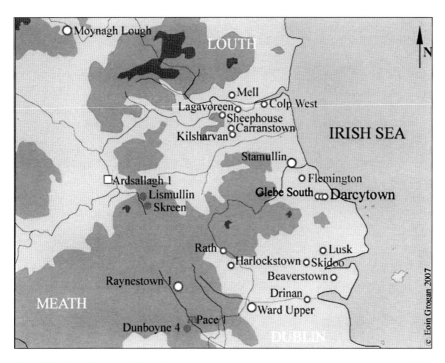

Fig. 2 The distribution of Late Bronze Age pottery in the Darcystown region of north Dublin, east Meath and south Louth

north Leinster area (Fig. 2). At a wider regional scale Late Bronze Age coarse ware comparable to that from Darcystown has also been found on settlement sites such as the hillforts at Freestone Hill, Co. Kilkenny (Raftery 1969, 86–96), and Rathgall, Co. Wicklow (Raftery 1976; 1995). Pottery of this type has been very securely dated at Rathgall, Haughey's Fort, Co. Armagh (Mallory 1995), and Mooghaun South, Co. Clare (Grogan 2005), to between 1100 BC and 800 BC. Dates from two of the burials at Priestsnewtown of 1300–1030 and 1490–1120 cal. BC (Beta–209723 and Beta–209722) suggest that plain coarse vessels were already current by c. 1300–1200 BC.

References

Carroll, J. 2004. The Excavation of a ring ditch at Darcystown 2, Balrothery, Co. Dublin (04E0741). Unpublished report by Judith Carroll and Company for Fingal County Council. National Monuments Service, Department of the Environment, Heritage and Local Government.

Case, H. 1961. Irish Neolithic Pottery: Distribution and Sequence. *Proceedings of the Prehistoric Society* 9, 174–233.

Davies, O. 1942. Excavations at Ballyreagh, Fermanagh, *Ulster Journal of Archaeology* 5, 78–89.

Davies, O. and Patterson, T.G.F. 1936–7. Excavations at Clontygora Large Cairn, Co. Armagh. *Proceedings and Reports of the Belfast Natural History and Philosophical Society*, 20–42.

Eogan, G. 1963. A Neolithic habitation site and megalithic tomb in Townleyhall townland, Co. Louth. *Journal of the Royal Society of Antiquaries of Ireland* 93, 37–81.

Eogan, G. and Roche, H. 1997. *Excavations at Knowth 2*. Royal Irish Academy Monographs in Archaeology, Dublin.

Evans, E.E. and Davies, O. 1934. Excavation of a chambered horned cairn at Ballyalton, Co. Down. *Proceedings of the Belfast Natural Historical and Philosophical Society* 1933–34, 79–104.

Gibson, A. 1995. First impressions: a review of Peterborough Ware in Wales. In I. Kinnes and G. Varndell (eds.), *Unbaked Urns of Rudely Shape*, 23–39. Oxbow Monograph 55, Oxford.

Gibson, A. 2002. *Prehistoric Pottery in Britain and Ireland*. Tempus, Stroud.

Gowen, M. and Tarbett, C. 1988. A Third Season at Tankardstown, *Archaeology Ireland* 8, 156.
Grogan, E. 1990. Bronze Age Cemetery at Carrig, Co.

Wicklow. *Archaeology Ireland* 16, 12–14.

Grogan, E. 2004. Middle Bronze Age burial traditions in Ireland. In H. Roche, E. Grogan, J. Bradley, J. Coles and B. Raftery (eds.), *From Megaliths to Metals. Essays in Honour of George Eogan*, 61–71. Oxbow, Oxford.

Grogan, E. 2005. *The later prehistoric landscape of south-east Clare*. Discovery Programme Monograph 6, Volume 1. The Discovery Programme/Wordwell, Bray, Wicklow.

Grogan, E. and Eogan, G. 1987. Lough Gur excavations by Seán P. Ó Ríordáin: further Neolithic and Beaker habitations on Knockadoon. *Proceedings of the Royal Irish Academy* 87C, 299–506.

Grogan, E. and Roche, H. 2004a. The prehistoric pottery from Site 6B, Priestsnewtown, Greystones, Co. Wicklow. Unpublished report for Judith Carroll and Company.

Grogan, E. and Roche, H. 2004b. The prehistoric pottery from Kilbane, Castletroy, Co. Limerick. Unpublished Report for Eachtra Archaeology Ltd.

Grogan, E. and Roche, H. 2005. The prehistoric pottery from Balregan 1, Co. Louth (03E0157). Unpublished Report for Irish Archaeological Consultancy Ltd.

Grogan, E. and Roche, H. 2006. The prehistoric pottery assemblage from Newtown Little, Stepaside, Co. Dublin (05E0665). Unpublished report for Margaret Gowen and Co. Ltd.

Hagen, I. 2004. Kilgobbin, Co. Dublin. Bronze Age cremation burials. In I. Bennett (ed.) *Excavations 2002*, 166. Wordwell, Bray, Wicklow.

Henry, S. 1934. A Find of Prehistoric Pottery at Knockaholet, Parish of Loughguile, Co. Antrim. *Journal of the Royal Society of Antiquaries of Ireland* 64, 264–5.

Herity, M. 1982. Irish Decorated Neolithic Pottery. *Proceedings of the Royal Irish Academy* 82C, 10–404.

Herring, I. 1941. The Tamnyrankin Cairn: west structure. *Journal of the Royal Society of Antiquaries of Ireland* 71, 31–52.

Liversage, G.D. 1968. Excavations at Dalkey Island, Co. Dublin, 1956–1959. *Proceedings of the Royal Irish Academy* 66C, 53–233.

Mallory, J. 1995. Haughey's Fort and the Navan Complex in the Late Bronze Age. In J. Waddell and E. Shee Twohig (eds.), *Ireland in the Bronze Age*, 73–89. Stationery Office, Dublin.

Ó Donnchadha, B. 2003. M1 Dundalk Western Bypass. Site 116, Balregan 1 and 2. Unpublished Report for Irish Archaeological Consultancy Ltd. National Monuments Service, Department of the Environment, Heritage and Local Government.

O'Callaghan, N. 2006. Kilbane, Castletroy, Bronze Age flat cemetery and *fulachta fiadh*. In I. Bennett (ed.), *Excavations 2003*, 309–10. Wordwell, Bray.

Ó Ríordáin, S.P. 1954. Lough Gur Excavations: Neolithic and Bronze Age Houses on Knockadoon. *Proceedings of the Royal Irish Academy* 56C, 297–459.

Phelan, S. 2005. Archaeological Excavation Report. Newtown Little, Stepaside, County Dublin (05E0665). Unpublished Report for Margaret Gowen and Co. Ltd. National Monuments Service, Department of the Environment, Heritage and Local Government.

Raftery, B. 1969. Freestone Hill, Co. Kilkenny: an Iron Age hillfort and Bronze Age cairn. *Proceedings of the Royal Irish Academy* 68C, 1–108.

Raftery, B. 1976. Rathgall and Irish Hillfort Problems. In D. Harding (ed.), *Hillforts: later prehistoric earthworks in Britain and Ireland*, 339–357. Academic Press, London.

Raftery, B. 1995. The conundrum of Irish Iron Age pottery. In B. Raftery (ed.), *Sites and Sights of the Iron Age*, 149–156. Oxbow Monograph 56, Oxford.

Raftery, J. 1944. A Neolithic burial in Co. Carlow. *Journal of the Royal Society of Antiquaries of Ireland* 74, 61–2.

Ryan, F. 2005. Excavations at Glebe South, Balrothery, Co. Dublin (04E0680). Unpublished report by Judith Carroll and Company for Fingal County Council. National Monuments Service, Department of the Environment, Heritage and Local Government.

Sleeman, M. and Cleary, R. 1987. Pottery from Athgarret, Co. Kildare. In R. Cleary, M. Hurley and E. Twohig (eds.), *Archaeological Excavations on the Cork–Dublin Gas Pipeline*, 43–44. Cork Archaeological Studies 1, Cork.

Tobin, S., Swift, D. and Wiggins, K. 2004. Greystones Southern Access Route (GSAR), Co. Wicklow. Sites 6/6a-g, Priestsnewtown. Excavation report. Licence no. 04E0401. Unpublished report by Judith Carroll and Company for Wicklow County Council. National Monuments Service, Department of the Environment, Heritage and Local Government.

Wiggins, K. 2006. Skerries Road, Balrothery. Bronze Age cremation cemetery. In I. Bennett (ed.), *Excavations 2003*, 107. Wordwell, Bray.

CATALOGUE

Where the pottery is listed in the catalogue the context numbers are in bold: *e.g.*: **71**.13. Numbers in square brackets (*e.g.* **71**.[12a–c]) indicate that the sherds are conjoined. The thickness refers to an average dimension; where relevant a thickness range is indicated. Vessel numbers have been allocated to all individual pots. In the Catalogue the excavation number 03E0067 is omitted throughout.
R = rimsherd   B = bodysherd

The Middle Neolithic pottery

Context 71
Vessel 8. A substantial portion of a Middle Neolithic broad rimmed bowl was recovered. This is represented by 30 sherds (3 rim- and 27 bodysherds: **71**.[R.1, 5, B.2a–d, 3a–b, 6, 9], R.4, B.7–8, 11, [12a–c], 14–15, [16, 19], 18, 20, [22–23], [24a–b, 26], [25a–b], plus 5 fragments: **71**.26–30). There is a broad, flat to gently curved, rim with a pronounced outward expansion; the rim is slightly inturned and beneath this the body expands slightly out into a deep rounded bowl. There is a large applied lug (45mm wide by 32mm high) on **71**.5 while a roughened and slightly raised patch on **71**.4 indicates the location of another detached lug. The well-fired and smoothly finished fabric is a slightly patchy red to pale buff with a brown-buff rim top, internal surface and core. There is a medium content of crushed, coarse-grained quartzitic granite inclusions (≤ 4 x 3mm, occasionally up to 6 x 6mm). There is sooting and occasional areas of burnt accretion on the inner surface of some of the bodysherds. Body thickness: 11.5–12.5mm; total weight: 849g.

Maximum external rim diameter: 29cm. Maximum internal rim diameter: 23.2cm; Estimated height: 20.7cm.

Decoration: There are four circumferential lines of fine whipped cord on the rim top. On the outer surface widely spaced broad, shallow, oblique scored lines extend to *c.* 60mm below the rim. On the upper body there are broad (*c.* 18–20mm) shallow (2–3mm) horizontal channels. While these may be a decorative feature they may also be a result of pinching together the coil joins (see especially **71**.[2a–c]).

Vessel 9. This is represented by a single rimsherd (**71**.13) from a simple Middle Neolithic bowl. The flat-topped rim has a pronounced inward expansion and a slighter external one. Beneath this the body is upright but may have had a deep rounded bowl profile. The fine compact and well-fired fabric is red-brown with a dark red to grey-brown inner surface and core. There is a medium content of crushed coarse-grained quartzitic granite inclusions (≤ 8 x 5mm, occasionally up to 9 x 6mm) that are occasionally exposed on the inner surface. Neck thickness: 8mm; weight: 12g.

Decoration: There s a shallow, pinched-in, channel immediately beneath the rim on the external surface.

Context 42
There are 5 much worn bodysherds (**42**.17a–b, 18–19, 16, plus 6 fragments: **42**.20–25) from a Middle Neolithic bowl, probably a broad-rimed vessel. The red-buff fabric has a dark grey inner surface and core. There is a medium content of crushed coarse-grained quartzitic granite inclusions (≤4 x 4mm, occasionally up to 7 x 5mm) and some small sandstone pebbles. Body thickness: 12.5–14mm; weight: 84g.

Probable Bronze Age pottery from Context C75

There are 9 much worn bodysherds (**75**.16–24, plus 6 fragments: **75**.25–30) of buff to pale buff fabric with a grey-brown internal surface and dark grey core. There is a medium to high content of crushed coarse-grained quartzitic granite inclusions (≤ 5 x 4mm) and some small sandstone pebbles. Body thickness: 8.5–10mm; weight: 43g.

Comment: The pottery is too poorly preserved to make any detailed assessment but the sherds are probably Bronze Age in date.

Middle to Late Bronze Age pottery from Context C73

This consists of a group of much degraded sherds mainly embedded in a clay matrix (**73**.1–14). Amongst this material there are 8 much worn bodysherds (**73**.1–8) of red-buff fabric with a grey-buff to dark grey core. There is a medium to high content of crushed dolerite inclusions (≤ 4 x 4mm, up to 7 x 5mm) and occasional small sandstone pebbles (≤ 3 x 3mm). Body thickness: 9.75–10.1mm; (total weight: 60g).

Comment: The pottery is too poorly preserved to make any detailed assessment but the sherds are of middle to Late Bronze Age date.

The Late Bronze Age

Vessels 1–7 had been consolidated and conserved prior to examination by Arch Con Labs Ltd. This has obscured some minor details. The Artefact Conservation Record is included for each vessel.

Area 3, F4 (03E0067/03E0067 extension)
Vessel 1. This is from the fill of a cremation pit (F4) (Wiggins 2006). The vessel was upright but only the base and the lower part of the body survived *in situ*.

This is a large domestic vessel with a flat footed base (17mm) high that swells out into the gently curved body. The slightly domed disc base was made separately and the lower coils of the body attached to the side of the disc. Externally there is a sharp junction where the base and body were pinched together. The fine-walled vessel is of cream-buff to buff fabric with a grey to dark grey-buff core. The surfaces are smooth but uneven and the outer surface had been finished with a fine paste or slurry. There is a high content of crushed dolerite inclusions (≤ 5 x 4mm, up to 12 x 6mm). There is possible sooting on the inner surface. Body thickness: 9–10mm. There are also several unconsolidated sherds.

Maximum external base diameter: 19cm.
Maximum surviving height: 12cm
Total weight: 1,000g
Artefact Conservation Record: C04–0170

Vessel 2 (52.4). This is from the fill (C052) of a cremation pit (C036). The vessel was upright but only the base and the lowermost part of the body survived *in situ*.

This is a large domestic vessel with a flat footed base (16mm) high, that swells out into the gently curved body. The domed disc base was made separately and the lower coils of the body attached to the side of the disc. Internally there is a shallow channel around the base where the disc and body were moulded together while externally there is a very slight foot where the base and body were pinched together. The vessel is of smooth buff fabric with a grey-buff core; some patches of red-buff occur internally on the base. The outer surface was finished with a fine paste of slurry and there are few protruding inclusions. There is a very high content of crushed dolerite inclusions (≤ 5 x 4mm, up to 12 x 8mm). Body thickness: 12.5–15mm. There are also two unconsolidated sherds.

Maximum external base diameter: 16.7cm.
Maximum surviving height: 3.5cm
Total weight: 400g
Artefact Conservation Record: C05–0167

Vessel 3 (47.3). This is from the fill (C047) of a cremation pit (C027). The vessel was upright but only the base and the lowermost part of the body, which had been compressed after disturbance to the grave pit, survived *in situ*.

This is a large fine-walled domestic vessel with a flat unfooted base that swells out into the gently curved body. The domed disc base was made separately and the lower coils of the body attached to the side of the disc. Internally there is a shallow channel around the base where the disc and body were moulded together while externally there is a sharp junction between the base and body. The vessel is of smooth, but uneven, buff to cream-buff fabric with a grey-buff core. The outer surface was finished with a fine paste of slurry but there are still frequently protruding inclusions. The inner surface is obscured by a burnt accretion. There is a high content of crushed dolerite and some quartzite inclusions (≤ 8 x 5mm). Body thickness: 8.8–10.5mm. There are also several unconsolidated sherds.

Maximum external base diameter: *c.* 13.8cm.
Maximum surviving height: *c.* 12cm
Total weight: 400g
Artefact Conservation Record: C05–0166

Vessel 4 (45.1). This is from the fill (C045) of a cremation pit (C025). The vessel was upright but only the base and the lowermost part of the body survived *in situ*.

This is a medium sized domestic vessel with a flat unfooted base and a splayed, straight sided, body profile. The domed disc base was made separately and the lower coils of the body attached to the side of the disc. Internally there is a deep channel around the base where the disc and body were moulded together. The vessel is of smooth cream-buff fabric with a grey-buff core. The outer surface was finished with a fine paste of slurry and there are few protruding inclusions but the internal face is rough probably a result of water damage. There is a high content of crushed dolerite, uncrushed sandstone pebbles and some quartzite inclusions (≤ 8 x 5mm, up to 10 x 7mm). Body thickness: 11.2–13.5mm.

Maximum external base diameter: 12.5cm.
Maximum surviving height: 7.5cm
Total weight: 400g
Artefact Conservation Record: C05–0165

Vessel 5 (89.1). This is from the fill (Co89) of a cremation pit (Co88). The vessel was upright but only the base and the lower part of the body survived *in situ.*

This is a large domestic vessel with a flat unfooted base. The lower part of the body is straight and splays out gently but above this it has a gently curved profile. The slightly domed disc base was made separately and the lower coils of the body attached to the side of the disc; externally there is a sharp junction between the base and body. The vessel is of smooth but unevenly finished cream-buff to buff fabric with a grey-buff core and a grey-buff to buff internal surface. The outer surface was finished with a fine paste of slurry and there are few protruding inclusions but the internal face is rough probably a result of water damage. There is a high content of crushed dolerite inclusions (≤ 5 x 3mm, up to 10 x 7mm). Body thickness: 14.3–14.8mm.

Maximum external base diameter: 19.5cm.
Maximum surviving height: 24cm
Total weight: 3800g
Artefact Conservation Record: C05–0170

Vessel 6 (41.1). This is from the fill (Co41) of a cremation pit (Co09). The vessel was upright but only the base and the lower part of the body survived *in situ*; it appears that only a small portion of the upper part of the vessel is missing.

This is a medium sized domestic vessel with a flat unfooted base. It has a gently curved biconical profile. The flat disc base was made separately and

the lower coils of the body attached to the side of the disc; externally there is a sharp junction between the base and body. This is a well-made vessel of very smooth compact fabric, buff to cream-buff with a grey-buff to dark grey core. Except where worn inclusions appear on, but do not protrude through, the surfaces. There is a burnt accretion on the inner surface. There is a medium to high content of crushed dolerite inclusions (≤ 4 x 3mm, up to 8.5 x 8.5mm). Body thickness: 9–9.5mm.

Maximum external base diameter: 18.5 x 19.5cm.
Maximum surviving height: 20cm
Total weight: 3600g
Artefact Conservation Record: C05–0164

Vessel 7 (85.1). This is from the fill (Co85) of a cremation pit (Co84). The vessel was upright but only the base and the lower part of the body survived *in situ.*

This is a large tall domestic vessel with a flat, gently domed, base and a slight, sharp, pinched out foot. The body splays outwards into a gently rounded profile. This is a well-made vessel is of smooth, but uneven, cream-buff to buff fabric with a grey to dark grey-buff core; there are few inclusions visible on the surfaces. A localised burnt accretion occurs on the inner surface on one side of the vessel. There is a high content of crushed dolerite, and some sandstone, inclusions (≤ 5 x 4mm, up to 15 x 7 x 7mm). Body thickness: 9.2–11.8mm.

Maximum external base diameter: 16.8cm.
Maximum surviving height: 21cm
Total weight: 900g
Artefact Conservation Record: C05–0169

Vessel 10. This is from the fill (Co83) of a cremation pit (Co82). The vessel is represented by 10 bodysherds (**83.**1–2, [3–4], [5–6], 7–10; plus crumbs: **83.**12) and single base-anglesherd (**83.**11); in the absence of any surviving rimsherds it is possible that the vessel was upright.

This is a large, tall domestic vessel with a gently rounded profile. This is a well-made vessel is of smooth, but uneven, pale buff to cream-brown fabric with a grey to dark grey-buff core; there are few inclusions visible on the surfaces. There is a medium content of crushed dolerite, and some sandstone, inclusions (≤ 6 x 4mm, up to 11 x 6.5 x 5mm). Body thickness: 10–11mm.

Maximum external body diameter: 26cm.
Total weight: 476g

APPENDIX IV

ANALYSIS OF CREMATED BONE FROM DARCYSTOWN 1, BALROTHERY, CO. DUBLIN (03E0067)

Jennie Coughlan

Introduction
This report details the results of the analysis of a group of Middle to Late Bronze Age cremated bone burials recovered during archaeological investigations outside the village of Balrothery in the townland of Darcystown [03E0067]. Excavations, directed by Kenneth Wiggins for Judith Carroll and Co. Ltd., were undertaken prior to the development of a new housing scheme in the locality.

Background
Archaeological investigations at Balrothery identified six distinct areas, documented as Areas 1-6, containing features of archaeological interest. In Area 2, the largest of the documented areas, a total of twenty-three pits were uncovered, a number of which contained cremated bone deposits and/or pottery vessels. A total of eight of the pits contained ceramic vessels that were in a relatively good state of preservation. These were excavated and removed from site by conservation specialists. During the off-site conservation process, burnt bone deposits contained within the vessels were removed and bagged for subsequent analysis.

In all, burnt bone assemblages from nine contexts were presented for osteological analysis (Table 1). Six of these came from ceramic vessels excavated under laboratory conditions. One came from a badly truncated pit which also contained two sherds of prehistoric pottery and two of the assemblages came from pits which did not contain any evidence for associated pottery. Analysis was undertaken to quantify and, where possible, identify the skeletal elements contained within the burnt bone assemblages. None of the bone deposits had been washed prior to analysis.

Materials and Process
The bone from each context was examined in accordance with recommended standards (Brickley and McKinley 2004). Each sample was sieved through laboratory-grade stack sieves of 2mm, 5mm and 10mm diameter mesh and the material from each sieve was weighed to the nearest 0.1gram. All material was examined macroscopically. Once the bone from each sample was sieved, each sieved portion of bone was weighed as a whole and examined for identifiable bone. All identifiable bone was described in detail and weighed separately.

Reasons for Analysis
Osteological analysis is undertaken to determine the demographic and pathological profile of an individual or population group. This is true of the analysis of both inhumation and cremation burials. The identification of demographic and pathological details are, however, more difficult in cremated remains as the fragmented and fire-damaged nature of the bone can limit the amount of information retrieved during analysis. In addition to individual details, the analysis of cremated remains can also reveal aspects of cremation ritual, including pyre technology and depositional processes.

Analysis of the burnt bone deposits from Balrothery sought to identify species represented, skeletal elements present, minimum number of individuals within individual deposits, age and sex profiles, pathological changes to the bone and the cremation technology employed.

Identification of Skeletal Material
The quantity of bone collected from each context varied considerably, ranging from a minimum of 3.7g to a maximum of 997.9g (Table 1). Of the nine assemblages presented for analysis all but one [pit 57, context 56] contained identifiable human skeletal elements. Pit [57] was truncated by a later cultivation furrow and produced only 3.7g of poorly preserved bone fragments. None were diagnostic of species. A single fragment of burnt animal bone, equating to 0.8% of the total weight of the deposit, was found associated with the cremated human remains from context 47 [pit 27].

In modern crematoria the weight of bone produced during the cremation process can range from approximately 1000.5g-2422.5g (McKinley 1993). Although burnt bone deposits from archaeological contexts can weigh considerably less, reflecting aspects of selective depositional practices and/or post-depositional disturbance, the quantity of bone retrieved from the majority of the cremation pits at Balrothery fell well below expected levels for

TABLE 1. TOTAL WEIGHT OF BURNT BONE BY CONTEXT

Cut	Fill	Weight of bone (g)	Area of context	Description	Associated vessel
5	37	12.2	2	cremation pit	no
6	38	36.2	2	cremation pit	no
9	41	54.2	2	cremation pit	yes
27	47	997.9	2	cremation pit	yes
36	52	11.1	2	cremation pit	yes
57	56	3.7	2	cremation pit	yes (2 pieces)
82	83	9.2	2	cremation pit	yes
84	85	26.1	2	cremation pit	yes
88	89	241.6	2	cremation pit	yes

individual burials. In all, only one pit [pit 27, context 47] contained a quantity of bone that could be considered representative of a complete individual.

The majority of bone fragments (61.4%) fell between 2mm and 10mm in diameter (Table 2). A total of 18.7% of elements were greater than 10mm in diameter with 19.9% less than 2mm in size. The maximum fragment length was 64.1mm, which came from the most complete assemblage (pit Co27).

Once identified, the human skeletal elements were divided into five main categories before being weighed separately and described in detail:

skull
axial
upper limb
lower limb
unidentified long bone

A sixth category ('other') was also used where elements were identified as human but could not be assigned to either the upper or lower limb. An example of this includes the identification of small fragments of bone that could be either from the distal portion of the metacarpal (hand) or metatarsal (foot).

Osteological Analysis

Despite the fragmentation of the bone it was possible to identify skeletal elements from all but one of the nine assemblages analysed with a total of 240.3g (14.7%) of the total weight of bone identifiable (Table 3). The majority of identifiable bone elements (5.8%) were cranial vault fragments (identified in eight assemblages) with a further 4.6% of identified elements from non-specific long bones.

TABLE 2. SUMMERY OF CREMATED BONE FRAGMENT SIZE

Cut	Fill	10mm	%	5mm	%	2mm	%	<2mm	%	Total
5	37	0.5	4.1	5.6	45.9	6.1	50.0	0.0	0.0	12.2
6	38	1.8	5.0	24.8	68.5	9.6	26.5	0.0	0.0	36.2
9	41	5.9	10.9	39.3	72.5	9.0	16.6	0.0	0.0	54.2
27	47	231.3	23.2	559.4	56.1	207.2	20.8	0.0	0.0	997.9
36	52	1.3	11.7	8.3	74.8	1.5	13.5	0.0	0.0	11.1
57	56	0.0	0.0	2.3	62.2	1.4	37.8	0.0	0.0	3.7
82	83	0.6	6.5	5.7	62.0	2.9	31.5	0.0	0.0	9.2
84	85	1.7	6.5	11.6	44.4	12.8	49.0	<0.1	-	26.1
88	89	17.8	7.4	197.6	81.8	26.2	10.8	0.0	0.0	241.6
	Totals	260.9	18.7	854.6	61.4	276.7	19.9	<0.1		1392.2

Table 3. Summary of identifiable skeletal elements

Cut	Fill		Skull	Upper Limb	Lower Limb	Unidentified Long Bone	Axial	Other Identifiable	Total Weight	Total
5	37	g	1.2	–	–	–	–	–	1.2	12.2
		%	(9.8)	–	–	–	–	(9.8)		
6	38	g	6.8	–	–	–	–	–	6.8	36.2
		%	(1.8)	–	–	–	–	(18.8)		
9	41	g	4.3	–	–	–	0.5	0.4	4.8	54.2
		%	(7.9)	–	–	(0.9)	(0.7)	(8.9)		
27	47	g	55.8	3.8	32.4	63.9	15.9	5.9	171.8	997.9
		%	(5.6)	(0.4)	(3.2)	(6.4)	(1.6)	(0.6)	(17.2)	
36	52	g	2.3	–	–	–	–	–	2.3	11.1
		%	(20.7)	–	–	–	–	(20.7)		
57	56	g	–	–	–	–	–	–	–	3.7
		%	–	–	–	–	–	–		
82	83	g	0.6	–	–	–	–	–	0.6	9.2
		%	(6.5)	–	–	–	–	(6.5)		
84	85	g	1.0	–	–	–	–	–	1.0	26.1
		%	(3.8)	–	–	–	–	(3.8)		
88	89	g	9.1	1.2	–	–	–	–	10.3	241.6
		%	(3.8)	(0.5)	–	–	–	(4.3)		
	Total		**81.1**	**5.0**	**32.4**	**63.9**	**16.4**	**6.3**	**204.3**	**1392.2**
			(5.8)	**(0.4)**	**(2.3)**	**(4.6)**	**(1.2)**	**(0.5)**	**(14.7)**	

Body part representation

The cremated bone assemblage from pit [Co27], context [Co47], will be dealt with in detail separately as it represents the most complete cremation burial from the site. The majority of identifiable cranial fragments from the remaining contexts consisted of vault elements, although fragments of the sphenoid bone [pit Co09] and mandibular body [pit Co88] were also represented. Post-cranial elements were only identified in the assemblages from pit [Co09] and pit [Co88]. A single fragment of radial head (0.5g), two partial hand phalanges and one complete distal hand phalanx (0.7g) were identified in pit [Co88] while in the assemblage from pit [Co09] there was a single distal hand phalanx (<0.1g), two fragments of distal MC/MT heads, a small fragment of a vertebral body and a single thoracic vertebral articular facet. Identifiable dental remains consisted of the roots of five teeth (four from the anterior dentition and one partial molar root) from pit [Co09].

Pit [Co27] contained a total weight of 997.9g of cremated bone of which 0.8g was identified as animal bone and 171.8g as human bone. The cranium was represented by fragments of the frontal bone, sphenoid, zygomatic process, mastoid and mandibular body. There were a total of eight tooth roots, six from the anterior dentition, one premolar and one molar. The upper limb was represented by four fragments of unsided proximal ulna and a single fragment of unsided radius. The majority of bone fragments identified as lower limb came from the tibia, represented by unsided anterior shaft fragments and an unsided partial distal epiphysis. Also identified were a single portion of the fibular shaft (in three pieces), three foot phalanges and a fragment of the tibial surface of the talus. The axial skeleton was poorly represented with only a small number of vertebral (cervical and thoracic/lumbar) and rib fragments, in addition to a single small fragment of the sternal body, identified. The bones of the axial skeleton, most notably the vertebrae and pelvis, contain a high percentage of cancellous bone, which is more likely to disintegrate in high temperatures. The majority of identifiable human bones (6.4%) in this burial were represented by non-specific long bones.

Minimum number of individuals

Analysis of the identifiable skeletal elements indicated that, where human skeletal material was identified, a minimum number of one individual was represented in each assemblage with no duplication of skeletal elements encountered.

Determination of age and sex

Methods used to assess age at death rely on characteristics of skeletal development through childhood, adolescence and early adulthood and, thereafter, on processes of degeneration. Although the specific skeletal and dental elements that provide the most accurate indications of age were not identified in the assemblages from Balrothery, the robusticity and cortical thickness of the identifiable long bone and cranial fragments suggest that, where present, these elements were from an adolescent or adult individual(s). The single exception to this was the assemblage from pit [Co05] where the cranial vault fragments appeared thinner than those found in the rest of the assemblages. Unfortunately only 12.2g of bone were recovered with this burial and there was no other skeletal evidence available to aid in assessment of age. This was one of the two burials interred without an associated funerary vessel.

In general, the pelvis is considered to exhibit the highest degree of sexual dimorphism, as it is adapted in females to allow for childbirth. Essentially a broad pelvic structure in the female skeleton contrasts with a narrow and high pelvis found in the male skeleton. The skull can also be used as a primary indicator of sexual differentiation in skeletal material and it is often found that males display more robust or prominent features than their female counterparts. No pelvic fragments were identified in any of the assemblages from Balrothery and, although the cranium was well represented, the majority of fragments were undiagnostic of sex. A

single partial orbital margin, identified in pit [Co27], provided the only sexually dimorphic element but unfortunately it was too distorted by heat to provide an accurate indication of sex.

Pathology

There are, relatively speaking, only a small number diseases that visibly affect bone. Most conditions that do affect the skeleton result from periods of long-standing disease and/or nutritional deficiency. In general, acute episodes of nutritional or pathological stress either resolve themselves, or result in death, before the bony elements become involved.

One of the most commonly encountered forms of pathology in archaeological material is joint disease and this proved to be the only evidence for pathology identified at Balrothery. The cremated bone assemblage from pit [Co27] contained a small number of vertebral fragments with mild osteophytes visible along the surviving portion of a single lower thoracic/lumbar centrum and possible intervertebral osteochondrosis identified on a second lower thoracic/lumbar centrum.

Osteophytes, visible as bony outgrowths along the margin of a joint, develop as a compensatory measure and, in the spine, act to increase the vertebral body surface during accumulated axial pressure. Intervertebral osteochondrosis affects the body of the vertebrae and is associated with degeneration of the intervertebral disc. This condition is visible in skeletal material as rugged crescentic lesions along the anterior aspect of the vertebral bodies. The presence of these pathological changes in a single assemblage suggests that this individual was affected by axial loading, probably

TABLE 4. SUMMARY OF DEMOGRAPHIC AND PATHOLOGICAL PROFILES

Cut	Fill	Total weight of bone	Maximum fragment length	Age at death	Sex	Pathology
5	37	12.2	14.8mm	?	–	
6	38	36.2	27.4mm	?Adult/Adolescent	–	
9	41	54.2	25.7mm	?Adult/Adolescent	–	
27	47	997.9	64.1mm	Adult	–	spinal joint disease
36	52	11.1	21.0mm	?Adult/Adolescent	–	
57	56	3.7	16.9mm	?Adult/Adolescent	–	
82	83	9.2	29.0mm	?Adult/Adolescent	–	
84	85	26.1	27.6mm	?Adult/Adolescent	–	
88	89	241.6	29.7mm	?Adult/Adolescent	–	

resulting from occupational stresses. Although only a small number of vertebral fragments were identified, making any conclusions as to the severity of vertebral disease difficult to predict, the visible changes were considered mild. This suggested that either the individual was young and/or was not involved in heavy activities.

Cremation technology

Bone colour

To achieve effective cremation a combination of high temperatures and continued maintenance of the pyre over a sustained period of time is required. Differences in colour, visible on cremated bone elements, can be used to indicate variations in pyre performance. Complete burning of an individual, resulting in the total loss of the organic portion of the bone, requires pyre temperatures of greater than 600°C maintained over a number of hours. Lesser temperatures produce variations in bone colour with a blue-grey colour produced when bone is subject to temperatures of approximately 600°C and blackened (charred) elements occurring at approximately 300°C.

At Balrothery the bone was well burnt with all but one unidentified fragment from context [C047] white in colour. The single small fragment had a slight blue-grey colour of the internal surface. This indicates that pyre technology was developed enough to produce an even and effective process of burning over a sustained period of time.

Fragmentation

Fragmentation of cremated bone can result from a number of different processes. The act of cremation itself causes the bones to warp and crack, leaving bone elements vulnerable to breakage along these weakened lines. In the immediate aftermath of the cremation raking of the remains can further damage the skeletal elements while post-depositional disturbance and erosion can further reduce the size of bone fragments. Commonly the fragment size of cremated bone deposits placed in the protective environment of a pottery vessel and/or cist is greater than that of bone that has been placed unprotected in a pit.

At Balrothery, six of the nine assemblages analysed came from an urned context indicating that they were in a protected environment. Despite this only one assemblage could be considered to represent a complete individual. This deposit contained the highest percentage of skeletal elements greater than 10mm in diameter (23.2%), contrasting with the other burials where a maximum of 11.7% of elements

were over 10mm in diameter. Surface and marginal erosion were slight to moderate throughout the assemblages suggesting that the burial environment provided some protection from outside agents. The most poorly preserved assemblage contained only 3.7g of bone with none of the fragments greater than 10mm in diameter. This poor preservation of skeletal elements in this assemblage can be explained by disturbance by later agricultural activity. The findings from Balrothery suggest that post-depositional disturbance contributed, at least partially, to fragment size.

Conclusion

Archaeological investigations at Balrothery identified a series of Middle to Late Bronze Age pits, a quantity of which contained cremated bone. The majority of these were associated with pots in varying degrees of preservation although two came from pits with no associated pottery. Osteological analysis of the cremated bone was undertaken in order to assess the nature of the deposits and, where possible, the demographic and pathological profile of the remains. Additional consideration was given to an assessment of the technological and ritual practices associated with the cremation process.

Although the quantity of cremated bone recovered at Balrothery varied considerably throughout the deposits, the presence of cremated bone placed deliberately in pits, and commonly within vessels, indicates that these represent a deliberate process of deposition.

Although the fragmented and incomplete nature of the deposits made a detailed demographic assessment difficult, the cortical thickness of the long bone and cranial fragments suggested that the individual/s interred were adolescent or adult at time of death. The identification of a variety of skeletal elements from the skull, torso and limbs indicates that there was no preferential collection of specific elements for deposition. There was no indication that more than one individual had been placed in a single burial although the identification of a burnt animal bone fragment associated with an urned cremation burial [pit C027] does indicate that the deliberate inclusion of animal remains formed a feature of the depositional process.

All bone fragments from Balrothery were well burnt and had a consistent white colour. This indicates that the pyre technology employed in the cremation process was developed enough to completely oxidise skeletal elements from all parts of the body.

References

Brickley, M. and McKinley, J.I. (eds.) 2004. Guidelines to the Standards for Recording Human Remains. Institute of Field Archaeologists. *Technical Paper No. 7* in association with BABAO.

McKinley, J.I. 1993. Bone fragment size and weights of bone from modern British nations and the implications for the interpretation of archaeological cremations. *International Journal of Osteoarchaeology* 3, 283-287.

CHAPTER 3

Excavation of a Late Bronze Age ring ditch and other features at Darcystown 2

Judith Carroll

The site, excavated under licence 04E0741 at Darcystown is referred to as Darcystown 2. *It comprised a ring ditch burial site of Late Bronze Age date in which a large amount of coarse pottery with some cremated bone was found. A cereal drying kiln of probable Late Iron Age date and two other pits, one post medieval, were found.*

BACKGROUND

The site was found during the monitoring of a housing development for Mullen Developments Ltd. During initial subsurface preparations monitored under Licence no. 02E0043, a group of cut features appeared under the topsoil. Excavation was proposed and took place under Licence 04E0741.

The site comprised a ring ditch and four smaller features which were found in close proximity. These included two pits, one small hearth and one corn drying kiln. These latter features were not closely associated with the ring ditch and their proximity may only be incidental, as a number of isolated features were found during the monitoring under licence no. 02E0043. The site was excavated within four weeks between June and July 2004.

C14 dating was carried out by Beta Analytic Inc (Appendix I); wood and charcoal analysis was carried out by Ellen O'Carroll (Appendix II); the prehistoric pottery from the site was examined by Eoin Grogan and Helen Roche (Appendix III); the animal bone was examined by Catherine Bonner (Appendix IV); the human cremated remains were examined by Patricia Lynch (Appendix V).

THE EXCAVATION

The Ring ditch

The ring ditch (Fig. 1; Plate 1) was a truncated roughly circular feature, 12.4m in diameter with a maximum depth of 0.9m. It was roughly V to U shaped in profile, 1.46m wide at the top and approximately 0.4m to 0.8m at the base (Plates 2-10).

Three distinct types of activity were identified in the excavation of the ring ditch and for ease of interpretation, the ring ditch has been divided into three separate areas, Area 1, 2 and 3 (Fig. 2).

The ring ditch contained layers of stone and clay containing prehistoric pottery, charcoal and cremated bone, as well as some animal bone and flint. A very large amount of prehistoric pottery – six hundred and ninety seven sherds – was found. This was concentrated in two small areas of the ditch. It was found in Area 2 on the east side of the ditch. This area comprised 1/7th to 1/8th part of the ditch, a stretch of about 4.5-5m. It was also found in Area 3 in the south-west of the ditch, for a stretch of 1.5m. The pottery was densely concentrated in both areas along with cremated bone and charcoal. Only a few isolated sherds of pottery and a few isolated fragments of cremated bone and charcoal were found outside these two concentrations.

In Area 2, the pottery and cremated bone was found associated with a dense concentration of sub-rounded stones. This dense concentration of stone was superimposed by a thick layer of compact grey-brown clay (C114) resembling redeposited natural, 3.6m in length, which ran from Section J (as C126) over Section M and towards Section Q, ending between Section M and Q on the east side of the ditch.

The northern part of the ring ditch, Area 1, which comprised a third part of the entire feature, was practically devoid of burial material. It contained only two sherds of prehistoric pottery, while several pieces of flint and a small number of animal bones were found in this area.

A summary of the three areas
Area 1 refers to the northern third part of the ditch which produced only two of the six hundred and ninety seven sherds of prehistoric pottery from the site and which may have been open for some time during the use of the site.

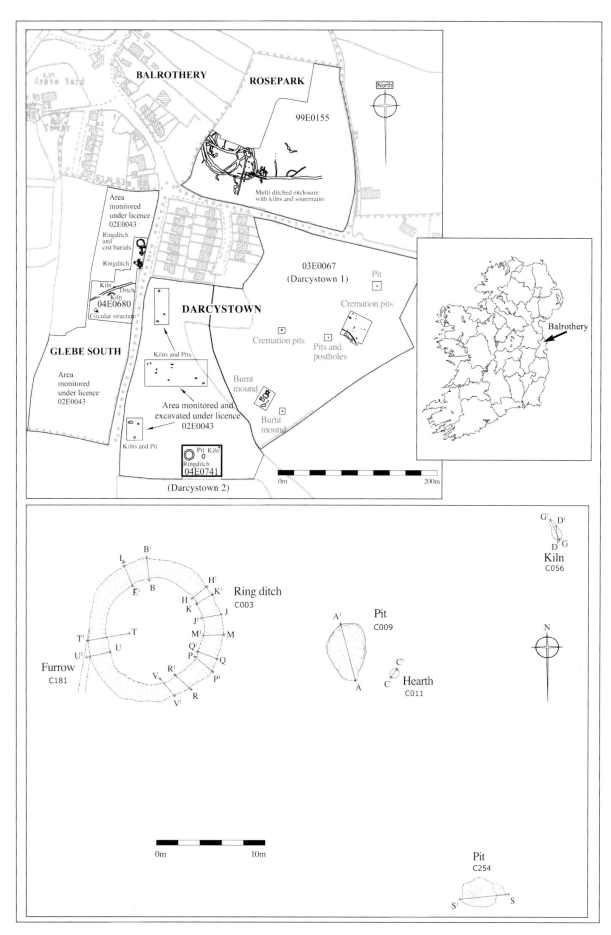

Figure 1: Darcystown 2, site location and plan of site

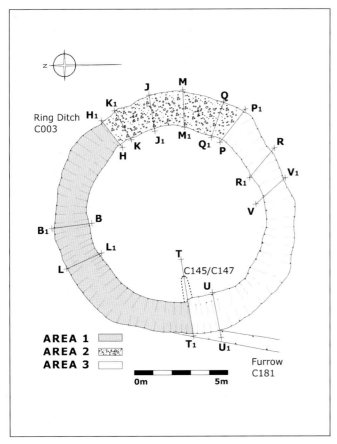

Figure 2: Ring ditch C003 showing location of Areas 1, 2 and 3

Area 2 refers to the eastern 6th-7th part of the ring ditch in which three phases of activity were identified. *Phase I* consisted of the deposition of a substantial amount of large sub-rounded stones which were concentrated within the entire cut of the ditch at Section M (Plate 5) and contained two hundred and nine sherds of prehistoric pottery, cremated bone and animal bone. These stones spread out to either side of Section M and were subsequently sealed by a very compact redeposited natural sand, *Phase II*.

Phase III consisted of the deposition of a very black charcoal-rich layer which contained two hundred and sixteen sherds of prehistoric pottery, cremated bone and animal bone. The pottery was contained in the uppermost deposit of the ditch and was noted to be of a somewhat different fabric to the pottery contained in the stony deposit in *Phase I*.

Area 3 refers to the the south-western third to half part of the ditch. As some of the deposits could be followed around from Area 2 to Area 3, it appeared that this part of the ditch was contemporary with *Phase III* of the stratigraphy in Area 2. Two hundred and ten sherds of prehistoric pottery, cremated bone, animal bone and eight pieces of flint were recovered

from Area 3. These were, however, almost all found only in a 1.5m area of the ditch at Section U to 1.5m south of Section U. The pottery sherds appeared to be similar to the pottery from *Phase III* in Area 2.

Area 1
The fills in Area I were all very compact and there was no evidence of deliberate backfilling of the ditch in this area. Only two sherds of pottery, some flints, a small number of animal bone fragments and occasional flecks of charcoal came from this area which comprised the northern third part of the ditch. No cremated bone was found in Area 1. Sections (T, L, B, and H) were cut at intervals across the ditch in Area 1.

Section T (Fig. 4) shows eight different deposits C146, C159, C160, C161, C144/C145, C142, C143 and C141. These can be described as very compact silty clays. They contained only occasional small stones and occasional charcoal flecks of oxidised clay.

Five different deposits were visible at Section L, C131, C129, C130, C128 and C100. The deposits at this section can be described as loose, fine sands with occasional small stones and silty clays with small stones and occasional charcoal flecks. It may be that the ditch had silted up naturally at this point. One piece of worked flint (04E0741:128:1) and occasional animal bone fragments came from C128.

Six different deposits were visible at Section B, C105, C104, C103, C102, C101 and C100.

These were moderately compact, gritty sands with moderate inclusions of sub rounded stones. The upper layers were more compact, coarse sands, the uppermost layer described as 'very compact'. Two sherds of prehistoric pottery (04E0741: 104:1,2) and eight pieces of worked flint (04E0741:104:3-10) came from C104.

Seven different deposits were visible at Section H, C139, C110, C108, C109, C138, C107 and C106. These were mainly composed of compact mid-brown to yellowish-brown, gritty medium sands, with moderate to frequent inclusions of sub rounded stones

Three pieces of worked flint were contained within the primary deposit, C139 (04E0741:139:1-3) and seven pieces of worked flint were contained within the uppermost deposit, C106 (04E0741:106:1-6). The remaining deposits were sterile.

Area 2
Area 2 refers to the south-east and eastern part of the ring ditch. It covered less than 1/6th of the total area of the ditch but most of the burial remains from the site were concentrated in this area. It is characterised

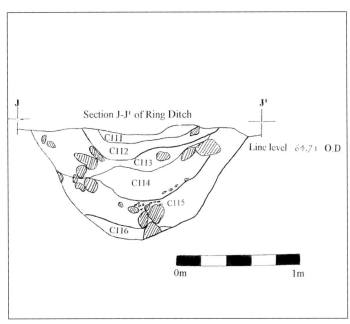

Figure 3: Section J -J1, Area 2 of ring ditch

by the deposition of large rounded stones mixed with pottery and cremated bone.

Three phases of deposition have been identified in this area: *Phase I*, which was the primary deposit and consisted of a substantial deposit of large rounded stones; *Phase II*, the deposition of a substantial layer of yellow sand (C114) resembling redeposited natural subsoil (Plates 4, 5, 6 and 9); *Phase III*, a superimposing black charcoal rich layer. There was no evidence of silting up in the bottom layers of the ditch.

Phase I, the stone deposit was characterised by a mid to dark brown, fine sand, containing very frequent sub-rounded pebbles and larger sub-rounded stones. The larger stones average 0.14m x 0.13m x 0.16m. The stone deposit (C115 and C117) filled the entire cut of the ring ditch at Section M and spread out at either side of this section for a distance of 4-5m. This stony layer was visible at Section J (C115), Section Q (C153) and Section P (C150). At Sections P and Q, the stone layer spread out over a layer of slip material, C149 (Section P) and C154 (Section Q). This indicated that the ditch was open and had started to silt up when the stones were deposited in the ditch. The length of this stone spread was 5.20m. It was a maximum of 1.69m wide and had a maximum depth of 0.65m.

A substantial amount of prehistoric pottery, two hundred and nine sherds, along with a large quantity of cremated bone, two worked flints and animal bone were retrieved from this layer. The cremated bone is likely to have been contained within the pottery vessels because it is closely associated with the sherds. The pottery sherds were predominantly located at the inner edge of the ditch among the stones, indicating that soil containing them was dumped into the ditch from the inside.

Phase II: following the deposition of the stone layer, a very compact yellow sand was deposited in the ditch. This layer extended through part of Area 3 also. It was given the following numbers in the various sections: J (C114); M (C127); Q (C151 and C152); P (C140, C148), and R (C140). All of these deposits were sterile, with

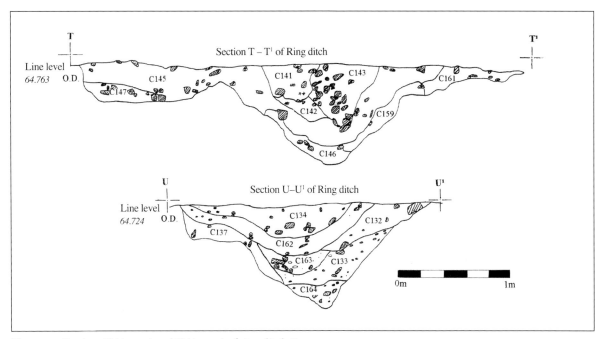

Figure 4: Sections T (Area 1) and U (Area 3) of ring ditch C003

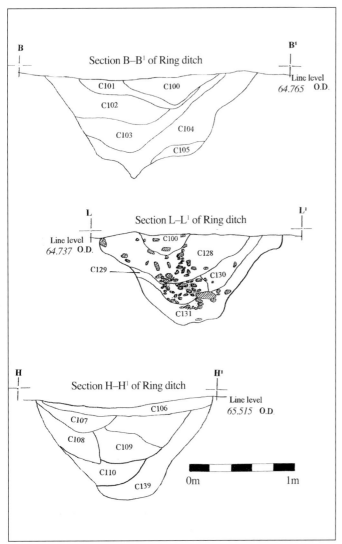

Figure 5: Sections B, L and H (Area 1) of ring ditch

the exception of C140 (in Area 3), which contained five pieces of prehistoric pottery, cremated bone and animal bone. It produced no finds or cremated remains. This sand layer extended for a length of approximately 8.40m and had an average depth of 0.26m. It is also described in relation to Area 3.

Phase III: the yellow sand of *Phase II* (C114, C127, etc.) was sealed by the black charcoal rich layer of Phase III. This layer respected the cut of the ditch and was given the following context numbers in the sections: Section J (C112 and C113); Section Q (C126), and Section P (C126).

The layer representing *Phase III* was approximately 8.40m in length, had an average width of 1.27m and a maximum depth of 0.26m. This charcoal rich layer contained significant amounts of prehistoric pottery but was not visible in the stoniest part of the ditch. *Phase III* contained two hundred and sixteen sherds of prehistoric pottery, animal bone and cremated bone.

Prior to excavation, it appeared there was a

gap/causeway in the south-east area of the ditch. A layer of brown sand which was visible in Sections J (C111) and Section M (C127) was directly above the stony area of the ring ditch (C117 in Section M). This layer had a length of 2.50m, was 1.50m wide and had a maximum depth of 0.14m. That C111 and C127 were broadly contemporary with the black charcoal layer seems likely. Twelve sherds of prehistoric pottery came from C111.

A total of six hundred and ninety-seven sherds of prehistoric pottery, along with cremated bone, were found in the ring ditch. Of this, a total five hundred and three sherds came from Area 2.

The five sections (K, J, M, Q, and P), which were drawn in Area 2, and are described as follows.

Section K: eight different deposits were identified at Section K, C124, C125, C123, C122, C121, C120, C119 and C118. The uppermost deposit C118 and the

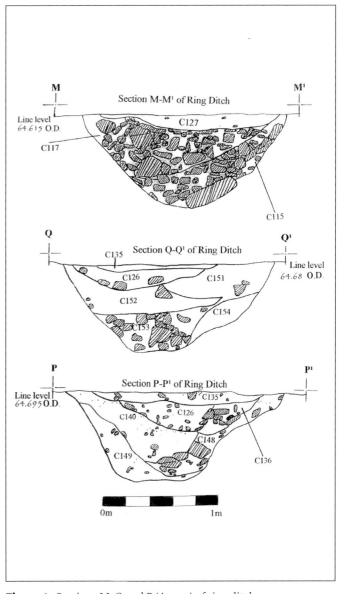

Figure 6: Sections M, Q and P (Area 2) of ring ditch

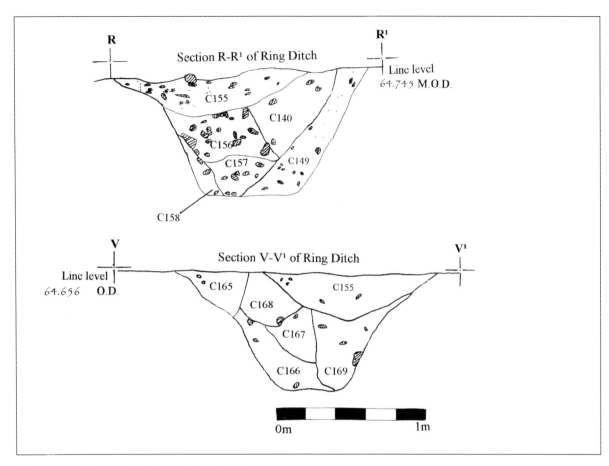

Figure 7: Sections R and V (Area 1) of ring ditch

deposit below it, C119, contained prehistoric pottery. C118 contained four sherds and C119 contained two sherds of prehistoric pottery, the rest of the fills in this section were sterile. The lower layers of the ditch at this point were comprised of compact medium or fine sands mainly with stone inclusions

Section J (Fig. 3; Plate 4) shows that six different deposits were identified at this section C116, C115, C114, C113, C112 and C111 and these contained a substantial amount of prehistoric pottery. C115, a compact, mid brown, fine sand, which was also identified at Section M, contained one hundred and eighty-eight sherds of prehistoric pottery (04E0741: 115:1-188) and two pieces of worked flint (04E0741:115:189,190). C115 was superimposed by C114, a compact, yellow, medium sand which contained fifty sherds of prehistoric pottery (04E0741:113:1-50) and one piece of worked flint (04E0741:113:51). C113, a black silty sand, contained cremated bone, eight rim sherds and forty-one body sherds and a base sherd, as well as animal bone and flint. This layer produced a radiocarbon date of 2600±50 BP, calibrated to BC 820-750, 690-660 and 640-590 (Beta-229063).

C112, a compact, grey-black, fine, sandy silt

containing charcoal, also contained two sherds of prehistoric pottery (04E0741: 112:1,2). Eight sherds of prehistoric pottery were contained within C111 (04E0741:111:1-8), a compact mid greyish-brown, fine, sandy silt – the uppermost deposit. Cremated bone was also found in these layers associated with the pottery.

Section M (Fig 6; Plate 5) reveals three deposits, C115, C117 and C127. A substantial amount of prehistoric pottery was contained within the fills at this section. C115 was a very compact, mid brown, fine sand, with frequent stone inclusions, which was also identified at Section J, contained at this point, one hundred and eighty-seven sherds of prehistoric pottery (04E0741:115:1-188) and two pieces of worked flint (04E0741:115:189, 190). A substantial quantity of cremated bone was also found with the pottery, which would suggest that the cremated bone was contained within the pottery. Twelve sherds of prehistoric pottery and cremated bone were contained within C117 (04E0741:1-12). C117 consisted of a moderately compact dark brown medium sand with frequent inclusions of sub-rounded and sub-angular stones of average size 0.12m by 0.08m by 0.04m.

C127, the uppermost deposit at Section M, was a very compact, mid brown, gritty, medium sand with infrequent inclusions of small rounded stones.

Section P (Fig. 6)
Seven different deposits can be seen in Section P: C149, C150, C148, C140, C136, C126 and C135. This area of the ring ditch also contained a substantial amount of prehistoric pottery, cremated bone and animal bone. These deposits were loose fine sands with large amounts of stone and gravels from all levels of the ditch.

Five body sherds of prehistoric pottery (04E0741:140:1-5), cremated bone and animal bone were retrieved from C140. C136 superimposed C140. Eleven base sherds (04E0741:136:1-2, 4-12), two rim sherds (04E0741:136:3,22), nine crucible sherds (04E0741:136:13-21) and eight body sherds (04E0741:136:23-30) of prehistoric pottery, cremated bone and animal bone came from C136,

At Section P, C126 superimposed C136 and was superimposed by C135. C126 was loose, dark, greyish-black, clayey sand with frequent pebble and assorted stones. Sixteen rim sherds (04E0741:126:1-6, 67-79) and one hundred and forty one body sherds (04E08741:7-66,80-162) of prehistoric pottery, cremated bone and animal bone came from C126.

C135 was the uppermost deposit at Sections Q and Section P. It was a moderately compact mid yellowish-brown, silty sand with occasional charcoal flecking and frequent inclusions of small pebbles. This deposit stretched between Section M in Area 2 and Section R (Area 3) and had a maximum depth of 0.12m. Two rim sherds (04E0741:135:1,2) and twenty-eight body sherds (04E0741:135:3-30) of prehistoric pottery were retrieved from C135.

Section Q (Fig. 6, Plate 6)
Six different deposits were revealed in Section Q: C154, C153, C152, C151, C126 and C135.

These were mainly compact sands with stones and charcoal flecking also containing pottery.

C153 had a large number of stones at a very low level, suggesting deposition of these at an early phase of the cutting of the ring ditch.

C152 superimposed C153 and was a very compact, sterile, yellow, medium sand with infrequent small stone inclusions. One piece of worked flint (04E0741:152:1) came from C152. C151 superimposed C152 and was overlain by C126. C126, also a stony layer, was 'a loose, dark, greyish-black, clayey sand with frequent pebble and assorted stone inclusions'. One hundred and forty-one body sherds

(04E08741:7-66,80-162) of prehistoric pottery, cremated bone and animal bone came from C126. C126 produced a radiocarbon date of 2740±50 BP, calibrated to BC 1010 to 810 (Beta-229064).

Area 3
Area 3, which covered over a third of the ditch, produced finds of cremated bone and pottery in two small areas. C140 (at Section R) produced five sherds of prehistoric pottery. The second area, approximately 1.5 metres in length (from the point of Section U to 1.5 metres south), produced cremated bone and one hundred and ninety-six sherds of prehistoric pottery. Outside this area, the deposits were almost sterile, yielding only charcoal flecks.

Three phases of activity were identified as follows in Area 3.

Phase I was a natural silting of the ditch which is indicated by the compact fine and silty sands of C149 at Section R and C166 at Section V.

Phase II: consisted of a very compact yellow sand resembling natural subsoil in the eastern half of Area 3. This layer was also visible in Area 2 as described above (C121; C114, etc.) and in Area 3 at Sections R (C140) and V (C167 and C168). C140 in Area 3 contained five pieces of prehistoric pottery, cremated bone and animal bone. This yellow sand layer extended for a length of approximately 8.40m (between Areas 2 and 3) and had an average depth of 0.26m.

Phase III in Area 3, which is probably contemporary with *Phase III* in Area 2, consisted of the layer, C155, a mid brownish-grey, medium, silty sand which had infrequent charcoal inclusions. This deposit had a width of 1.31m, was visible between Section P and V and was 0.3m in depth.

A furrow (C181) cut through the upper deposit of the ring ditch at Section U. The fill of the furrow, C134, contained fourteen sherds of prehistoric pottery, five pieces of worked flint, cremated bone and a clay pipe stem. This feature is interpreted as a modern feature which cut through the fill of the ring ditch at this point. One hundred and ninety-six sherds of prehistoric pottery, cremated bone, animal bone, and three pieces of worked flint, were contained within a metre and a half south of Section U. Most of the pottery, one hundred and forty-six sherds, was contained within deposit, C133, which was very close to the base of the ring ditch. This indicated that the ditch must have been open to quite a depth when the pottery was deposited. This pottery was noted to be different to that recovered from the stony layers associated with Phase I in Area

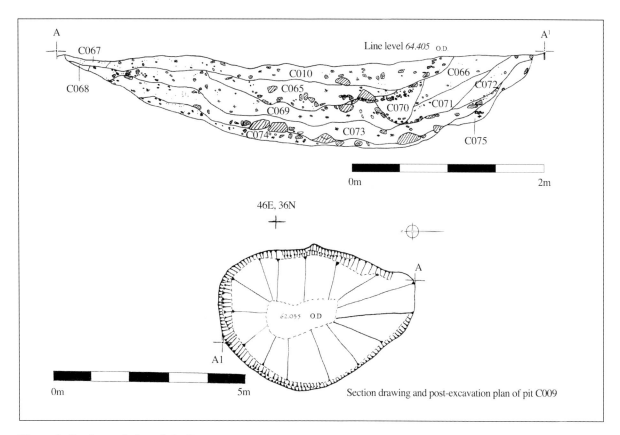

Figure 8: Section and plan of pit, C009

2, and was very similar to the pottery contained within the black, charcoal-rich layers associated with Phase III.

Section R (Fig. 7; Plate 9) shows that above C158, a mid brown, silty sand and a compact, orange-yellow fine sand, C149, were C155, C156 and C157, all mid brown to brownish-grey, silty sands. C140 (which produced 5 sherds of prehistoric pottery) was a compact, yellow, fine sand.

Five body sherds of prehistoric pottery (04E0741:140:1-5), cremated bone and animal bone were retrieved from C140, which had a width of 1.12m and a depth of 0.36m. C140 ran between Section P (Area 2) and Section V.

Section U (Fig. 4; Plate 8): at this point, one hundred and ninety-four sherds of prehistoric pottery were recovered from the deposits from this section to 1.5m south.

C137 superimposed C164 and was abutted by C133. C137 was a loose, mid brownish-yellow, fine sand with pebble and stone inclusions average size 0.07m by 0.05m. One sherd of prehistoric pottery (04E0741:137:1), cremated bone and one piece of worked flint (04E0741:137:2) came from C137. This deposit had a width of 0.90m, terminated between Section T (Area 1) and Section V, and was 0.3m deep.

C133 was a loose, mid yellow, coarse sand with frequent pebble and gravel inclusions. Three rim sherds (04E0741:133:1-3) and one hundred and forty two body sherds (04E0741:133:5-148) of prehistoric pottery were contained within this deposit. Cremated bone, animal bone and two pieces of worked flint (04E0741:133:147 and 148) also came from C133.

C163, which superimposed C133, was a moderately compact, light greyish-yellow, clayey sand with frequent pebble and stone inclusions average size 0.10m x 0.05m.

C132, which superimposed C163, was a moderately compact, light yellowish-brown, gravelly sand. Two rim sherds (04E0741:132:1,2), two base sherds (04E0741:132: 3,4), one shoulder sherd (04E0741:132:5) and twenty-nine body sherds (04E0741:132:6-35) of prehistoric pottery were contained within C132.

Cremated bone also came from C132. C162, which superimposed C132, was a loose mid orange-brown, clayey sand with a moderate amount of pebble and stone inclusions.

C134 was the fill of a furrow, which cut the ring ditch at this section only. This fill was a loose, mid orange-brown, clayey sand with moderate pebble and stone inclusions. One base sherd (04E0741: 134:1), thirteen body sherds of prehistoric pottery

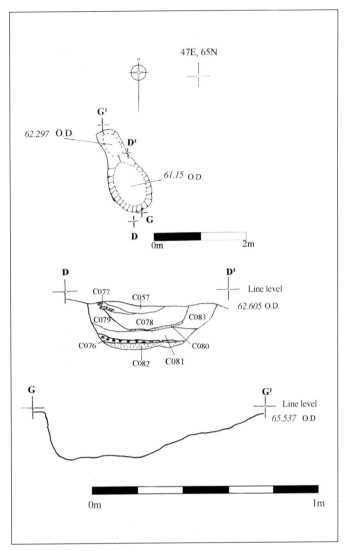

Figure 9: Plan, section and profile of kiln, C056

(04E0741:134:2-14), cremated bone, animal bone, five pieces of flint (04E0741:134:15-19) and a fragment of clay pipe (04E0741:134:20) came from C134 which had a width of 1.43m and a maximum depth of 0.28m.

Section V (Fig. 7; Plate 10) shows six different deposits, C166, C167, C168, C165, C169 and C155. The fills in this part of the ditch were sterile except for the occasional charcoal fleck and were mainly composed of compact silty sands.

Features outside the ring ditch

Pit 1, C009 (Fig. 8; Plates 11 and 13)
Situated to the east of the ring ditch was a large pit, C009. This pit was roughly oval to pear shaped, 5.06m north-north-west/south-south-east by 1.2m-3.50m in width. It had a maximum depth of 0.93m. C009 had a sharp break of slope at top of the cut. The

sides were steeply sloped except at the southern end where they were more gradually sloped. The break of slope at the base was imperceptible and the base itself was uneven and oval in shape. It was filled by deposits, C010, C065, C066, C067, C068, C069, C070, C071, C072, C073, C074 and C075. The main deposit at the base of the pit, C074, produced friable, dark grey, sandy clay with stones and a small amount of heat-shattered stone, as well as a number of animal teeth fragments. C075, also at the base, was a light, brownish-yellow, medium sand with occasional charcoal flecking. Above these two primary deposits was C073, a friable, dark grey, sandy clay with frequent charcoal inclusions, stones, animal teeth. A small amount of heat-shattered stone was also contained within this deposit. C073 was 4.50m north/south, 3.80m east/west and had a maximum depth of 0.2m. Overlying C073 was C069, a compact mid brownish-grey, clayey sand with frequent charcoal flecking. Animal bone, mainly teeth, was also contained within this deposit. A report on the animal bone from these contexts is appended (Appendix IV).

C071 lay directly over C072 at the northern end of the pit and was a compact, light greyish-yellow, gravelly sand with frequent pebble inclusions. Overlying C071 was C066 which was a compact, light greyish, clayey sand with frequent pebble and stone inclusions. C070 was a small cut into C069, C066 and C071 and could possibly be interpreted as a post-hole. Its fill was a moderately compact, light yellowish-grey, clayey sand which had frequent pebble inclusions and occasional charcoal flecking. C065 also contained badly preserved animal bone and animal teeth. The uppermost deposit was C010, a light yellowish-brown, clayey sand of firm compaction, which had frequent charcoal flecking and frequent small stone inclusions. Occasional fragments of heat-affected stone and a moderate amount of animal bone (mainly teeth) were contained within this deposit.

Kiln 1, C056 (Fig. 9; Plates 14 and 15)
Situated in the eastern end of the site was C056, a keyhole shaped cut of a cereal drying kiln. This kiln was located on an east facing slope, orientated north-west/south-east, with the narrow and shallow end, probably the flue, at the north-west of the feature. The kiln was 1.90m north-west/south-east. The 'bowl' was 0.88m wide and the 'flue' 0.46m in width. The bowl had a maximum depth of 0.4m and the flue had a maximum depth of 0.18m. The cut of C056 had a sharp break of slope at the top, on all sides except at the north-west end where it was imperceptible. The

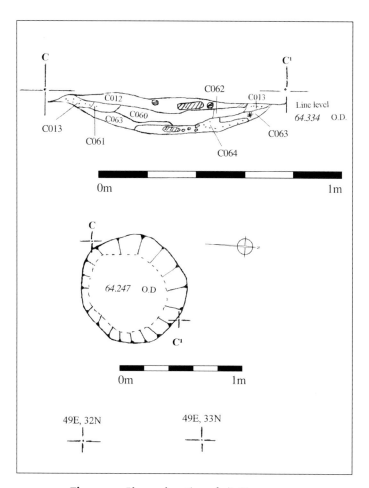

Figure 10: Plan and section of pit, Co11

sides were steeply sloped in the 'bowl' area and they were more moderately sloped at the 'flue' end. The break of slope at the base of Co56 was imperceptible. The base of the kiln was regular, oval and slightly concave. The base at the 'flue' end was slightly concave and sloped to the south-east.

Co56 contained nine deposits and two phases of activity were associated with it.

Phase I: Co82 was the primary deposit of the kiln, a moderately compact, red, medium sand with occasional small sub-rounded stone inclusions and very occasional charcoal flecking. Co82 was 0.72m north/south and had a maximum depth of 0.06m. It was a layer of oxidization confined to the bowl of the kiln. Overlying this deposit was Co76 a moderately compact, black, fine silty sand with very frequent charcoal inclusions. Co76 was 0.72m north/south and had a maximum depth of 0.06m. Co81, which was confined to the bowl area, was a moderately compact, greyish-brown, medium, gritty sand with moderate charcoal flecking and a moderate number of angular stone inclusions.

Charcoal from Co76 produced a radiocarbon date of 1680±50 BP, calibrated to AD 230 to 430 (Beta-229062).

Phase 2: Two deposits, Co83 and Co79, which appear to be contemporary, mark the second phase of kiln use and seem to have been deliberately packed in to the sides of the kiln to create a narrower bowl. Co79 consisted of a moderately compact, mid yellowish-brown, medium sand with a moderate amount of tiny grit inclusions. Co83 was a moderately compact, mid brown, medium sand with a moderate amount of sub rounded stone inclusions. Both these layers sealed the first phase of kiln use. Co80 was the first deposit within the new kiln bowl area. This was a moderately compact, red, medium sand with no inclusions, probably indicating oxidisation.

Overlying the *in situ* burning was Co78 which was a moderately compact mid brown silty sand. Co77 superimposed Co78 and consisted of a moderately compact, mid yellowish-brown, medium sand. This deposit was only contained in the southern end of the kiln bowl. Co57 was the uppermost deposit of the kiln. This deposit was a loose, mid brown/grey, fine sand with infrequent tiny stone inclusions. Co57 was 0.5m north/south and had a maximum depth of 0.07m. Co57 was contained within the southern end of the kiln bowl.

Pit Co11 (Fig. 10; Plates 17 and 17)
Slightly to the south-east of Co09 was a small pit, Co11, 0.93m east/west by 0.89m north/south with a depth of 0.14m. Co11 had a sharp break of slope at the top on all sides and the break of slope at the base was imperceptible. The sides of the cut were moderately sloped and the base was regular and concave. Co11 contained nine different deposits many of which contained burnt bone fragments.

The primary deposit within Co11 was Co64. This deposit was a light reddish-brown, loose, medium sand which had occasional charcoal flecking and moderate stone inclusions. Co64 was a layer of oxidisation at the base of Co11 which indicated *in situ* burning. Burnt bone fragments were also contained within Co64. Directly above this deposit was Co63, which was a black, loose, fine sand with frequent charcoal pieces and occasional small pebble inclusions. Above Co63 was Co13, a layer which consisted of a mid reddish-brown, fine sand of firm compaction with occasional charcoal flecking and a moderate amount of small stone inclusions. Co13 was a layer of oxidisation indicating *in situ* burning which was not associated with Co64, the initial *in situ* burning at the base of the hearth. Co62 overlay Co13 and was a light orange-brown, loose, fine sand with occasional charcoal flecking and a moderate number of small pebble inclusions. Co60 was contained

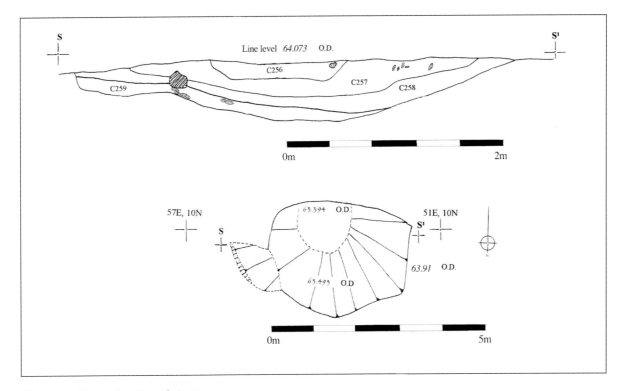

Figure 11: Plan and section of pit, C254

within the centre of the hearth and superimposed C062. This deposit was a light yellowish-brown, silty clay of firm compaction which had occasional charcoal flecking and a moderate number of small stone inclusions. Occasional fragments of bone were contained within this deposit.

Directly above C060 was C061 which was a light orange-brown, loose, fine sand which had occasional charcoal flecking and a moderate number of small stone inclusions. Occasional fragments of bone were contained within C061. The uppermost deposit of C011 was C012 which consisted of a mid grey-brown, fine sand of firm compaction with occasional charcoal flecking and a moderate number of small stone inclusions. Small fragments of animal bone were contained within this deposit.

Post-medieval pit, C254 (Fig. 11; Plate 12)
C254 consisted of an east/west orientated pit, 2.62 by 3.20m and 0.55m deep. It had concave sides and a rounded base and contained four deposits. C259, the lowermost deposit, consisted of a compact, rich, yellow, silty clay. This deposit was contained throughout the base of the feature to a depth of 0.13m. The recovery of a sherd of black glazed ware from this layer indicated a post medieval date for this feature. Overlying C259 was C258, a disturbed, dark brown, stony, silty clay which had moderate charcoal inclusions. Overlying C258 was a stony, light brown-yellow, silty clay, C257. This deposit was

concentrated mainly in the centre of the feature and was 0.33m deep. The uppermost horizon of this feature was C256, a dark yellow-brown, sandy clay. C256 was contained within the centre of the feature. It was 1.29m in width and 0.16m in depth.

DISCUSSION

The ring ditch burial site
The site excavated under this licence was composed of the ring ditch and other four features, a hearth, two pits and a kiln.

The ring ditch was an important find in the context of the other burial sites and features found in this area. This site was in the same townland as the Late Bronze Age cemetery of Darcystown 1, about 230m to the north-east. It was also about the same distance (roughly 230m) to the cemetery in Glebe South in which cremation and inhumation burials from the Bronze Age to the early medieval period were found (see Chapter 4). It was closer still, about 100-112m, to the two burnt mounds of Areas 4 and 5 of Darcystown 1, two of which yielded a Late Bronze Age date (see Chapter 2).

The ring ditch appeared as a truncated feature during monitoring, recognisable only by its cut in the natural subsoil. It was found to be a relatively substantial burial monument, containing cremated human bone and a total of six hundred and ninety-seven sherds of prehistoric pottery. The assemblage contained at least 19 Late Bronze Age vessels, all of which were coarse, domestic, flat-bottomed pots, while sherds from at least seven crucibles, one of which was substantially represented, were found (report by Eoin Grogan and Helen Roche, Appendix III). No complete vessels were found accompanying the cremations and thirteen different pots were represented by sherds from a single context.

It is suggested by Grogan and Roche that broken sherds of incomplete pots were brought to site to accompany the cremation burials. They also suggest that the selective deposition of broken pottery may mirror the selective nature of most cremations of the period which generally consist of only a small portion of the skeletal remains (Appendix III).

It was, however, noted by the excavators that the pottery and bone gave the distinct impression of having been tipped into the ditch along with the pile of stone in the area of Sections P and J (Figs. 3 and 6; Plate 4). The stone material, which may have been deliberately deposited in one area of the ditch, probably to form a causeway, was mixed with pottery and cremated bone as well as charcoal. The cremated bone was clearly associated with the pottery. A difference was noted in the pottery within the stony layer and that outside it, the pottery within the stony layer being very black in section. At the point of the stony layer, the pottery finds were extremely dense. From a total of six hundred and ninety-seven sherds of prehistoric pottery, two hundred and nine were found in the stony layer at the point between Section J and Section P.

It is a possibility, therefore, that the ring ditch, sited on a hill overlooking the countryside, was cut around an earlier burial cairn such as that at Carrig, Co. Wicklow (Grogan 1990, 12). The elevated siting for such a cairn would be typical. At Carrig, a burial cairn, a 'low circular pile of field stones and small boulders with no formal edging to the cairn' yielded a number of cremation burials, including a cremation associated with Late Bronze Age coarse ware. It is suggested that the ditch at Darcystown 2 might be secondary and that there may have been an earlier unenclosed burial on the site.

If there was such a burial cairn at Darcystown 2, some of the stone material of the cairn may have been used for a ring ditch causeway. The large number of deposited layers in the ring ditch do not necessarily suggest phases and may merely represent spadefuls. Interestingly, two deposits in the upper layers of the ditches produced C14 dates. Charcoal from C113 produced a radiocarbon date of 2600±50 BP, calibrated to BC 820-750, 690-660 and 640-590

(Beta-229063) while charcoal from C126 produced a radiocarbon date of 2740±50 BP, calibrated to BC 1010 to 810 (Beta-229064). This may further strengthen the suggestion that there are two separate periods of burial and that a 'renovation' of an older burial site, marked by a cairn, took place about 600 BC to facilitate the new burial marked by a ring ditch.

The excavation of this site has added greatly to our limited knowledge of burials of Late Bronze Age date in Ireland, in particular to Late Bronze Age burials in ring ditches of which there are few known in Ireland.

At Rathgall, Co. Wicklow, the large V shaped ring ditch produced Late Bronze Age pottery at all levels. Cremation burials in the interior of the enclosure included an upright pot containing the cremated remains of an adult and a child (Cooney and Grogan 1994, 145; Raftery 1973, 294).

At Mullaghmore, Co. Down (Mogey and Thompson, 1956), a ring ditch produced a burial in a Late Bronze Age coarse ware pot in the centre of the cairn and 300 sherds of Late Bronze Age coarse ware as well as a blue glass bead. It is suggested by Newman that there may have been two phases of prehistoric burial activity at this site, the central burial deposit masking an earlier pit (Newman 1997, 158).

The ring ditch excavated in Kilmahuddrick, Co. Dublin, in 2000, yielded, in one of the basal layers of the ditch, an Early Bronze Age date from an ash charcoal sample, while a Late Bronze Age date of 1208-935 cal BC came from oak charcoal at the base of the ditch. A human skull fragment produced a Late Bronze Age date of 911-802 AD in the upper layers of the ditch while other upper ditch fill contexts produced Iron Age C14 dates between the 2nd and 4th century BC from cremated bone. Two Late Bronze Age dates (1012-819 cal BC and 992-822 cal BC) were obtained from bone from cremation pits in the interior of the site (Doyle 2005, 43-75).

At Priestsnewtown, Co. Wicklow, a group of five upright coarse ware vessels containing cremations, and a number of cremation pits, were excavated in 2004. Four of these were found in an area enclosed by a shallow ditch with a flat to 'U' shaped base and vertical edges. It is probable that this feature is not a ring ditch. The excavators suggest, from the shape of the ditch, that it was a mortuary house (Tobin, Swift & Wiggins 2004, 21-23, 29). C14 dates were obtained from two of the burials here. These were 1300-1030 BC and 1490-1120 BC (Beta-209723 and Beta-209722).

All the Late Bronze Age burial sites above, apart from the site of this report, produced cremation burials, with or without pots, in the interior of the ring ditch or trench and it is interesting that no such features were dug into the interior of the Darcystown 2 ring ditch. It is possible that C145 (see Fig. 2), so close the ditch, was a pit and the linear trench, C181, at right angles to it, were deliberate features. However, it may also be the case that C145 represents a plough cut. C181, which contained sherds of prehistoric pottery, cremated bone and a clay pipe stem, has been interpreted as a cultivation furrow which disturbed the upper cremation layers. The lack of features cut into the enclosure may also be due to the ring ditch being significantly truncated. It was invisible above ground and only just recognisable when it appeared on the surface during soil stripping.

The Late Iron Age to early medieval period
The small keyhole shaped cereal drying kiln (C056) is comparable in type to a number of other kilns found during excavations in the townland under licence 04E0043.

C056 was a small corn drying kiln of keyhole shape yielding a radiocarbon date from C076 of 1680±50 BP, calibrated to AD 230 to 430 (Beta-229062). During monitoring in Darcystown under licence 02E0043, a total of 10 cereal drying kilns and five pits were identified throughout the field, concentrated in groups. Most of the kilns were very close in form to the kiln of this report. Two of them were radiocarbon dated and both produced dates with ranges between the early 4th and late 6th centuries and the early 4th and mid 7th centuries respectively (Carroll 2004). Kiln C056 of this report is particularly close in shape to two kilns in Rosepark which yielded very similar dates to it between the mid-third and early fifth centuries AD (Carroll 2002).

The kilns found on the Balrothery sites are earlier than those usually assigned to corn-drying kilns of keyhole shape (Monk and Kelleher 2005, 105-7). However, a corn drying kiln very similar in shape to the kilns found at Darcystown and Rosepark was found at Balriggan townland north-west of Dundalk and was dated to AD 60-250 (Roycroft 2006, 9). In 1984, a corn-drying kiln at Ballyman, Co. Dublin was excavated and dated to the early 5th century (O'Brien 1985, 214).

It is interesting that the inner enclosure at the top of the Rosepark hill gave a date of BP 1693±22 calibrated at two sigma to 255-411 AD (UB 4808) and that in the cemetery of Glebe South, a token cremation pit cut into Ring ditch 1 yielded a date of 1690 ±50 BP, calibrated to AD 240 to AD 430 (Beta-229059). A relationship between the Darcystown 2 kiln and the occupation and burial relating to Rosepark and Glebe South around the early 4th century AD cannot but be put forward.

References

Carroll, J. 2002. Report on archaeological monitoring at Rosepark, Balrothery, Co. Dublin, 2000-2001. Licence no. 99E0155. Two volumes. Unpublished report by Judith Carroll & Co. Ltd. National Monuments Service, Department of the Environment Heritage and Local Government.

Carroll, J. 2004. Report on archaeological excavations at Darcystown and Glebe South, Balrothery, Co. Dublin, 2004. Licence no. 02E0043. Unpublished report by Judith Carroll & Co. Ltd. National Monuments Service, Department of the Environment Heritage and Local Government.

Cooney, G. and Grogan, E. 1994. *Irish prehistory: a social perspective*. Bray, Wicklow.

Doyle, I. 2005. Excavation of a prehistoric ringbarrow at Kilmahuddrick, Clondalkin, Dublin. *The Journal of Irish Archaeology* XIV, 43-76.

Grogan, E. 1990. Bronze Age cemetery at Carrig, Co. Wicklow. *Archaeology Ireland* 4 (4), 12-14.

Grogan, E. and Roche, H. 2004. The prehistoric pottery from Site 6b, Priestsnewtown, Greystones, Co. Wicklow (04E0401). Unpublished report for Judith Carroll & Co. Ltd. National Monuments Service, Department of the Environment Heritage and Local Government.

Mogey, J. M. and Thompson, G. B. 1956. Excavation of two ring barrows in Mullaghmore townland, Co. Down. *Ulster Journal of Archaeology* 19, 11-28.

Monk, M. 1981. Post-Roman drying kilns and the problem of function. In D. O'Corrain (ed.), *Irish Antiquity*, 216-230. Cork.

Monk, M. and Kelleher, E. 2005. An assessment of the archaeological evidence for Irish corn-drying kilns in the light of the results of archaeological experiments and archeobotanical studies. *The Journal of Irish Archaeology* XIV, 77-114.

Newman, C. 1997. *Tara: an archaeological survey.* Discovery programme monograph 2. Dublin.

O'Brien, E. 1985. In Youngs, S. M. *et al* (eds.), Medieval Britain and Ireland in 1984. In *Medieval Archaeology* 29, 214.

Raftery, B. 1973. A Late Bronze Age Burial in Ireland. *Antiquity* 47, 293-5.

Roycroft, N. 2006. Iron Age patterns: silent sites. In *Seanda*. National Roads Authority magazine, Issue 1, 9.

Wiggins, K. and Swift, D. 2004. Greystones Southern Access Route (GSAR), Co. Wicklow. Kilpedder East, Priestsnewtown, Farrankelly. Monitoring report. Licence no. 04E0128. Unpublished report by Judith Carroll & Co. Ltd. for Wicklow County Council. National Monuments Service, Department of the Environment Heritage and Local Government.

Wiggins, K. 2005. Darcystown, Skerries road, Balrothery, Co. Dublin. Excavation report. Licence no. 03E0067 (ext.), Judith Carroll & Co. Ltd for Wicklow County Council. Unpublished report. National Monuments Service, Department of the Environment Heritage and Local Government.

Tobin, S., Swift., D., Wiggins, K., 2004. Greystones Southern Access Route (GSAR), Co. Wicklow. Sites 6/6a–g, Priestsnewtown. Licence no. 04E0401. Unpublished excavation report by Judith Carroll & Co. Ltd. for Wicklow County Council. Unpublished report. National Monuments Service, Department of the Environment Heritage and Local Government.

APPENDIX I

RADIOCARBON RESULTS FROM DARCYSTOWN 2, BALROTHERY, CO. DUBLIN (04E0741)
Beta analytic

Feature	Description code	Material	Sample	Results	2 sigma calcibration
C076	Fill of Kiln C056	Charcoal	229062	1680 ± 50 BP	230-430 cal. AD
C113	Fill of ring ditch	Charcoal	229063	2600 ± 50 BP	820-750 cal. BC and 690-660 cal. BC and 640-590 cal. BC
C126	Fill of ring ditch	Charcoal	229064	2740 ± 50 BP	1010-810 cal. BC

APPENDIX II

ANALYSIS OF CHARCOAL FROM DARCYSTOWN 2, BALROTHERY (04E0741)

Ellen O'Carroll

Introduction

Four charcoal samples from an excavation at a site on the Lusk road, Darcystown, Balrothery, Co. Dublin were submitted for analysis. The site comprises a ring ditch and four small features which were found in close proximity. These included two pits, one small hearth and one possible kiln. These smaller features were not closely associated with the ring ditch and their proximity may only be incidental, as a number of isolated features were found during the monitoring of this site, while the general area is rich in archaeology. The charcoal was sent for species identification prior to 14C dating, and also to obtain an indication of the range of tree species which grew in the area, as well as the utilization of these species for various functions. Wood used for fuel at prehistoric sites would generally have been sourced at locations close to the site. Therefore, charcoal identifications may, but do not necessarily, reflect the composition of the local woodlands. Larger pieces of charcoal, when identified, can provide information regarding the use of a species. The charcoal sampled and analysed from Darcystown was excavated from the tertiary fill of the ring ditch (C113 & C126), Phase

1 of a cereal drying kiln (C076) and the secondary deposit of a hearth (C063).

Methods

The process for identifying wood, whether it is charred, dried or waterlogged is carried out by comparing the anatomical structure of wood samples with known comparative material or keys (Schweingruber 1990). The identification of charcoal material involves breaking the charcoal piece so as a clean section of the wood can be obtained. This charcoal is then identified to species under an Olympus SZ3060 x 80-zoom stereomicroscope. By close examination of the microanatomical features of the samples, the species were determined. The diagnostic features used for the identification of charcoal are micro-structural characteristics such as the vessels and their arrangement, the size and arrangement of rays, vessel pit arrangement and also the type of perforation plates. All samples were suitable for species identification.

A small amount of elm (*Ulmus sp.*) was identified from C113, the ditch deposit. The elm from this sample is bagged separately and should not be sent for dating as it is a relatively long living species.

The elm identified suggests that there was a supply of elm in the surrounding environment. English elm *(Ulmus procera)* and wych elm *(Ulmus glabra)* cannot be separated by their wood structure. As suggested by Mitchell (1986), elm declined with the advent of farming and the dutch elm disease around 3700BC. It generally prefers damp woods particularly on limestone.

Hazel (*Corylus avellana*) was identified from C076 or Phase 1 of the kiln activity. Hazel rods from a coppiced wood may have been selected for use at this kiln. The hazel tree was very common up to the end of the 17th century and would have been used for the manufacture of many wooden structures such as wattle walls, posts, trackways and baskets. McCracken (1971, 19) points out that 'it was once widespread to a degree that is hard to imagine today'.

Results

TABLE 1: RESULTS FROM CHARCOAL IDENTIFICATIONS AT DARCYSTOWN 2, BALROTHERY, CO. DUBLIN

Site number/ Feature no.	Feature type no.	Sample	Species	Weight
03E0741/63	Deposit of hearth	4	All Pomoideae*	35g
03E0741/76	Phase 1, Kiln material of kiln C056	10	All hazel	140g
03E0741/126	Phase 3, Ditch deposit, charcoal layer	42	All blackthorn	239g
03E0741/113	Phase 3, Ditch deposit, charcoal layer	23	Blackthorn and one piece of elm (bagged separately)	68g

Pomoideae includes apple, pear, hawthorn and mountain ash. It is impossible to distinguish these wood species anatomically.

TABLE 2 SPECIES REPRESENTED IN THE IDENTIFIED

Botanical name	Species
Corylus avellana	Hazel
Prunus spinosa	Blackthorn
Ulmus sp.	Elm
Pomoideae	Apple type

Discussion

There are four species types present in the charcoal remains. The range of species identified from the feature analysed includes large (elm) and smaller scrub like (blackthorn, hazel and pomoideae) trees.

With the introduction of brick, steel and slate, the crafts associated with hazel became obsolete, and today the woods that supplied hazel have diminished rapidly. Hazel is normally only about 3-5m in height and is often found as an understory tree in deciduous woods dominated by oak. It also occurs as pure copses on shallow soils over limestone as in The Burren in Co. Clare and survives for 30 to 50 years. Its main advantage is seen in the production of long flexible straight rods through the process known as coppicing.

Blackthorn *(Prunus spinosa)* was identified from the ditch layer, C126. It is a very durable wood and is as strong as oak. It is a thorny shrub found in woods and scrub on all soil types. In a woodland situation it is more likely to occur in clearings and at the woodland edges.

Pomoideae was identified from the hearth deposit, C063, and includes apple, pear, hawthorn and mountain ash. It is impossible to distinguish these wood species anatomically, but as wild pear is not native and crab apple is a rare native species to Ireland, it is likely that the species identified are hawthorn or mountain ash (rowan) (Nelson 194-200, 1993). Hawthorn (*Crataegus*) is native, and is found in many hedgerows throughout Ireland. Mountain ash (*Sorbus aucuparia*) is also a common tree to Ireland, growing particularly well in rocky and hilly mountainous places.

Conclusion

Four species were identified from the features investigated. The species identified are more indicative of a dryland terrain where scrub material prevailed. A coppiced hazel wood may have been associated with the period of use of the cereal drying kiln. The elm points to the presence of woodlands and indicates that open conditions did not prevail throughout the Darcystown area of Co. Dublin during the period of use the ring ditch. The pomoideae from the hearth material may have been scrub-like material such as hawthorn, collected from nearby to the site and subsequently used as kindle for the fires. Coppiced hazel from the surrounding environment is most likely to have been used as raw material for processes associated with the kiln. The

blackthorn may have grown locally in hedgerows or in the ditches associated with the ring ditch feature.

Advice for radiocarbon dating

The best material to send for dating is short lived species such as blackthorn and pomoideae and hazel. Therefore the elm identified from the proposed 14C sample has been separated out and should not be sent for dating.

References

Beckett, J.K. 1979. *Planting Native Trees and Shrubs.* Jarrold & Sons Ltd. Norwich.

Nelson E.C. 1993. *Trees of Ireland.* The Lilliput Press. Dublin.

Warner, R.B. 1987. A proposed adjustment for the 'Old-Wood Effect'. In W. Mook and H. Waterbolk (eds). *Proceedings 2nd Symposium of 14C & Archaeology, Groningen 1987*, 29, 159-172.

Webb, D.A. 1977. *An Irish Flora.* Dundalgan Press Ltd. Dundalk.

Schweingruber, F.H. 1990. *Microscopic Wood Anatomy.* 3rd edition. Birmensdorf: Swiss Federal Institute for Forest, Snow and Landscape Research.

APPENDIX III

THE PREHISTORIC POTTERY ASSEMBLAGE FROM Darcystown 2, BALROTHERY, CO. DUBLIN (04E0741)

Eoin Grogan and Helen Roche

Summary

The site produced a large assemblage consisting of 411 sherds (plus 237 fragments) representing at least 19 domestic vessels (nos. 1–19; total weight: 5,570g) from a Late Bronze Age ring ditch cemetery. The pottery came from the ring ditch fill associated with cremations: all of the vessels had been broken prior to deposition. Portions of seven crucibles (nos. A–G) also came from the ditch fill.

The Late Bronze Age pottery

This assemblage contains the remains of at least 19 Late Bronze Age vessels (nos. 1–19); all of these are coarse, domestic, flat-bottomed pots, re-used in burial contexts. The Darcystown vessels had all been broken prior to deposition and were associated with cremations in the fills of a ring ditch. Substantial

portions of Vessels 1–2, 4–6, and 14–17 were recovered but the other pots, nos. 3, 7–9 and 10–13, were represented by only a few sherds. The circumstances of deposition indicated that the pottery accompanied cremation burials and functioned as gravegoods. In this context it is interesting that some vessels may have been broken on site while others appear to have been brought to the site from domestic contexts as sherds only. Burnt accretions on Vessels 2, 10, 12, 15 and 18, and sooting on nos. 5–6, indicate that these seven vessels had been used for cooking, but it is probable that other pots, such as that represented by 112.1, had a similar use history. The presence of sherds from at least seven crucibles, only one of which (G. 136.13–21) was substantially represented, suggest material was also brought from an industrial context for deposition with the burials.

While there is some variation in the form, quality and size, the assemblage is reasonably homogenous and, from a ceramic perspective, the material appears to be contemporary. The pottery is, in general, in good condition although there is some surface wear that suggests the vessels had been used extensively prior to breakage and deposition. The Darcystown assemblage is made up of domestic pottery derived ultimately from settlement contexts. The fabric is similar in most of the pots. Local clays were combined with inclusions of crushed dolerite and occasionally small, water-rolled, sandstone pebbles; generally these were ≤ 5mm in maximum dimensions although occasionally larger pieces up to 14mm in length are present. However, the make-up of Vessel 9, which contains quartzite and mica inclusions, is significantly different although the ultimate finish is similar to that of the other pots. The pottery was well-fired and is compact with a generally hard smooth finish. Generally, the Darcystown 2 pottery is of medium to good quality within the overall Late Bronze Age range. Vessels 1–3 and 14–15 have unusually thin walls (8–10mm) and nos. 1 and 2 are of very fine quality. The body thickness of most of the other vessels is c. 13.8-17mm, similar to that of most Late Bronze Age domestic pots, while nos. 8, 13 and 18–19 (11.2-13.5mm) are only slightly finer that is common. It is probable that most of the pots were coil built although breakage patterns on nos. 1 and 15 indicate that at least part of these were slab built. The bases are generally simple angular junctions but Vessels 4–5, 9, 11, and 15–16 have a low vertical foot.

Vessels 1, 7, 11–13 and 18 have upright, open (where the rim is widest portion of the pot), profiles with gently curved bodies and slight footed bases (Fig. 1) while nos. 2 and 14 have more biconical, slightly closed, profiles. These vessel types are the most common within the Irish Late Bronze Age repertoire and occur, for example, at Lough Gur and Kilbane, Co. Limerick, Priestsnewtown, Co. Wicklow, and nearby at Darcystown Site 1, Co. Dublin, and Stamullin, Co. Meath (Fig. 1; Ó Ríordáin

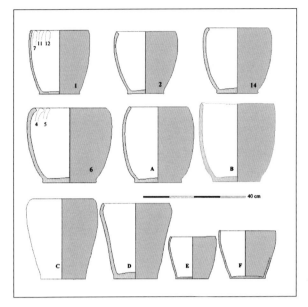

Figure 1: Conjectural reconstruction of Vessels 1, 2, 6 and 14 from Darcystown with (in red) rim profiles of Vessels 4, 5, 7 and 11–12; comparative vessels from: **A.** Mooghaun, Co. Clare (Vessel 1, Grogan 2005, Fig. 2.6), **B.** Lough Gur, Site C, Co. Limerick (Ó Ríordáin 1954, Fig. 16.1), **C.** Knockaholet, Co. Antrim (Henry 1934, Fig. 28.2), **D.** Circle P, Lough Gur (Grogan and Eogan 1987, Pl.23), **E–F.** Priestsnewtown, Co. Wicklow (Grogan and Roche 2004b).

1954; Grogan and Eogan 1987; O'Callaghan 2006; Grogan and Roche 2004a; 2004b; 2007a; 2007b). The more closed profiles of No. 4–6, 8 and 10, with a distinctive bulbous upper section, occur at a smaller number of sites including Knockaholet, Co. Antrim, Circle P, Lough Gur, Co. Limrick, Mooghaun, Co. Clare (Fig. 1; Henry 1934; Grogan and Eogan 1987; Grogan 2005), and Priestsnewtown (Tobin et al. 2004; Grogan and Roche 2004b, Fig. 1.1). Although the upper portions of the vessels from Darcystown Site 1 had been removed by agricultural activity it may be that some of these had similar upper profiles (Grogan and Roche 2007a). The Darcystown vessels have generally simple rounded rims. No. 2 (Fig. 1) has an gently concave internal bevel. These are a feature of Middle to Late Bronze Age vessels and probably accommodated a lid, of pottery, wood or stone. In discussing bevelled rims from other sites, including Rathgall, Raftery (1995, 154-55, Fig. 76) noted the similarity to the rims of stave-built wooden vessels, such as the Iron Age examples from Corlea, Co. Longford; similar Late Bronze Age vessels came from Lough Eskragh, Co. Tyrone (see Waddell 1998, Fig. 124:A5). Echoing Case (1961, 196), Raftery suggested that these might have been designed to support lids.

Context

All of the pottery came from fills within the ring ditch associated with cremations; similar examples occur at Shanaclogh, Co. Limerick (Gowen 1988, 68–72), and at Raynestown, Co. Meath (Stuart Elder pers comm.). This type of funerary deposit is one major element of Middle to Late Bronze Age burial traditions as is the contrasting custom of cremations contained in intact domestic vessels as at Darcystown Site 1 (Grogan 2004; Wiggins 2005). Despite the complexity of the fill sequences in the east and south-west segments, which produced most of the pottery, the ceramic analysis indicates that the fills were made up of discreet, individual, deposits. Thirteen vessels were represented by sherds from a single context (nos. 1, 3–9, 12, 14, 16, 18, 19) while nos. 2 (C115/117), 1, 13 (C111/113), 15 (C132/133) and 17 (C118/119) came from successive fills that probably indicate subtle differences rather that separate layers. No. 15 from two successive layers (C132/133) and a furrow (C134) that cut these fills. This suggests that individual vessels, or perhaps in the case of nos. 2–9, 11-14, 15–16 and 18–19, for example, groups of pots, accompanied each episode of burial. This may well reflect the type of burial practice at flat pit cemeteries, such as Darcystown 1, where intact vessels accompanied each burial (Grogan and Roche 2007a). At Darcystown 2, however, as noted above, it is clear that no complete vessels were involved; this suggests that the broken sherds of incomplete pots were brought to the site to accompany the burials. Some of the pots, such as nos. 2, 10, 12, 15 and 18 (see above) had already been used in domestic contexts. The selective deposition of broken pottery may mirror the selective nature of most cremations during the period which generally consist of only a small portion of the skeletal remains (Grogan et al. forthcoming). This evidence highlighted by the fragmentary crucibles that also appear to have been deposited in a broken condition as grave goods. One unusual example amongst the Darcystown vessels (no. 14) was represented by a sizeable portion of the pot and this appears to have no pre-deposition evidence for wear or usage. This is an exceptionally crude vessel with very considerable variation in the wall thickness giving it an extremely uneven appearance; in addition, the junction between the body and the exceptionally thick base does not appear to have been cleanly finished. Nevertheless, both surfaces retain evidence for burnishing, a very rare finish for Late Bronze Age pottery. It is possible that this pot was made specifically for inclusion with a burial although it too was only partly deposited in sherds.

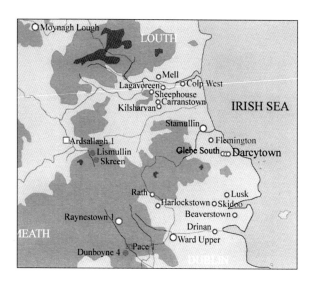

Figure 2: The distribution of Late Bronze Age pottery in the Darcystown region of north Dublin, east Meath and south Louth.

The regional context

Until very recently there were surprisingly few discoveries of Late Bronze Age pottery in the north Leinster region. Settlement evidence at Dalkey Island, Co. Dublin, and Moynagh Lough, Co. Meath, and burials at Athgarret, Co. Kildare, and Carrig, Co. Wicklow, were exceptions although a recent re-evaluation of the ceremonial enclosure at Lugg, Co. Dublin, has indicated that the pottery at this site is also of this period (Liversage 1968; Bradley 2004; Sleeman and Cleary 1987; Grogan 1990; Roche and Eogan forthcoming). A series of major infrastructural schemes in the region in the past 10 years has revealed an intensively settled landscape although there is a noticeable gap in the area now occupied by the metropolitan Dublin area (Fig. 2). Important new sites include the large enclosure at Stamullin, Co. Meath, the complex ring ditches at Raynestown, Co. Meath, and Priestsnewtown, Co. Wicklow, the ceremonial enclosure at Ward Upper, Co. Dublin, and several settlement sites at Charlesland, Co. Wicklow (Gil McLoughlin pers comm.; Grogan and Roche 2007b; Stuart Elder pers comm., Tobin et al. 2004; Grogan and Roche 2004b; Roche and Grogan 2005a; Grogan 2004b; Roche and Grogan 2005b).

References

Case, H. 1961. Irish Neolithic Pottery: Distribution and Sequence. *Proceedings of the Prehistoric Society* 9, 174–233.

Gowen, M. 1988. *Three Irish Gas Pipelines: New Archaeological Evidence in Munster*. Wordwell, Dublin.

Grogan, E. 1990. Bronze Age cemetery at Carrig, Co. Wicklow. *Archaeology Ireland* 4 (4), 12-14.

Grogan, E. 2004a. Middle Bronze Age burial traditions in Ireland. In H. Roche, E. Grogan, J. Bradley, J. Coles and B. Raftery (eds.), *From Megaliths to Metals. Essays in Honour of George Eogan*, 61–71. Oxbow, Oxford.

Grogan, E. 2004b. The prehistoric pottery assemblage from Charlesland, Co. Wicklow. Sites 1B, J, K, R.M.P, Area 5 and GC 1. Unpublished Report for Margaret Gowen and Co. Ltd.

Grogan, E. 2005. Appendix C. The pottery from Mooghaun South. In E. Grogan *The later prehistoric landscape of south-east Clare*, 317–28. Discovery Programme Monograph 6, Volume 1. The Discovery Programme/Wordwell, Dublin.

Grogan, E. and Eogan, G. 1987. Lough Gur excavations by Séan P. Ó Ríordáin: further Neolithic and Beaker habitations on Knockadoon. *Proceedings of the Royal Irish Academy* 87C, 299–506.

Grogan, E., O'Donnell, L. and Johnson, P. 2007. *The Bronze Age archaeology of the Gas Pipeline to the West*. Margaret Gowen and Co. Ltd./Wordwell, Dublin.

Grogan, E. and Roche, H. 2004a. The prehistoric pottery from Kilbane, Castletroy, Co. Limerick. Unpublished Report for Eachtra Archaeology Ltd.

Grogan, E. and Roche, H. 2004b. The prehistoric pottery from Site 6B, Priestsnewtown, Greystones, Co. Wicklow. Unpublished report for Judith Carroll and Company.

Grogan, E. and Roche, H. 2007a. The prehistoric pottery assemblage from Darcystown 1, Balrothery, Co. Dublin (03E0067/ 03E0067 extension). Unpublished report for Judith Carroll and Company.

Grogan, E. and Roche, H. 2007b. The prehistoric pottery assemblage from Stamullin, Co. Meath (05E1271/05E0962). Unpublished Report for Arch-Tech Ltd.

Henry, S. 1934. A Find of Prehistoric Pottery at Knockaholet, Parish of Loughguile, Co. Antrim.

Journal of the Royal Society of Antiquaries of Ireland 64, 264–5.

Liversage, G.D. 1968. Excavations at Dalkey Island, Co. Dublin, 1956–1959. *Proceedings of the Royal Irish Academy* 66C, 53–233.

O'Callaghan, N. 2006. Kilbane, Castletroy - Bronze Age flat cemetery and *fulachta fiadh*. In I. Bennett (ed.). *Excavations 2003*, 309–10. Wordwell, Dublin.

Ó Ríordáin, S.P. 1954. Lough Gur Excavations: Neolithic and Bronze Age Houses on Knockadoon, *Proceedings of the Royal Irish Academy* 56C, 297–459.

Raftery, B. 1995. The Conundrum of Irish Iron Age Pottery. In B. Raftery (ed.), *Sites and Sights of the Iron Age*, 149–156. Oxbow Monograph 56, Oxford.

Roche, H. and Eogan, G. forthcoming. A re-assessment of the enclosure at Lugg, Co. Dublin, Ireland. In C. Gosden *et al.* (eds.), *Communities and Connections: Essays in Honour of Barry Cunliffe*. Oxford University Press, Oxford.

Roche, H. and Grogan, E. 2005a. N2 Finglas – Ashbourne. Ward Upper, Co. Dublin (Site 6, 03E1358). Unpublished Report for CRDS Ltd.

Roche, H. and Grogan, E. 2005b. The prehistoric pottery assemblage from Charlesland, 'Durkin', Co. Wicklow. Sites C and D: Areas 1 and 4. Unpublished Report for Margaret Gowen and Co. Ltd.

Sleeman, M. and Cleary, R. 1987. Pottery from Athgarret, Co. Kildare, 43–44. In R. Cleary, M. Hurley and E. Twohig (eds), *Archaeological Excavations on the Cork–Dublin Gas Pipeline*, Cork Archaeological Studies 1, Cork.

Tobin, S., Swift, D. and Wiggins, K. 2004. Greystones Southern Access Route (GSAR), Co. Wicklow. Sites 6/6a-g, Priestsnewtown. Licence no. 04E0401. Unpublished report by Judith Carroll and Company for Wicklow County Council.

Waddell, J. 1998. *The Prehistoric Archaeology of Ireland*. Galway University Press, Galway.

Wiggins, K. 2005. Darcystown 1, Skerries Road, Balrothery. Licence no. 03E0067. Unpublished report by Judith Carroll and Company for Fingal County Council.

Plate 1: Post-excavation view of ring ditch, C003, facing south-east

Plate 2: East facing Section B of ring ditch

Plate 3: North-west facing Section L of ring ditch

Plate 4: North facing Section J of ring ditch

Plate 5: North facing Section M of ring ditch

Plate 6: South-west facing Section Q of ring ditch

Plate 7: North facing Section T of ring ditch

Plate 8: South facing Section U of ring ditch

Plate 9: South-east facing Section R of ring ditch

Plate 10: South-west facing Section V of ring ditch

Plate 11: East facing section of C009

Plate 12: North facing section of C254

Plate 13: Post-excavation view of C009, facing west

Plate 14: East facing section of kiln, C056

Plate 15: Post-excavation view of C056, facing south

Plate 16: South-east facing section of C011

Plate 17 Post-excavation view of C011, facing south

Plate 18: Late Bronze Age pottery from C113, fill of the ring ditch

Plate 19: Late Bronze Age pottery from C126, fill of the ring ditch

Plate 20: Late Bronze Age pottery from C126, fill of the ring ditch

CATALOGUE

Where the pottery is listed in the catalogue the context numbers are in bold: *e.g.*: **126**.1. Numbers in square brackets (*e.g.* **126**.[67–8]) indicate that the sherds are conjoined. The thickness refers to an average dimension; where relevant a thickness range is indicated. Vessel numbers have been allocated to pottery where some estimation of the form of the pot is possible, or where the detailed evidence of featured sherds (*e.g.* rims, bases) or fabric indicates separate vessels.

The excavation number 04E0741 is omitted throughout; only the context number, followed by the find number, is included.

The site produced 411 sherds (42 rim-, 55 base- or base angle-, 317 bodysherds and 237 fragments) representing at least 19 domestic vessels (weight: 5,570g). The pottery came from 15 contexts in the fill of a ring ditch. The pottery was broken prior to deposition and was associated with cremations. Seven crucibles are also present in these deposits (weight: 100g).

Context 115
Vessel 1. This is represented by 51 sherds (5 rimsherds: **115**.[79, 80, 107], 81, 1; 7 base- base-anglesherds: **115**.2, 82–5, 164–5; 39 bodysherds: **115**.[3–6], 7–12, 86–93, [108–9], 110–17, 120, [166–71], 172–5) from a fine, medium sized, vessel with a rounded upright rim; externally there is a broad shallow channel immediately beneath the rim. There is a flat base with a slight protruding foot that expands out sharply into the lower body. The grey to dark grey fabric is compact and slightly brittle with very smooth surfaces. There is a medium content of crushed dolerite inclusions (≤ 5 x 4mm). Thickness: 8.5mm. Weight: 400g.

Vessel 2. This is represented by 88 sherds (4 rimsherds: **115**.[75–6], 77–8; 7 base- base-anglesherds: **115**.[67–8], 13–15, 118–9; 67 bodysherds: **115**.16–51, [69–70], 71–4, 125–43, 176–84; **117**.1–10; 13 fragments: **117**.11–13) from a medium sized vessel with a rounded inturned rim and a gently concave internal bevel. The rounded and inturned upper body gives the vessel a bulbous profile. There is a flat, apparently unfooted, base that expands out gently into the lower body. The grey to dark grey fabric is hard and compact. The upper body has generally smooth surfaces but the exterior is rougher towards the base. There is a medium content of crushed dolerite inclusions (≤ 5 x 4mm, up to 6 x 5mm). There is a burnt accretion on the upper external surface and over much of the interior. Thickness: 8.5–10mm. Weight: 800g.
Maximum external rim diameter: *c.* 23cm.

A further 52 fragments and crumbs (**115**.52–66, 97–1-6, 121–4, 144–63, 185–8) are from Vessels 8 or 9 (Weight: 100g).

Context 117
This produced 10 sherds (plus 13 fragments) from Vessel 2 (see Context 115 above: weight 90g).

Context 140
Vessel 3. This is represented by 5 sherds (1 base anglesherd: **140**.5; 4 bodysherds: **140**.[1–4]) from a medium sized vessel of compact grey- to brown-buff fabric with smooth but uneven surfaces. There is a medium to high content of crushed dolerite inclusions (≤ 4 x 3mm, up to 9 x 8mm in the base). Thickness: 8.8mm. Weight: 115g.

Context 126
Vessel 4. This is represented by 12 sherds (5 rimsherds: **126**.57, [1, 58–60]; 7 bodysherds: **126**.7–8, 61–5; plus fragments: **126**.66, 15g) from a large domestic vessel with an inturned, flat topped, bulbous rim. The upper body has a bulbous profile. The distinctive brown- to grey-buff crumbly fabric has frequent surface and internal cavities. Where preserved the surfaces are smooth with some visible but not protruding inclusions. There is a high content of crushed dolerite inclusions (≤ 9.5 x 4.5mm, up to 8 x 8mm). Thickness: 17mm. Weight: 150g.

Vessel 5. This is represented by 11 sherds (3 rimsherds: **126**.[67–8], 2; 8 bodysherds: **126**.82–9) from a medium sized domestic vessel with an inturned rounded rim; there is a slight internal expansion. The upper body has a bulbous profile. The compact, well-fired, fabric is grey-buff to buff externally with a buff interior and a grey-buff core. The surfaces are very smooth with some visible but not protruding inclusions. There is a medium content of crushed dolerite inclusions (≤ 7.5 x 3.5mm, up to 8.5 x 8.5mm). Thickness: 13–4mm. Weight: 225g.

Vessel 6. This is represented by 21 sherds (6 rimsherds: **126**.[3–4], 5, 69–71; 1 basesherd: **126**.100;14 bodysherds: **126**.[9–11], 12, [90–1], 92–9) from a large domestic vessel with flat-topped inturned rim. The upper body has a bulbous profile. The compact, well-fired, fabric is brown-buff with a grey-buff core. The surfaces are very smooth with some visible but not protruding inclusions. There is a medium to high content of crushed dolerite inclusions (° 6 x 4mm, up to 11 x 6mm). There is external sooting along the upper 20mm of the body immediately beneath the rim. Thickness: 16mm. Weight: 500g.

Maximum external rim diameter: c. 28cm.

Other sherds

There are 48 bodysherds (**126**.25–39, 101–33; 230g) and 24 fragments (**126**134–62; 130g) from Vessel 5 or 6.

Vessel 7. This is represented by 6 sherds (4 rimsherds: **126**.6, 72–4; 2 base anglesherds: **126**.[75–6]) from a medium sized domestic vessel with rounded to slightly pointed upright rim, a gently rounded body profile and a flat unfooted base. The smooth fabric is red-buff to red with frequently protruding inclusions. There is a medium to high content of crushed dolerite inclusions (up to 8 x 6mm). There is a 10mm high band of external sooting immediately beneath the rim. Thickness: 16mm. Weight: 75g.

Maximum external base diameter: c. 11cm.

Vessel 8. This is represented by a single rimsherd (**126**.77) from a medium sized vessel with a pointed rim and an irregular internal bevel; the vessel has an inturned upper profile. The compact fabric is buff throughout with smooth but uneven surfaces. There is a medium content of crushed dolerite inclusions (≤ 4 x 3mm, up to 8 x 5mm). Thickness: 11.2–13.5mm. Weight: 40g.

126.80–1. Two base anglesherds from a flat unfooted base of buff fabric with a grey-buff core and a medium content of crushed dolerite inclusions. Weight: 10g. These may be from Vessel 8.

Vessel 9. This is represented by 5 bodysherds (**126**.15–9; 5 fragments: **126**.20–4) from a vessel of compact buff fabric with a low content of crushed quartzite and mica inclusions (up to 5 x 4mm); there are no sherds with both surfaces intact. Weight: 25g.

Crucibles

D. This is represented by a single rimsherd (**126**.78) from a crucible or possibly a very small vessel with a rounded rim and an upright profile. The compact fabric is buff throughout with smooth surfaces. There is a medium content of crushed dolerite inclusions (≤ 4 x 3mm, up to 8 x 5mm). Thickness: 10.2mm. Weight: 5g.

E. This is represented by a single worn bodysherd (**126**.79). The compact red-buff fabric has a smooth outer surface, the inner is not preserved. There is a medium content of crushed dolerite and uncrushed sandstone inclusions (up to 6x 5mm).

126.13–14 are pieces of hard buff to red-buff fabric similar to that of crucible D. These appear to have been small balls or folded pieces of clay attached to a vessel by pressing them onto the surface: possibly lugs or stabilisers from a crucible.

Other material

There are 5 pieces of very compact clay (**126**.134-8) containing small fragments and crumbs of pottery.

Context 135

Vessel 10. This is represented by 7 sherds (1 rimsherd: **135**.1; 4 base-, base anglesherds: **135**.[2–3], 4–5; 2 bodysherds: **135**.6–7; detached outer paste layer: **135**.8; 29 fragments: **135**.9–24) from a vessel with a round topped inturned rim and a bulbous upper body profile. The fabric is buff- to red-brown with smooth but uneven surfaces. The outer surface was finished with an unusually thick paste layer (2.5–5mm; see **135**.8) which has become detached from some of the surviving sherds. There is a medium to high content of crushed dolerite inclusions (≤ 5 x 3mm, up to 8.5 x 8mm) and some small sandstone pebbles (4 x 2mm). A burnt accretion forms a 15mm high band immediately beneath the rim on the external surface. Thickness: 13.8mm. Weight: 175g.

Crucibles

F. This small bowl or crucible is represented by 4 sherds (1 rimsherd: **135**.25; 3 bodysherds: **135**.26–8; 2 fragments: **135**.29–30) with a rounded rim and curved profile. The compact buff fabric is smooth but uneven with a medium content of crushed dolerite inclusions (≤ 4 x 3mm, up to 6 x 6mm). Thickness: 7.5–8.5mm. Weight: 25g.

Context 136

Vessel 18. This is represented by 3 sherds (1 rimsherd: **136**.1; 2 base anglesherds: **136**.[2–3]) from a medium sized vessel with a rounded upright rim and a rounded unfooted base that expands out sharply into the lower body. The red-buff fabric has smooth but uneven surfaces. There is a medium to high content of crushed dolerite inclusions (≤ 6 x 4mm). A burnt accretion forms a 15mm high band immediately beneath the rim on the external surface. Thickness: 12mm. Weight: 25g.

Vessel 19. This is represented by 3 bodysherds (**136**.4–6; 6 fragments: **136**.7–12) from a medium sized vessel of smooth buff fabric with a dark grey core. There is a high content of crushed dolerite inclusions (up to 14 x 6 x 4mm). Thickness: 11.5–14.2mm. Weight: 75g.

Other sherds

136.22 is a base anglesherd (plus 8 fragments: **136**.23–30) from a flat base with a slight, pinched-out, foot that expands sharply out into the lower body. The buff fabric has a smooth but uneven external surface. Weight: 50g.

Crucibles

G. Substantial refitting portion from a small crucible (**136**.13–21) with a rounded rim and curved profile: it is sub-rectangular with a shallow bowl-shaped profile. The buff fabric has a red-buff core: the inner part of the core has been heat affected and is pink. There are smooth but uneven surfaces. There is a medium content of crushed dolerite, sandstone and quartzite inclusions (up to 6.5 x 5 x 4mm). Dimensions: 37.5 x 35 x 24mm. Thickness: 7.6–10.2mm. Weight: 35g.

Context 113/111

Vessel 11. This is represented by 20 sherds (2 rimsherds: **113**.1, **111**.2; 3 base anglesherds: **113**.[9–11]; 15 bodysherds: **113**.[12–3], [21–22], 14–20; **111**.3–6; 2 fragments: **111**.7–8) from a medium-sized vessel with a flattened rim with a rounded outer face and a slightly expanded inner. The compact slightly friable fabric is buff to cream-buff with a grey-buff core. The outer surface has sheared-off nos. **113**.14–18. The slightly footed base expands gently into the straight to gently rounded body profile. There is a medium to high content of crushed dolerite inclusions (≤ 4 x 3mm, up to 9 x 7mm). Body thickness: 13.8mm. Weight: 260g.

Vessel 12. This is represented by 20 sherds (2 rimsherd/bodysherd: **113**.[2, 23]; 5 bodysherds: **113**.24–28]; **111**.3–6; 2 fragments: **113**.29–30) from a medium-sized vessel with a rounded rim and a flat internal bevel. The smooth cream-buff fabric has a grey-buff core; there are some patches of burnishing on the outer surface. A band of burnt material occurs on the outer surface 20mm below the rim. There is a high content of crushed dolerite inclusions (≤ 7 x 5mm, up to 10 x 8mm). Body thickness: 17mm. Weight: 65g.

Vessel 13. This is represented by 9 sherds (4 rimsherds: **113**.3–5, **111**.1; 5 bodysherds: **113**.31–35];

13 fragments: **113**.47) from a small to medium vessel with a rounded upright rim. The smooth buff fabric has a grey-buff core. There is a medium content of crushed dolerite inclusions (≤ 4 x 3mm, up to 8 x 5mm). Body thickness: 11mm. Weight: 25g.

Other sherds

There are a further 5 bodysherds (**113**.42–6) and 7 fragments (**113**.48–50) probably from Vessels 11–13.

Crucibles

A. This is represented by 3 sherds (**113**.36–8) with a pointed rim of fine buff fabric with a medium content of crushed dolerite inclusions (≤ 4 x 3mm). It appears to have a shallow profile. Weight: 5g.

B. This is represented by a rounded rimsherd (**113**.39) of hard buff fabric. Thin-walled (7mm) with deep U-shaped profile. Weight: 10g.

C. This is represented by 2 sherds (**113**.40–1) with a pointed rim of fine buff fabric with a low to medium content of crushed dolerite inclusions (≤ 3 x 2mm). Weight: 10g.

Context 112

112.1 is a bodysherd of compact buff to cream-buff fabric with a dark grey core and grey-buff inner sooted surface. There is a medium content of crushed dolerite inclusions (up to 10 x 8mm). Body thickness: 14mm. Weight: 20g.

112.2 is a bodysherd of compact buff to cream-buff fabric with a dark grey core. There is a medium content of crushed dolerite inclusions (up to 5 x 4mm). Body thickness: 12mm. Weight: 10g

Context 137

This produced a single worn bodysherd. Weight: 5g.

Context 133

Vessel 14. This is represented by 44 sherds (4 rimsherd: **133**.1–4; 8 base-, base anglesherds: **133**.[16–17], 25, 33, 34–35, 44; 32 bodysherds: **133**.5–9, 13–15, 26, 37, 39–42, 51–58, 67–70, 131–34, 136–37; 48 fragments: **133**.10–11, 18–24, 27–32, 43, 47–50, 60–64, 71–85, 135, 138–42) from a vessel with a rounded, slightly flattened, inverted rim with a gently curved closed profile and an unfooted domed base. The buff to red-brown-buff fabric is well-fired but rather crudely finished with a smooth but very irregular surface; both surfaces may have been burnished. The fabric is friable but there is no evidence for pre-depositional wear or use.

TABLE 1 VESSELS AND OTHER SHERDS

Vessel No.	Old Vessel No.	Context/feature	Area	Phase	Number of sherds	Rimsherds	Base-, baseangle	Bodysherds	Fragments	Inclusions	Vessel size	Weight (g)	Pottery type
1	8	115	2	I	51	5	7	39	0	D	M	400	LBA
2	9	115	2	I	78	4	7	67	0	D	M	800	LBA
2	9	117	2	I	10	0	0	10	13	D	Rim 23cm	90	LBA
	Other	115	2	I	0	0	0	0	52			100	LBA
		115/17	2	I	139	9	14	116	65			1390	LBA
3	13	140	2	II	5	0	1	4	0	D	M-L	115	LBA
4	1	126	2	III	12	5	0	7	0	D	M	150	LBA
5	2	126	2	III	11	3	0	11	0	D	M	225	LBA
6	3	126	2	III	21	6	1	14	0	D	Rim 28cm	500	LBA
7	4	126	2	III	6	4	0	2	0	D	M	75	LBA
	Other	126	2	III	33	0	0	33	0	D		230	LBA
	Other	126	2	III	0	0	0	0	24			130	LBA
8	5	126	2	III	1	1	0	0	0	D	M	40	LBA
9	7	126	2	III	5	0	0	5	5	Q	M	25	LBA
	Other	126	2	III	2	0	2	0	0	D	?	10	LBA
		126			91	19	3	72	29			1385	LBA
10	10	135	2	III	7	1	4	2	29	D S	M	175	LBA
11	14	113/111	2	III	20	2	3	15	2	D	M	260	LBA
12	15	113	2	III	6	1	0	5	2	D	M	65	LBA
13	16	113/111	2	III	9	4	0	5	13	D	S-M	25	LBA
	Other	113	2	III	5	0	0	5	7			15	LBA
	Other	112	2	III	2	0	0	2	0	D	M	30	LBA
14	17	113	2	III	44	4	8	32	48	D	Rim 24.5cm	930	LBA
		111/12/13			86	11	11	64	72			1325	
15	18	132/33/34	2	III	61	0	12	49	11	D	Body 19cm	625	LBA
16	19	132	2	III	3	0	2	1	0	D	Body 19cm	200	LBA
17	20	118/19	2	III	3	0	0	3	3	D	-	30	LBA
		132-4, 118-9			67	0	14	53	14			855	
18	11	136	2	III	3	1	2	0	0	D	M	25	LBA
19	12	136	2	III	3	0	0	3	6	D	?	75	LBA
	Other	136	2	III	1	0	1	0	8	D	L	50	LBA
		136	2	III	7	1	3	3	14			150	LBA
	Other	104	B		2	0	2	0	0	D	?	25	LBA
		104/136			16	2	8	6	28			325	
		Crucibles											
D	6	126.78			1	1	0	0	0		?	5	LBA
E		126.13–14										10	LBA
F		135.25–30										25	LBA
G		136.13–21									37 x 35mm	35	LBA
A		113.36–38										5	LBA
B		136.39										10	LBA
C		136.40–41										10	LBA
												100	

TABLE 2 TOTAL SHERD COUNT

Vessel No.	Old Vessel No.	Context/feature	Area	Phase	Number of sherds	Rimsherds	Base-, baseangle	Bodysherds	Fragments	Inclusions	Vessel size	Weight (g)	Pottery type
		115/17			139	9	14	116	65			1390	LBA
13		140	2	II	5	0	1	4	0	D	M-L	115	LBA
		126			91	19	3	72	29			1385	LBA
10		135	2	III	7	1	4	2	29	D S	M	175	LBA
		111/12/13			86	11	11	64	72			1325	
		132-4, 118-9			67	0	14	53	14			855	
		104/136			16	2	8	6	28			325	
					411	42	55	317	237			5570	

There is a medium content of crushed dolerite inclusions (up to 10 x 8mm) with occasional pieces of uncrushed rounded quartzite (≤ 5 x 4mm). Body thickness: 12.2–13.2mm; base: 19–22mm. Weight: 930g.

Maximum external rim diameter: *c.* 24.5cm.
Maximum external body diameter: *c.* 26.5cm
Maximum base diameter: *c.* 16c

Context 132/133/134

Vessel 15. This is represented by 61 sherds (12 base-, base anglesherds: **133**.65–66, **132**.[1, 6, 7], 2, 4–5, 7–10, **134**.1; 49 bodysherds: **133**.12, 38, 45–46, 59, 130, 135, 143, **132**.3, 11–28, **134**.[2–5], 6–12; 11 fragments: **133**.144–6, **132**.30–33) from a vessel with a low (10mm) upright foot that expands very gently into a straight to gently curved body. The smooth buff to grey-buff fabric is compact and well-fired with a grey to grey-buff inner surface; the external surface is rougher towards the base. A burnt accretion occurs on the inner surfaces of **133**.130, **132**.3, 11–14. There is a medium content of crushed dolerite inclusions (≤ 3 x 2mm; up to 8 x 5mm). The refitting sherds **134**.[2–5] indicate that at least part of the vessel was slab, rather than coil, built. Body thickness: 8–10.5mm. Weight: 625g.

Maximum external body diameter: *c.* 19cm
Maximum base diameter: *c.* 8cm

Context 132

Vessel 16. This is represented by 3 sherds (2 base-, base anglesherds: **132**.34–35; 1 bodysherd: **132**.29) from a vessel with a low (10mm) upright foot that expands

sharply into a gently curved body. The smooth buff to grey-buff fabric is compact with smooth but uneven surfaces. There is a medium content of crushed dolerite inclusions (up to 8 x 5mm). Body thickness: 10mm. Weight: 200g.

Maximum external body diameter: *c.* 19cm
Maximum base diameter: *c.* 14.5cm

Context 134

The fill of this furrow produced 12 sherds (**134**.1–12) from Vessel 18 (see above).

Context 118/19

Vessel 17. This is represented by 3 bodysherds (**118**.1, **119**.1–2; 3 fragments: **118**.2–4) from a vessel of smooth buff to cream-buff fabric with a high content of crushed dolerite inclusions (≤ 8 x 8mm). Body thickness: 12mm. Weight: 30g.

Section B

Context 104

There are 2 basesherds (**104**.[1–2] from the disc base of buff-brown fabric with a medium content of crushed dolerite inclusions. Weight: 25g.

APPENDIX IV

THE ANIMAL BONES FROM DARCYSTOWN 2, BALROTHERY, CO. DUBLIN (04E0741)

Catherine Bonner

The animal bones which were retrieved from Balrothery Site 2 are fragmented and poorly preserved, and indicate that soil conditions at the site were unfavourable to bone preservation. The extremely high proportion of teeth encountered in the samples also suggests poor bone preservation properties, as teeth have a better survival rate than that of other bones due to their protective enamel. The eroded surfaces of the bones hindered the identification of butchery marks, but none were encountered in the analysis. Pathological lesions were also absent.

It can be seen from Table 1 that the three main domesticates (cattle, pig and sheep/goat) were identified, as well as horse. The vast majority of bones were those of cattle. Few epiphyses were preserved in the samples, and the vast majority of these were of mature individuals. It should be noted that the high proportion of mature individuals

suggested in the samples is unlikely to represent an accurate age profile, but rather to indicate poor bone preservation. This is because in areas of poor bone preservation fused bones survive better than their unfused counterparts because they are less porous. The only unfused specimen came from pig (Context 74) and represents an individual of less than twenty-four months of age (Silver 1969, 285-286).

Bibliography

Driesch, A. von den, 1976. *A Guide to the Measurement of Animal Bones from Archaeological Sites.* Peabody Museum Bulletin, Harvard.

Silver, I. A. 1969. The ageing of domestic animals. In D. Brothwell and E. Higgs (eds.), *Science and Archaeology*, London (2nd edition), 283-302.

Table 1 Fragments distribution for faunal material from Darcystown 2, Balrothery. Metrical information after von den Driesch (1976)

Context	No. fragments	Species	Anatomy	Details
10	12	Cattle	Tooth	Fragments
	1	Cattle	Humerus	Fragment
	1	Cattle	Femur	Shaft
	1	Cattle	Metatarsal	L, P
	4	S/G	Tooth	Fragments
	50	Unid.		
12	1	Unid.		
65	9	Cattle	Tooth	Fragments
	3	Cattle	Radius	Shaft fragments
	7	Unid.		
69	20	Cattle	Skull	Fragments
	87	Cattle	Tooth	Fragments
	1	Cattle	Mandible	Fragment
	1	Cattle	Scapula	Fragment
	1	Pig	Tooth	M3
	3	LM	Longbone	Fragment
	39	Unid.		

Key: S/G=sheep or goat; LM=large mammal (cattle or horse); MM=medium mammal (pig, sheep or goat); Unid.=unidentifiable; L=left; R=right; P=proximal end; D=distal end; FU=fused epiphysis; UN=unfused epiphysis.

Table 1 (contd.) Fragments distribution for faunal material from Darcystown 2, Balrothery. Metrical information after von den Driesch (1976)

Context	No. fragments	Species	Anatomy	Details
73	1	Cattle	Skull	Fragment
	66	Cattle	Tooth	Fragments
	1	Cattle	Metacarpal	Shaft
	1	Cattle	Metatarsal	Shaft
	2	Horse	Tooth	Fragment
	1	Pig	Skull	Fragment
	2	Pig	Scapula	1L(FU). GLP=35.1, LG=26.7
	17	Unid.		
74	11	Cattle	Tooth	Fragments
	1	Cattle	Humerus	Shaft
	1	Cattle	Ulna	Fragment
	1	Cattle	Tibia	Fragment
	1	Pig	Metatarsal IV	R, D (UN)
	1	LM	Longbone	Fragment
	1	LM	Rib	
	202	Unid.		
111	1	Horse	Tooth	Molar
112	20	Cattle	Tooth	Molar fragments
113	98	Cattle	Tooth	Fragments
	1	Cattle	Mandible	Right symphysis
	2	Horse	Tooth	Molar fragments
	2	Pig	Tooth	Molar fragments
	1	LM	Longbone	Shaft
	16	Unid.		
115	18	Cattle	Tooth	Fragments
	1	Cattle	Mandible	Fragment
	6	Cattle	Humerus	1R, D (FU)
	1	Cattle	Metacarpal	D (FU)
	1	Cattle	Pelvis	Fragment
	83	Unid.		
117	2	Cattle	Humerus	1R, D
	3	Cattle	Pelvis	1L (FU)
	51	Unid.		
119	28	Cattle	Tooth	Molar fragments
126	106	Cattle	Tooth	Fragments
	5	Pig	Tooth	Molar fragments
	2	Unid.		
128	3	Cattle	Tooth	Fragments
133	15	Cattle	Tooth	Fragments
134	13	Cattle	Tooth	Fragments
	4	LM	Longbone	Fragments
136	46	Cattle	Tooth	Molar fragments
	2	Pig	Tooth	Molar fragments
140	3	Cattle	Tooth	Fragments
	6	Pig	Tooth	Fragments

Key: S/G=sheep or goat; LM=large mammal (cattle or horse); MM=medium mammal (pig, sheep or goat); Unid.=unidentifiable; L=left; R=right; P=proximal end; D=distal end; FU=fused epiphysis; UN=unfused epiphysis.

APPENDIX V

OSTEOARCHAEOLOGICAL REPORT ON HUMAN CREMATED BONES RECOVERED FROM
DARCYSTOWN 2, BALROTHERY, CO. DUBLIN, EXCAVATION LICENCE NO. 04E0741

Patricia Lynch B.A. M.Sc. M.I.A.I.

Introduction

The cremated human bone in this report was recovered from Darcystown 2, Balrothery, Co. Dublin. The preservation of the bone was very poor with all of the bones in a very fragmentary condition. As a result of this only circa 30% of the recovered bone was identifiable.

The data in this report is recorded as an inventory of the identifiable bone.

The presence of any pathology and non-metric trait are recorded, and described.

Where possible age-at-death and species estimation are also recorded.

The estimation of the number individuals present is by counting the minimum amount of bones from each individual, not per find.

While some individual bones and tooth roots were identified, *Plate 1*, the cremated bone was too fragmentary to further identify sex estimation or a more specific age at death.

The density of the bones from each context suggests an adult.

There was no evidence of pathologies and non-metric traits in the assemblage, but this was probably as a result of the fragmentary condition of the bone fragments.

The animal tooth fragments recovered were unburnt.

In summery, the remains of ten human skeletons were identified.

See inventory opposite.

Discussion and Conclusion

These cremated bone fragments were recovered from an excavation at Darcytyown, Balrothery, Co. Dublin.

The bones were in a very fragmentary condition and as a result of this it was only possible to identify 30% of the bone.

The bone samples were recovered from C60, 61, 111, 112, 113, 115, 126, 132, 133 and 136

In all 505.75g of cremated human bone was recovered.

The Minimum Number of Individuals of the analysis is further summarized as follows:

C60	1 Adult
C61	1 Adult
C111	1 Adult
C112	1 Adult
C113	1 Adult & 1 Cow
C115	1 Adult
C126	1 Adult & 1 Cow
C132	1 Adult
C133	1 Adult
C136	1 Adult

CONTEXT NO.	INVENTORY	COMMENTS
C060, Sample # 2.	2g of cremated bone fragments 1.77mm - 11.18mm including: 3 articular surface fragments Remains representing one Adult.	No pathologies present. No post-mortem trauma present. Insufficient bone to estimate sex.
C061, Sample # 3.	0.75g of cremated bone fragments 2.56mm - 8.93mm. No post-mortem trauma present. Insufficient bone to estimate sex. Remains representing one Adult.	No pathologies present.
C111, Sample # 22.	4g of cremated bone fragments, 3.96 - 13.54mm, including; 1 skull fragment, 1 tooth crown fragment. Insufficient bone to estimate sex. Remains representing one Adult.	No pathologies present. No post-mortem trauma present.
C112, Sample # 21.	3g of cremated bone fragments, 2.03mm – 16.31mm. No post-mortem trauma present. Insufficient bone to estimate sex. Remains representing one Adult.	No pathologies present.
C113, Sample # 16.	68g of cremated bone fragments, 3.63mm - 30.68mm, and one unburnt animal tooth fragment including: 3 skull fragments, 1 tooth root, 1 coracoid process of ulna, 1 rib shaft fragment, 5 pelvis fragments, 3 articular surfaces. Remains representing one Adult human and one Cow.	No pathologies present. 1 unburnt Cow tooth fragment No post-mortem trauma present. Insufficient bone to estimate sex.
C115, Sample # 15.	159g cremated bone fragments, 2.95mm - 40.81mm, including: 35 skull fragments including L orbit with supraorbital notch and occipital fragments, 2 tooth roots, 1 metacarpal shaft fragment, 5 rib shaft fragments, 3 vertebra fragments, 3 femur shaft fragments, 1 tibia shaft fragment, 1 fibula shaft fragment.	No pathologies present. No post-mortem trauma present. Insufficient bone to estimate sex. Remains representing one Adult.
C126, Sample # 34.	87g of cremated bone fragments, 1.86mm - 28.90mm, and 23 animal tooth root fragments including: 5 skull fragments, 1 tooth root fragment, 1 pisiform (carpal bone) fragment, 3 rib shaft fragments, 4 articular surface fragments. 23 fragment unburnt Cow tooth.	No pathologies present No post-mortem trauma present. Insufficient bone to estimate sex. Remains representing one Adult human and one Cow. .
C132, Sample # 26, 31, 39.	160g of cremated bone fragments, 3.19mm - 54.40mm, including: 55 skull fragments including 1 R petrous portion of temporal, maxilla, occipital fragments, 2 scapular axillary border fragments, 5 rib shaft fragments, 3 vertebra fragments including body, 4 pelvis fragments, 1 fibula shaft fragment.	No pathologies present. No post-mortem trauma present. Insufficient bone to estimate sex. Remains representing one Adult.
C133, Sample # 40.	18g cremated bone fragments, 2.92mm - 26.79mm, including: 10 skull fragments, 2 vertebral body fragments. Insufficient bone to estimate sex. Remains representing one Adult.	No pathologies present. No post-mortem trauma present.
C136, Sample # 35.	4g cremated bone fragments, 3.19mm – 15.61mm. No post-mortem trauma present. Insufficient bone to estimate sex. Remains representing one Adult.	No pathologies present.

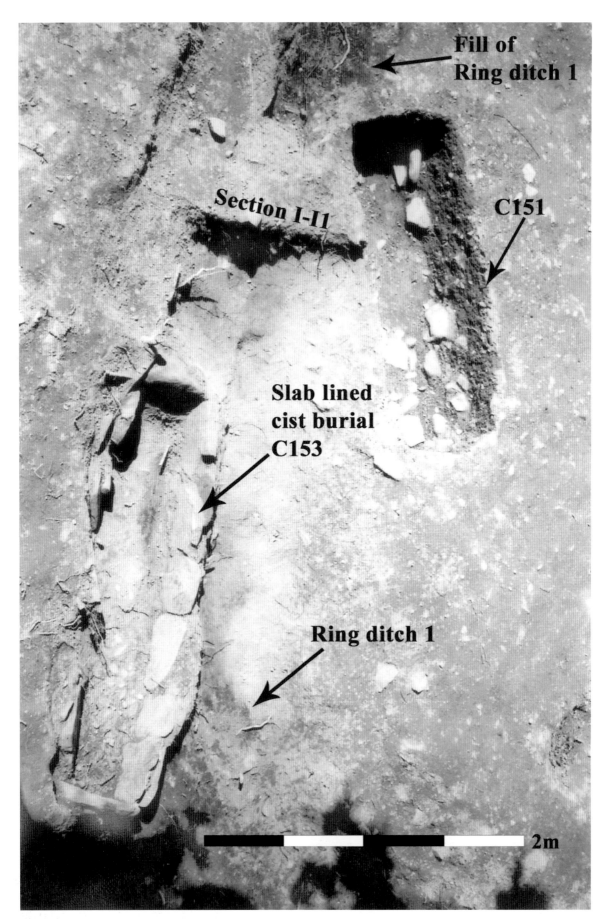

Plate 1: Slab lined cist burial, C153, of early medieval date and Late Iron Age inhumation grave cut, C151, cut into Ring ditch 1

CHAPTER 4

Excavation of Iron Age ring ditches, cist burials and features relating to habitation at Glebe South

Frank Ryan

The site, excavated under licence 04E0680, at Glebe South, comprised two Iron Age ring ditch burial sites (Ring ditches 1 and 2) in a cemetery also containing cremation pits of Bronze Age date; cremation burials of the early centuries AD; associated inhumation cist burials of probable Iron Age to early medieval date; a medieval ditch with cereal-drying kilns and a round house of Early to Middle Bronze Age date with a pit containing grains.

BACKGROUND

Prior to application for planning permission for a housing development within parts of two townlands, Darcystown and Glebe South, this company was asked to carry out an archaeological assessment by the developers, Mullen Developments Ltd in 2002.

Planning permission was granted by Fingal County Council for a housing development on the site in 2004, subject to archaeological monitoring and resolution of any archaeological features found. Monitoring of topsoil removal from the site prior to ground preparation works was undertaken in April 2004 under licence number 02E0043 by Judith Carroll & Company.

Several archaeological features were identified during monitoring in the two large fields which comprised the area of the development. The features, found in the west field (in Glebe South townland), were grouped quite closely together and were deemed sufficiently significant to warrant a separate license for excavation (see extent of excavation Figs. 1 and 2). A licence (04E0680) was granted for excavation of the complex of sites and features in Glebe South. These included two ring ditches, an associated inhumation cemetery, several related cremation pits, a linear ditch which ran through the site, cereal drying kilns and a structure. Initially it was not clear how these features related to each other and they were treated as a complex. The excavation took place over six weeks, between June and July 2004. Beta Analytic Inc. carried out the C14 dating for the site (Appendix I). The pottery from the site was examined by Eoin Grogan and Helen Roche (Appendix II). The osteological analysis was carried out by Patricia Lynch (Appendix III and IV) and the

charcoal from the site was examined by Ellen O'Carroll (Appendix V). Meriel McClatchie carried out environmental analysis of material from a pit C011 related to the Bronze Age hut site (Appendix VI).

THE SITE

The site was located in a long field, in which the west half of the area of the development was located. The field rose as a hill from the north to the south, with the neighbouring hill of Rosepark to the north. The burial sites were found in the south half of the field on its east border by the townland boundary of Glebe South which was delineated on the east side by the road to Lusk (Fig. 1). The road ran north and circled around to the west. North of the site, and within the sharp curve formed by the road, is a recent housing estate which is part of Glebe South and would have originally been part of the land to the south of the medieval church. The medieval church is directly north-west of the curved line.

THE EXCAVATION

When the features were revealed during monitoring, their relationship to each other was not immediately apparent. What came to light initially was a very concentrated group of burials on the south side of the site, at its east edge. These were located close to edge of the field by the townland boundary. The burials comprised two ring ditches, some cremation pits and at least 17 inhumation burials in cists which were related to the ring ditches. Some walls and trenches running across Ring ditch 2 were found to

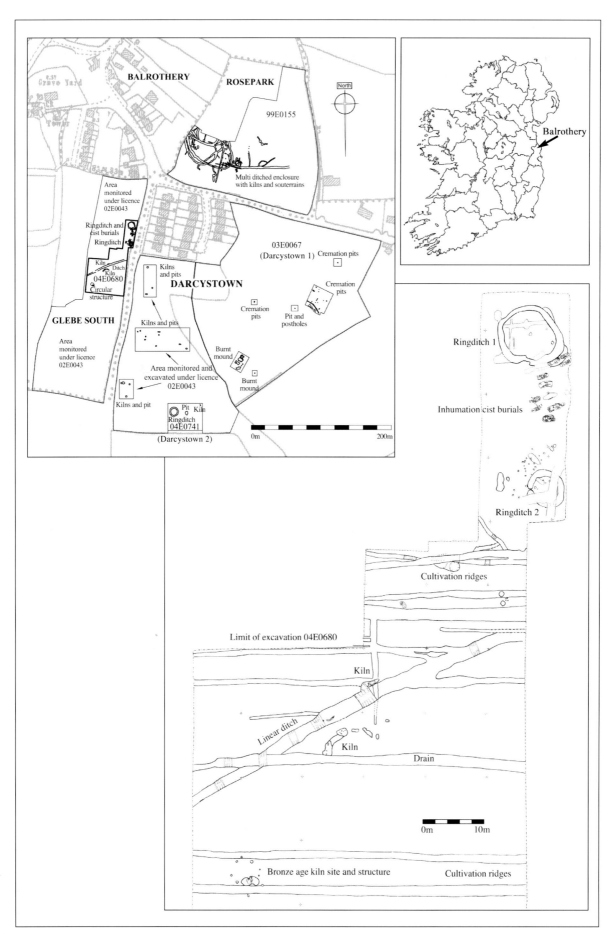

Figure 1: Glebe South, site location and plan of site.

relate to a post-medieval structure superimposing it.

To the south of the ring ditches, a linear ditch, aligned north-east/south-west, ran across the site. This ditch was superimposed by kilns relating to cereal drying activity. On its south-west side was a structure of post-holes containing a pit in which Early to Middle Bronze Age pottery was found.

RING DITCH 1

The ring ditch

A dark band of organic clay (C166) came to light during the removal of topsoil in this area. It was approximately. 0.5m in width and enclosed a roughly

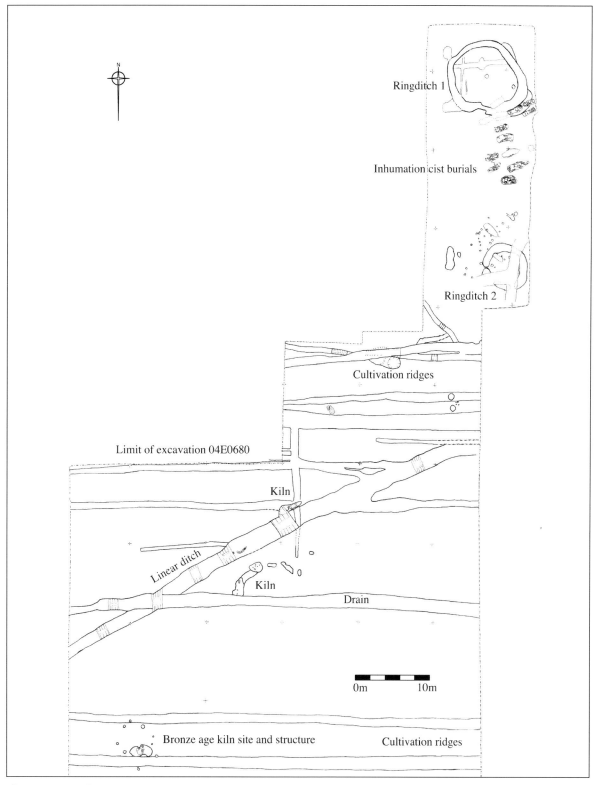

Figure 2: Plan of archaeological features at Glebe South

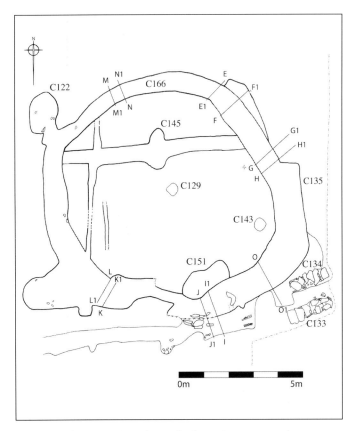

Figure 3: Plan of Ring ditch 1 prior to excavation

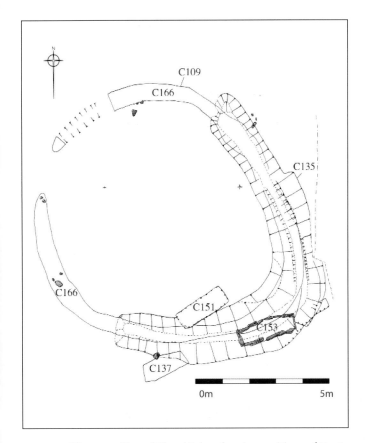

Figure 4: Plan of Ring ditch 1 showing positions of C116 (cut C109) and cut, C135

circular area of about 10m in diameter (Fig. 3; Plate 4 and 5).

The organic clay, C166 was part of the upper fill of a ditch cut (C109). C109 was cut through a wider ditch cut (C135) which contained a cremation deposit. C135 did not form a full circle. It was best described as a roughly semi-circular to 'boomerang' shape (Fig. 4).

One arm of C135 (Fig. 4), was aligned east-west for about 7.5m, curving northwards for a further approximate 8.5m. C135 may be an earlier cut as its north terminus was well defined and this was cut through by C109 (fill C166). However, there was no clear edge on the south-west end due to disturbance by later inhumation burials. The later cut, C109, which was a narrow penannular ditch, cut through C135, but may not be significantly later. There appeared to be no cremation deposits associated with cut C109 or its fills.

The base of C135 was flat and up to 0.7m in width, at the north end (Fig. 6). C109, which was a much narrower and shallower cut, was U to V shaped in most places, 0.3m-0.35m in maximum width of its main primary fill, C170.

The base of C135 contained a number of stony, sand fills. C210, was located on its east side (Section H-H1, Fig. 7) and extended to the north where a similar basal layer, C203, contained less stones (Sections F-F1 and G-G1, Fig. 7).

At the south end of the base of the trench was C181, a very stony sand, and C183, a less stony silty of loose compaction. Overlying C181 on the south-east side was a layer of loose silty sand, C184. C183, on the north-west side immediately underlay the later ditch cut, C109, and its fill C166 (Section 0-01, Fig. 6).

C183 was overlain by a deposit of light brown sand, C182, which contained a layer of stones within its fill. Further west, the primary fill C205, contained small patches of charcoal and cremated bone within a silty sand layer, 0.8m in maximum width by 0.26m in depth (Sections I-I1 and J-J1). A sand deposit, C206 (Section J – J1), containing occasional pebbles overlay this layer and may have extended east for at least 3m where it was recorded in section as C184 (Section 0 – 01). The north end of the primary cut C135 contained C208, a stony, clayey sand which superimposed C203. This deposit was 0.19m in depth. C208 was overlain by C211.

Above the primary deposits was a spread of charcoal-rich soil, C178, containing cremated bone. This layer became thinner and more widely spread towards the north. It extended from the north edge of the ditch cut, C135, but was more concentrated at a distance of 3m from the north edge where it was

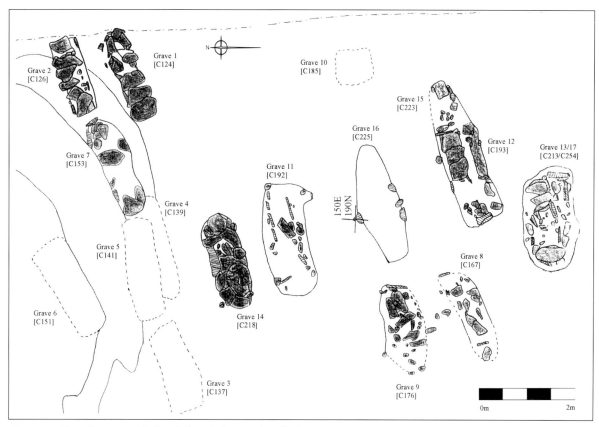

Figure 5: Plan of graves with lintels in relation to Ring ditch 1

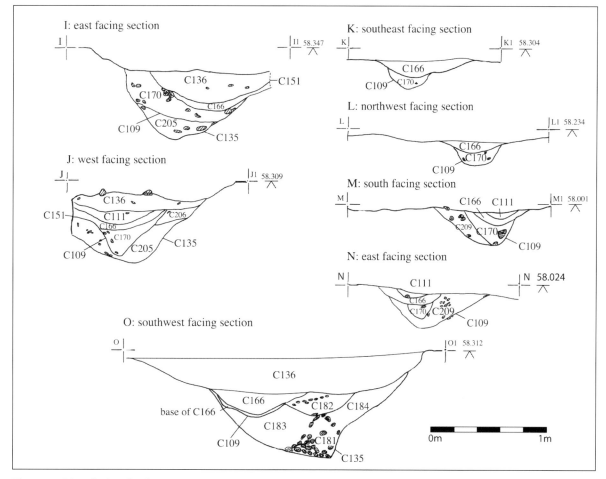

Figure 6: Ring ditch 1, Sections I – O

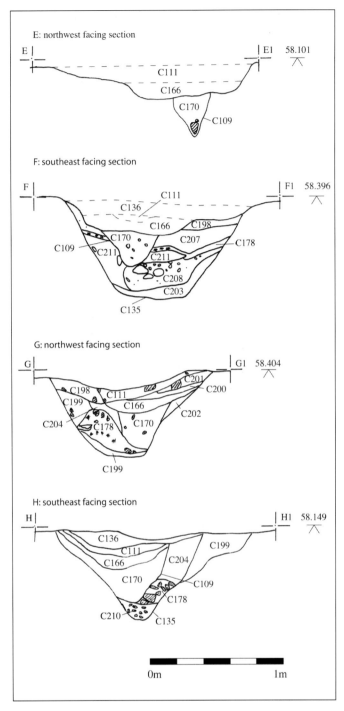

Figure 7: Ring ditch 1, Sections E – H

0.52m in width and 0.25m in depth (Sections F-F1, G-G1 and H-H1, Fig. 6). C178 produced a radiocarbon date of 2060±40 BP, calibrated to 200 BC to AD 10 (Beta-229060). It also produced three very small copper alloy fragments of a probable fibula (Plate 22), possibly of Navan type (04E0680: 178: 1-3). One of the fragments was a bar with a slight ball head (Plate 21) resembling those illustrated by Hawkes from Navan, Co. Armagh (Hawkes 1982, 63, Fig. 10). A glass bead (Plate 16) was also found in this context (04E0680: 178: 4).

C178 was overlain by a sandy, stony layer (C199) in which was found a small, fragmentary, thin, rolled over bronze plate (04E680: 199: 1, Plate 19). C178 was also overlain by a C204, a layer composed of orange-brown sand containing flecks of charcoal and this abutted C199 (Section H-H1, Fig. 7). A mid brown to yellow coarse sand, C207, superimposed the cremation layer, C178, further north of C204 and C199. C207 was overlain by a thin layer of pebbly sand, 0.4m in width and 0.08m in depth (Sections F-F1, G-G1, H-H1, Fig. 7).

A shallow cut, C369 (Section N-N1, Fig. 6), was found close to the north terminus of the ditch cut, C109, on the west side of the ring ditch. This feature was 0.87m north-west/south-east and contained one fill, C209, a light brown medium sand of moderate compaction with frequent small sub-angular stones, 0.3m in depth. This feature, which may be coeval with ditch cut C135, was cut through by C109.

C109, the stratigraphically later cut, was narrower throughout and irregularly 'V' shaped. It enclosed a circular area, approximately 8m in diameter and was shallowest on the west side, where the ring ditch was more truncated.

The primary fill, C170, of C109, was contained throughout the base of the penannular cut, apart from a patch in the south-east area (Section O-O1, Fig. 6) where C170 was not detected. C170 comprised silty sand with occasional charcoal flecks. Some small unidentified copper alloy flakes probably from a bronze object were found in this layer (04E0680:170:1). The layer was widest and deepest on the east side, reaching the upper level of the cut on the inner edge of the ring ditch (Section H-H1, Fig. 7) and the outer edge of the cut on the south side (Section J-J1, Fig. 6).

C170 was superimposed by C166 (Plate 4), a dark-brown/ black silt which appeared in many areas on the surface when the topsoil was removed. A quartz crystal (04E01680:166:1, Plate 23) and a piece of worked flint (04E01680:166:2) were found within the fill at the north end of the ditch in this layer.

Superimposing C166, in areas, was a layer of very stony dark brown silty sand (C111), a loose sand (C200) and a redeposited natural subsoil (C201).

These two latter deposits may represent slippage from the inner edge of the ring ditch on the east side (Section G-G1, Fig. 7). C111 was not present on the west side of the ring ditch and it would appear that the layers above C166 were disturbed in this area. A thick, loose layer of sandy soil with moderate stone inclusions (C136) formed the upper ditch fill layer on the east half of the ditch where the stratigraphy was better preserved (Section H-H1, Fig. 7; Section O-O1, Fig. 6).

Features cut into Ring ditch 1, including cremation pits

There were five pit-type features cut into the ring ditch. Four were situated within the circumference of the ring ditch. One was cut into the outer edge of the ditch on the north-west side (Fig.3)

Cremation deposit in pit C122

C122 was a sub-oval in plan, 1.45m north-east/south-west by 1.3m north-west/south-east. It was 0.15m in depth. C122 was cut into the outer slope of the ring ditch on its north-west side. It contained one fill, C123, an ashy, grey, silty sand with brown mottling. C123 was of moderate compaction with occasional charcoal flecks and occasional sub-angular and rounded stones. It also contained bone and five iron fragments. The ashy grey silt and bone would suggest the contents of the pit comprised a cremation deposit.

Pit C129

C129 was cut into the south half of the ring ditch, close to the centre. It was sub-circular in plan, 0.43m in diameter by 0.15m in depth. It contained one fill (C130), a light brown, medium sand of moderate compaction with frequent charcoal in the upper area, reddish sand in the lower area and occasional sub-circular and sub-rectangular stones.

Pit, C143

C143 was cut into the south-east side of the area inside the ditch. It was circular in plan, 0.47m in diameter by 0.09m in depth. It was a shallow feature with steep sides, containing one fill (C144), a dark brown, charcoal stained, medium sand. C144 also contained frequent sub-angular stones and a single piece of bone, indicating a probable token cremation pit, with large charcoal fragments which formed a layer at the base of the fill. Charcoal from C144 produced a radiocarbon date of 1690±50 BP, calibrated to AD 240 to 430 (Beta-229059).

Pit, C145

C145, a long, shallow pit of irregular shape, was disturbed by a furrow. It was 1.5m north/south by 0.9m east/west and 0.08m in depth. Its break of slope was gentle and uneven. It contained one fill (C146), a greyish dark brown silty sand of loose compaction with occasional charcoal and moderate sub-rounded small stones. An unidentified iron object (0E0680:146:1) was found in this pit.

Inhumation burials cut into Ring ditch 1 and located to the east of it

A total of 17 inhumation burials were excavated within, or to the south of, Ring ditch 1. All were closely spaced within an area of 11.5m (Fig. 5). Of these, one was located within the area enclosed by the ring ditch and six were cut into, or located at the edge of, the southern side of the enclosing ditch

There were sixteen stone-lined cists of slate, limestone or shale. Only one inhumation burial, that within the ring ditch itself (Grave 6, C151), was not stone-lined, but the base of the grave appeared to be flagged, suggesting a difference between Grave 6 and the other graves.

The condition of the stone-lined cists varied (Fig. 8). Some were very fragmentary, if present at all, with only a few stones remaining. Eight bore evidence of lintels. Three of the cists (Graves 4, 15 and 17) were cut by later cists (Graves 5, 12 and 13 respectively).

The articulated remains were generally extended supine in the graves which were orientated roughly east/west, or, as in the case of Grave 6, north-east/south-west, with the heads to the west or south-west.

The human remains found among the 17 burials were in a poor state of preservation and very fragmentary. Disturbance, due to later farming activity, roots of trees and animal burrows caused considerable damage to some of the graves. Grave 10 was so badly damaged that the extreme east end of the grave was defined only by a few round stones enclosing an arc 0.6m in length by 0.3m in width (Figs. 5 and 8).

The burials are described briefly as follows with details of the human remains in the osteological report (Appendix III).

Grave 1

Grave cut C124 was rectangular in plan, 1.9m east/west by 0.6m north/south and 0.21m in depth. The stone cist was well constructed and well preserved, covered with capstones of assorted size, 0.2m - 0.55m, sub-rectangular to irregular flat slate slabs. It was lined on all sides with stone slabs. Ten stones lay vertically directly up against sides of cut (124): three on the south side, five on the north side and one at each end. The partial remains of an articulated adult female skeleton was extended within, supine, east/west, head to west. The north-west corner of the grave was cut into C136, the upper ring ditch fill.

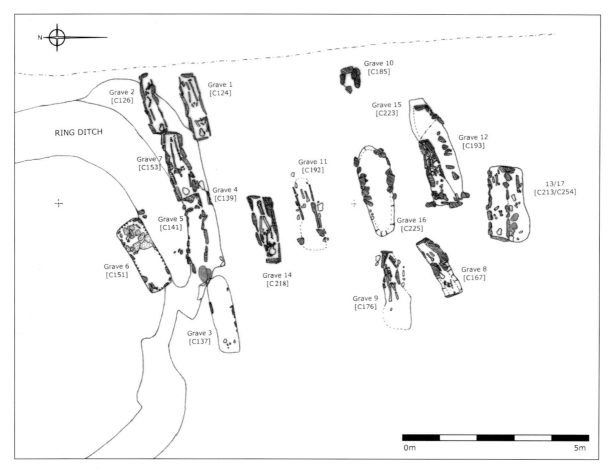

Figure 8: Plan of graves with capstones removed

Grave 2

Grave cut C126 was a long rectangle in plan, with the west end slightly rounded. It was 1.6m east/west by 0.42m north/south and 0.18m in depth. The stone cist was well constructed and, though capstones were missing on the south side, fairly well preserved. The cist was covered with capstones of assorted size, 0.2m - 0.4m, angular to sub-rectangular slate slabs. It was lined on all sides with stone slabs and fourteen stones lay vertically against sides of the cut (C126). The partial remains of an adult male skeleton lay east/west, head to west on the right side. The skeleton was in poor condition and had been disturbed by root and animal activity. The grave was cut into C136, the upper ring ditch fill.

Grave 3

Grave cut C137 was a long sub-rectangle in plan, with rounded corners. It was 1.6m east/west by 0.74m north/south and 0.19m in depth. The stone cist was very badly preserved. Only five slate side stones placed vertically around edges remained of what was probably a similarly constructed grave to *Graves 1* and *2* above. There were three vertical slabs on the north side, one on the east and one on the

south. The very fragmentary remains of an adult consisting of nine fragments of the cranium and 23 long-bone fragments survived. The cranium fragments were found in the west end of the cist. The north-east corner of C137 abutted, but did not appear to cut, C136, the upper ring ditch fill.

Grave 4

Grave cut C139 was sub-rectangular with rounded corners, where these survived on the south half of the cut. It was heavily disturbed by Grave 5 (C141) which cut into the north half of the grave, except for the north-east corner, which was cut by Grave 7 (C153). C139 was 2m in length east/west and, as far as could be established, 0.4m north/south and 0.1m in depth. The stone cist was very badly preserved. Only two slate side stones, placed vertically on the south side of the cut, indicated that the cist was similar in type to the others of the group. Behind these stones lay three small sub-rounded stones which seemed to support the vertically placed stones. Only one fragment of temporal bone of an adult survived.

Grave 5

Grave cut C141 was a long, irregularly shaped cut, with rounded corners on the east end, indistinct on the west. It was 2.1m east/west by 0.45m north/south and 0.20m in depth. The sides were steep and the stone cist was formed of fifteen large, sub-rectangular, flat stones of various types, from 0.15m – 0.45m in diameter, placed vertically along sides and ends of the cut.

The very fragmentary remains of an adult consisting of 10 femur fragments survived. The grave cut into C136, the upper ring ditch fill.

Grave 6

Grave cut C151 (Plates 1, 4 and 6) was a long sub-rectangle in plan, with rounded corners. It was 1.98m north-east/south-west by 0.7m north-west/south-east and 0.49m in depth. The sides of the cut were sharp and vertical, the base flat. Sixteen, mainly flat, stones (C162) were found at the base, 0.1m – 0.35m in diameter. These stones were found in the north-east half of the grave cut only and were lying directly on the base of the cut. Eighteen small side stones of various shapes and sizes, 0.1m - 0.3m in diameter were placed up against the side and on top of the base stones.

The very fragmentary remains of an adult consisting of one cranium fragment and one long bone fragment survived.

The cranium fragment was found in the south-west end of the cut.

A glass bead (04E680: 152: 1, Plate 7) was also found in the fill (C152) at the north-east end of the cut. C151 was cut into the south end of the enclosure of Ring ditch 1. It also partly cut into the fill of the ditch.

Grave 7

Grave cut C153 (Plates 1 and 8) was roughly rectangular in plan, its longer sides curving slightly, particularly on the south side. It was 2.11m east/west by 0.68m north/south and 0.28m in depth. The stone cist was well constructed and well preserved, partly covered with capstones of assorted size, averaging 0.5m by 0.4m by 0.1m, sub-angular in shape. These appeared to be missing in the centre of the east half of the burial and it is interesting that this is where parts of the skeleton are missing also. Fifteen large sub-angular stones, with average dimensions of 0.4m by 0.24 by 0.07m, lay vertically against the inner sides of the cut. The partial remains of an articulated adult was extended within, supine, east/west, head to west. The grave was cut into C136, the upper ring ditch fill. A pre-molar from the inhumation, C153,

provided a C14 date of 1440±40 BP calibrated to AD 430 to 640 at 2 sigma range (Beta 243093).

Grave 8

Grave cut C167 may be described as an irregular, elongated pear shape in plan, but the stone cist was a roughly rectangular shape in plan before excavation (Fig. 8). It was orientated north-east/south-west, its longer sides curving slightly to the north. It was 2m north-east/south-west by 0.6m north-west/south-east and 0.2m in depth. The stone cist was badly preserved, though some lintel stones remained *in situ*. Four sub-rectangular, flat covering stones, averaging 0.2m by 0.22m by 0.02m, survived only on the east portion of the grave. Only five sub-rectangular stones, with average dimensions of 0.27m by 0.26 by 0.04m, were set vertically against the inner sides of the cut, three on the south edge, one on the east, one on the north. The partial remains of an adult male was extended within, supine, head to west.

Grave 9

Grave cut C176 was an irregular, elongated shape with rounded ends in plan. The stone cist within the cut was originally a narrow rectangular shape but had been badly disturbed at the west end. It was orientated east/west and was 2.07m east/west by 0.72m and 0.15m in depth. The stone cist was badly preserved, though some lintel stones remained *in situ*. Seven sub-rectangular, flat covering stones, averaging 0.1m -0.5m in diameter, survived only on the east portion of the grave. Only eight sub-rectangular slate stones, with average dimensions of 0.40m by 0.30 by 0.03m, were set against the inner sides of the cut which had collapsed slightly inwards. These also were preserved only on the east. Human remains were present only on the east end. The partial remains of an adult *in situ* was extended within, supine, orientated with head (absent) to west.

Grave 10

Grave cut C185 was the cut of a stone cist which had survived only on the east end. It was, by its dimensions and the setting of its stones, one of the group of east/west orientated long stone cists. East/west, 0.73m of the cut survived by 0.74m north/south. It was 0.2m in depth. Five roughly square sub-angular stones 0.20m – 0.32m in length and 0.12m – 0.18m in width, were set vertically into the cut, one in the east end, two in the north and two in the south. Two covering stones, 0.18m x 0.14m and 0.28m by 0.12m remained *in situ*. No human remains were present.

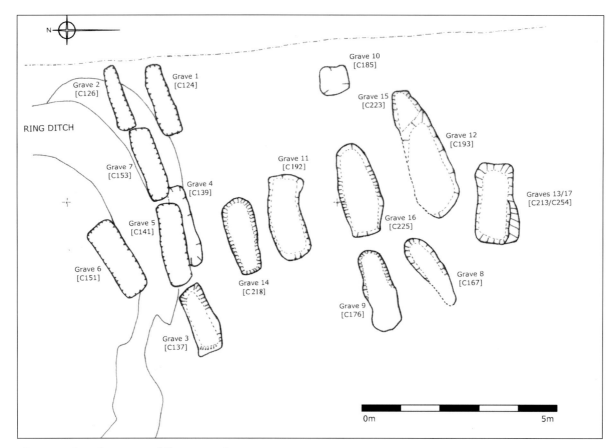

Figure 9: Plan of grave cuts fully excavated

Grave 11

Grave cut C192 was roughly rectangular in plan, its corners rounded. The north and south sides, curved slightly southwards, particularly on the east side. The cut was 1.9m east/west by 0.70m north/south and 0.3m in depth and contained a stone cist in a poor state of preservation. There were no covering stones and only eight side stones, sub-angular and sub-rounded, which were set vertically against the inner north and south sides of the cut. No stones survived at the east or west end. The stones averaged 0.7m by 0.2m by 0.1m for sub-angular stones and 0.17m by 0.12m by 0.08m for sub-rounded stones. The partial remains of an adult male *in situ* survived in the east half of the cut only. The remains were extended supine, east/west, head (absent) to west.

Grave 12

Grave cut C193 was a long, irregular, oval shape, wider at the west end and abutting cut C223. It is likely that, as it may have had a secondary cist grave inserted within it, the stone cist containing human remains in Grave 12 was located at the north side of the grave cut, while a row of disturbed stones (C212) may represent an earlier construction. The cut, C193, was 2.5m east/west by 1.05m north/south and 0.24m in depth. The stone cist (C195) set east/west along the

north side of the cut was a long, trapezoidal shape with the west end wider than the east. It was 1.75m east/west, 0.25m north/south at its east end and 0.6m north/south at its west end. The cist was constructed of sub-rectangular, flat stones set vertically, averaging 0.24m by 0.44m by 0.05m, and was disturbed at the west end. Three sub-rectangular flat stones averaging 0.38m by 0.34m by 0.05m covered the cist at the east end. Within the grave cut, to the south of the cist, was a loose, scattered line of stones (C212) which may relate to the stone cist construction, C222, in cut C223 (Grave 15).

C195 may, therefore, be a secondary cist construction replacing C212/C222. No human remains were found relating to C212 in Grave 12 or C222 in Grave 15. However, in the cist C195, there were the disarticulated and mixed remains of two adults, a male and a female.

Grave 13

Grave cut C213 was rectangular in plan with rounded corners, 1.8m east/west by 0.65m north/south and 0.27m in depth. It contained a stone cist in moderate condition with eighteen irregularly shaped stones set in a vertical position lining the grave cut. These averaged 0.4m by 0.47m by 0.07m. Only fragmentary remains of the covering stones of the cist survived. There were six irregularly shaped, flat slate covering stones, averaging 0.4m by 0.4m by 0.06m, which showed evidence of decay. Most of these stones were situated in the eastern part of the grave. Grave 13 cut another grave, Grave 17 (C254) and superimposed it.

The fragmentary remains of two adults, one male and one female were found within the cist. The female skeleton was extended *in situ* east/west with the head to west.

Grave 14

Grave cut C218 was 1.9m east/west by 0.75m north/south at the east end where it was wider and rounded in shape. It was 0.5m north/south at the west end where the side of the cut was straight with gently rounded corners. It was 0.45m in depth.

The stone cist was well constructed and well preserved, covered with 14 large covering stones. These were sub-rectangular flat slate slabs averaging 0.4m by 0.3m by 0.05m. These covered the whole of the grave. There was one large granite stone near centre on the south edge. Ten roughly square flat stones were set vertically around the grave cut. These averaged 0.3m by 0.42m by 0.05m.

The remains of an articulated adult female skeleton was extended within, supine, east/west, head to west.

Grave 15

Grave cut C223 was roughly trapezoidal in plan, 0.7m-1m in length east/west and 0.28m – 0.75m wide north/south by 0.18m in depth. It contained part of a stone cist in a poor state of preservation. This consisted of two large sub-rectangular stones laid perpendicularly and vertically up against the grave cut in the east and south edges of the cut (C222). Also present along the south edge were a number of smaller, sub-rounded and sub-angular stones averaging 0.16m by 0.09m by 0.05m. This cut may have been part of Cut C193 and the stones (C212) along the south edge of that cut may have related to the cist construction, C222. There were no human remains present and it is suggested that Grave 12, which contained the remains of two disarticulated skeletons, may be a secondary construction and may contain human remains which were once in Grave 15.

Grave 16

Grave cut C225 was 2.32m east/west by 1.06m north/south towards the centre where it was wider and rounded in shape. It was 0.7m north/south at the west end where the side of the cut was straight with gently rounded corners. It was also approximately

0.7m north/south at the east end which was rounded. It was 0.25m in depth.

Irregularly shaped, sub-angular and angular stones, averaging 0.24m by 0.2m by 0.18m, were laid in two lines along the north and south edges in the centre and east end of the cut. There were no stones at either end. There were no human remains present.

Grave 17

Grave cut C254 underlay and was cut by Grave 13 (C213). It was 0.8m in length east/west and 0.6m wide north/south by 0.45m in depth. Only the east end and part of the south side survived. It contained part of a stone cist in a very poor state of preservation. This consisted of three stones set vertically in the east and south sides of the cut. There was one sub-rounded stone on the north edge and two sub-rectangular slate stones on the east and south edges. One flat slate covering stone, 0.43m by 0.16m by 0.05, related to the cist, C256. The cist had been superimposed by the cist, C214, of Grave 13 (cut C213). A small number of disarticulated human bones were situated in the east end of grave cut. These represented one adult and one juvenile.

RING DITCH 2

The ring ditch

A second ring ditch, sub-circular in plan, was found 17m to the south of Ring ditch 1 and approximately 7.5m south of the group of cist burials. It was 6m in diameter north-south and 5.8m east-west (Plate 9). The ditch had a wide 'U' shape with a flat to concave base. It was 0.98 to 1.35m in width with a depth of 0.44m-0.53m in most areas. The ring ditch was superimposed by walls and a cobbled area (Plate 10) and cut by a later medieval ditch, C238, and post-medieval ditch, C240, which disturbed the ring ditch layers in many areas. Whether or not the ring ditch was penannular was unclear. The ditch terminated in two rounded ends only about a centimetre apart on the west side. There was no causeway and it is possible that these features were ditch cuts, not terminals. At the south end of the ring ditch, there were what appeared to be the bases of two rounded ditch terminals about 0.45m apart. However, these were heavily cut through by the post-medieval ditch and it was not entirely clear, again, there was a causeway between them. The difficulty in separating sequential ditch cuts from deliberately created ditch terminals is evidenced in the south-west quadrant of the ring ditch. Here, a cremation, C272, is contained

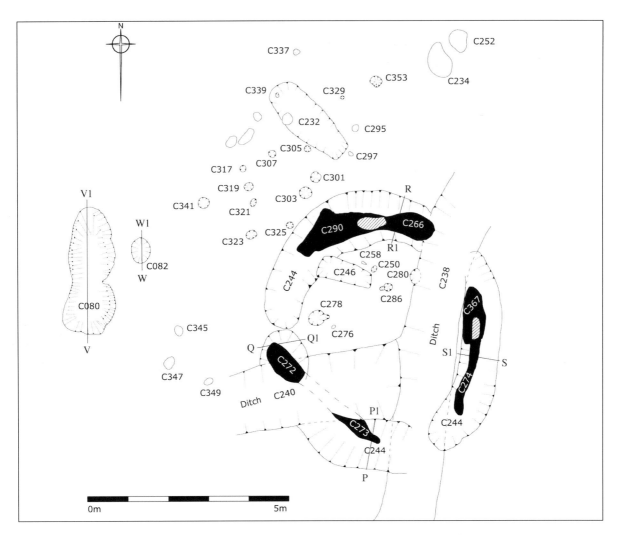

Figure 10: Ring ditch 2 showing cremation deposits and adjacent features with positions of sections

within a cut which is part of the ring ditch (Fig. 10). It is not clear whether or not the rounded cut containing the cremation on its north side is a ditch terminal, as there is only about a centimetre between this terminal and the opposing one to the north of it.

A number of intact layers and least four cremation deposits were recorded from within the ring ditch. A charcoal rich layer C272/273 containing cremated bone was located at the south-west quadrant of the ditch to the west of the intrusive later medieval north-south trench, C238. A second cremation deposit, C274 was spread to the east of this in the ring ditch. From C274, came a fragment of a small corroded iron ring or curved object (04E0680:274:1, Plate 20) and three small blue glass beads (04E0680:274:2, Plate 15).

Above C274 and extending from the south-east to the intersecting later medieval ditch, C238, was a third cremation deposit, C367.

A cremation deposit extended from the west side of the north-south post-medieval trench at the same level as C367. This was C290. This may be a continuation of C367 (cut by ditch C238) or it may be a separate deposit. Above this was another deposit of charcoal rich cremated bone, C266, which superimposed C290 but may relate to it. An analysis of the cremated bone has been undertaken (Appendix IV).

An amber toggle bead came from one of the upper layers of the ring ditch, C242 (04E680: 242:1, Plate 14) as did some worked flints (04E680: 242:2-6) and a small unidentified iron object (04E680: 242:7).

Ring ditch cremation deposit C272/C273
In the south-west quadrant of the ring ditch, on the south side of the possible terminal cut by the post-medieval ditch, C240, was cremation deposit C272.

The primary fill, C268, underlying C273, was 0.6m in width by 0.23m in depth and comprised a dark brown-grey, stony, silty sand with occasional charcoal. This abutted a mid brown, silty sand of medium compaction with occasional small pebbles, which may be a natural slip (C275 and C267). These layers were superimposed by cremation deposit

C273, This deposit was part of cremation deposit C272 on the other side of the post-medieval ditch, C240, which cut it. C272/273 was spread over 3m within the ditch fill above the primary fill. Charcoal from the cremation, C272, provided a C14 date of 2160±40bp calibrated to 360-90 BC at 2 sigma range (Beta 239118). The cremation layers were superimposed by deposits C270, a dark brown-yellow, silty sand of medium compaction containing frequent pebbles averaging 0.03m, and C269, a dark brown-grey, silty sand of medium compaction with moderate pebble inclusions averaging 0.02m.

Ring ditch cremation deposit C274
C274 (Fig. 11, Section S-S1), was spread on the inner south-east edge of the ring ditch for a distance of 2.3m reaching a depth of 0.2m. This layer superimposed C268, a dark brown-grey, silty sand of medium compaction with occasional charcoal flecks and frequent stone inclusions. C268 abutted deposits C292 and C293, which were, respectively, dark brown, medium sand and yellow-brown, medium sand containing occasional charcoal flecks, both of firm compaction. Both may be primary natural slump layers. C274 was superimposed by C291 described below.

Ring ditch cremation deposit C367
A cremation deposit, C367 (Fig. 11, Section S-S1), a black, charcoal-rich, fine, silty sand was found in the east quadrant of the ditch. It was separated from cremation deposit C274 by C291 and C368, two very stony compact light sand layers (Section S-S1, Fig.11).

Deposit C367 was spread 0.6m east/west by 1.80m and was 0.05m in thickness. It extended west to where it was truncated by later medieval ditch cut, C238. It may possibly relate to cremation deposit C290/266.

Ring ditch cremation deposit C290/266
Towards the base of the ditch, on the north side of the ring ditch (Section R-R1, Fig. 11), was cremation deposit, C290. C290 was approximately 2.8m in length east/west and was a maximum of 0.9m in width north/south. This cremation deposit contained 14 small blue glass beads (Plate 17), three of which were fused together, probably by heat (04E0680:290:1). Also from C290 came a small unidentified iron object (04E0680:290:2). C290 was separated from cremation deposit, C266, by C358, a grey-brown, fine, stony sand. Cremation deposit, C266 may have been related to it and was 0.75m in length and 0.30m-0.58m in width north/south. It was cut off on its east side by the later medieval ditch,

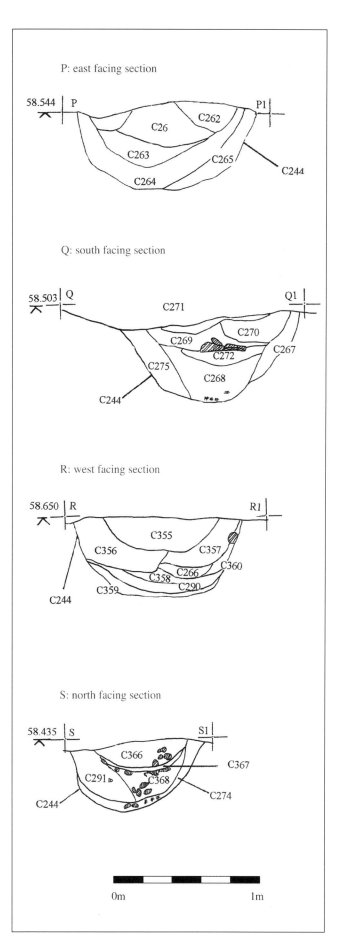

Figure 11: Ring ditch 2, Sections P – S

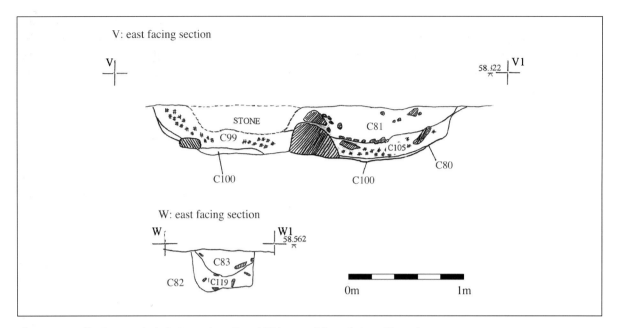

Figure 12: Kiln C080 and pit C082 sections V and W (see position of pit on Fig. 10)

C238. C266 was superimposed by later deposits, C357, a dark grey-brown, silty sand containing occasional charcoal flecks, C356, a mid brown sand of moderate compaction containing occasional charcoal flecks and stone and C355, a grey-brown sand of firm compaction.

Features, including cremation pits and post-holes, adjacent or cut into, to Ring ditch 2 (Fig. 10)

Cremation pit C278
C278 was 0.45m diameter by 0.13m in depth. The sandy silt fill (C279) contained frequent charcoal flecks and occasional cremated bone and is interpreted as a cremation pit. It was located on the west interior side of the ring ditch, adjacent to the closely spaced terminus ends of the ditch (Fig. 10). Charcoal from the fill of the pit (C279) produced a radiocarbon date of 2820±40 BP, calibrated to 1040-840 BC (Beta-229061).

Pit 280
C280 was cut by linear ditch, C238, and only the west half remained. It was 0.47m in diameter and 0.18m in depth. It contained a mottled fill of sandy silt, C281.

Pits/stake-holes C250 and C258
C250 was 0.26m in diameter and 0.08m in depth. It produced a silty sand fill as did C258, a small cut, 0.07 in diameter and 0.2m in depth, which was formed by a stake inserted at an oblique angle.

Pits /stake-holes C276 and C282
C276 was a circular to oval cut, 0.1m by 0.07m and 0.07m in depth. Its silty, sand fill contained occasional charcoal flecks. It was interpreted as a stake-hole as was C282, 0.22m in diameter and 0.08m in depth, and C286, 0.18m in diameter and 0.06m in depth. Both contained silty sand fills.

Pit C080
C080, a long irregularly shaped, figure-of-eight, pit was located approximately 5m west of the ring ditch (Figs. 10 and 12; Plate 13). It was 3m in length north-south by 1.2m in maximum width east/west descending to 0.7m in the centre. The slope of the sides here were curved, with sides graduating towards a flat base. It appeared to be separated into two bowl-shaped halves. Two large stones which had been placed in the centre of the pit separated the north and south ends. The base was fire reddened and contained oxidised sand and fire cracked stones (C100). Oxidisation was more evident in the north half of the pit.

A layer of charcoal-rich, clayey sand (C105), containing burnt, fired clay, suggesting high temperature, and fragmentary bone, overlay C100 to a depth of 0.16m in the north half of the pit. This layer was the same as that in the southern half of the pit where C099 was up to 0.18m in depth and contained burnt organic soil which was turf-like in texture. The upper fill (C081) covered the north half of the pit to a depth of 0.19m. It extended into the south half of the pit superimposing a large stone at the south end of the pit. Charcoal from the pit produced a radiocarbon date of 1640±50 BP, calibrated to AD 330 to 550 (Beta-229058).

The nature of the pit is unknown. Its proximity to the ring ditch and a rough arc of post-holes and stake-holes is, however, interesting. A piece of burnt human bone was found in the fill. A possible whetstone and four fragments of worked flint were recorded from the upper layer, C081.

Pit C082
C082, a small oval pit, was located immediately to the east of pit C080. It was 0.6m north/south and 0.43m in depth with sharp sides and a flat base. The primary sand fill, C119, had a maximum depth of 0.15m. Above this was a silty sand layer containing heat shattered stones and some charcoal.

Pit C234
C234, a sub-circular pit, 3m to the north of the ring ditch, was 0.55m north-west/south-east by 0.5m and 0.23m in depth. It had steep concave sides and base. It contained a single fill (C235) of dark, sandy clay of firm compaction, containing angular stones, at the base of which were found sherds of pottery covered by stones. Fragments of base, sides and rim were present. This has been identified as a fine Late Neolithic/Early Bronze Age Beaker and a Late Bronze Age domestic vessel (Appendix II).

Cremation pit C252
A third pit, C252, immediately to the north of C234 was sub-circular in shape and was 0.6m north-west/south-east by 0.51m and 0.32m in depth. It contained a lower sterile layer of compact sand, C228, 0.3m in depth. This extended from the top of the cut and covered the base of the pit to a depth of 0.2m.

Overlying C228 was C253, a charcoal-rich, silty sand layer, up to 0.2m in depth. It contained a small quantity of cremated bone, an elongated round stone, which may have been used as a sharpening stone, as well as occasional fire-cracked stones. This pit, and pit C234, were disturbed by rodent activity, as evidenced by burrows on the north and west sides of the features. The burrows extended north-west and cut through a small surface area of oxidised clay which indicated *in-situ* burning adjacent to the pits.

Post-holes and stake-holes relating to the ring ditch

On the west and north side of the ring ditch were a group of 21 post-holes (Fig. 10; Pl. 11). They were located within 3.6m of the outer edge of the ring ditch, with seven of the nine largest post-holes possibly enclosing a roughly circular or oval area immediately north-west of the ring ditch. These included the following:

C341, at 2.2m north-west of the ring ditch, which was 0.25m in diameter and 0.14m in depth, with a fill, C342, a greyish brown clay sand of moderate compaction.

C315, at 1.6m north-west of C341, was oval in shape, 0.3m by 0.25m and 0.2m in depth with a fill, C316, described roughly as above.

C351, 1.5m east-north-east of 315, was 0.35m in diameter and 0.35m in depth, with a fill, C352. Its fill could also be described as above, though it contained a small amount of charcoal. It was partly truncated to the north by rectangular feature, C232.

C301, C303 and C323 were stake-holes which could be described roughly as above. These enclosed an oval area of approximately 2.5m by 1.9m. Three post-holes C311, C305 and C325 were on the perimeter of this oval area. A further four post-holes, C307, C321, C319 and C317, were contained within this area. Two post-holes, C337 (1.6m to the north of C351), and C295 (1.6m to the east of C351), were of similar size to the post-holes within the oval area.

A stake hole, C329, was located 0.7m north-north-west of C295. A large oval post-hole, C353, was located 1.2m north-north-east of C295.

A further three post-holes were located within 2.5m of the west perimeter of the ring ditch. These were C345, C347 and C349 which were respectively 0.22m in diameter by 0.27m in depth; 0.4m by 0.38m by 0.15m in depth and 0.28m by 0.24m by 0.09-0.04m in depth. They all contained similar sand fills.

Two stake-holes, C297 and C339, were located at either end of the rectilinear feature, C232, a later feature, which partly truncated stake hole, C351.

No finds were recorded from any of these features. Little charcoal was recorded. While some attempt has been made to form a shape from the pattern of the post-holes, it was not possible to establish either the shape or the function of the structure they supported or the function they performed.

Possible inhumation burials relating to Ring ditch 2

To the south of the main group of inhumation burials which seemed to be associated with Ring ditch 1, two rectilinear cuts closely resembling grave cuts were found in relation to Ring ditch 2 (Fig. 10). One, C246, was cut within the ring ditch, in its north-west quadrant, partly into the upper ring ditch fill, on the inner side of the ditch. It was 1.56m north-west/south-east by 0.6m and 15m in depth. It had step sides and a flat base with a gentle slope east/west.

The second rectilinear cut was cut only 0.75-0.8m north-west of Ring ditch 2 and was 2.30m in length north-west/south-east. It was wider at the west end, 0.85m, while at the east end it was 0.47m in width. It was 0.15-0.2m in depth with steep, concave sides and a flat base. Neither of these two cuts contained human remains, or stones, suggesting a burial, while they were differently orientated to the group of east/west aligned burials to the north.

Both C232 and C246 were, however, very similar in shape to the group of grave cuts and they were orientated roughly north-west/ south-east. The fact that they did not contain any bone and were not stone-lined does not rule out the possibility that they were inhumation cuts similar to the group associated with Ring ditch 1. Burials were not found in all the graves of the group, while the skeletal remains surviving were in very poor condition. Grave 6, which (as discussed below) appeared to be earlier in type, produced only two, very small, bone fragments. This may suggest the earlier the burial the poorer the survival of remains. Also, the stone lining of the cists of the group of burials did not survive in all cases. It therefore not unlikely that these two cuts associated with Ring ditch 2 were for inhumation burials of possibly early date.

Later ditches, walls and a cobbled area superimposing Ring ditch 2

The ring ditch was cut by two later ditches (Fig. 10). One (C238), orientated north/south was 1.25m in width and 0.34m-0.26m in depth and was located east of the centre of the ring ditch. A single sherd of medieval pottery was recorded from the fill. The north end of the second linear ditch (C240), which was orientated east-west, adjoined the first trench south of centre of the ring ditch. It was 1.8m in width and was dug to a depth of 0.67m. Finds from the ditch fill indicated that it was post-medieval in date and might be a field boundary ditch. This indicated that the walls and cobbled areas exposed above this ditch were post-medieval.

The bases of two stone walls (C229 and C237), which were built at right angles to each other, were orientated east/west and north/south respectively (Fig. 16, Plate 10). A possible third wall, orientated east/west at the south end of C237, demarcated the southern limit of the cobbled area (C231) which was contained within the walls. The walls were constructed of stone which was faced on both sides and contained a rubble core. Wall 1 (C229) was orientated east/west and was 3.5m in length by 0.6m in width, expanding to 0.7m, due to dislodgement of the stones. The wall appeared to be of dry stone construction. The base was quite narrow and contained stones with a maximum of 0.4m in diameter while the average diameter was about 0.2m.

The walls enclosed an area of 4.8m by 3.5m. Wall 2 (C237) contained a gap, 1.28m in width, at the south end, indicating a probable entrance facing the present road. Over half of the area enclosed by the walls was paved with round cobble stones (C231). The remainder contained no cobbles and these may have been removed during more recent disturbance of the site. The west end of the area was disturbed by recent ploughing so that its width at this point was less than 4.7m from the east face of Wall 2, C237, to the west end of the cobbles.

Finds from within and below Wall 2 (C237) included a door key, glass and clay pipe indicating a date in recent centuries for its construction.

THE LINEAR DITCH

The ditch

Approximately 18m south of Ring ditch 2, a linear ditch, C041, 60m in excavated length, ran north-east/south-west across the site (Fig. 2,13, Plate 2b).

The ditch (Plate 2b) was narrower and shallower in the west, 0.95m in width by 0.46m in depth, getting gradually wider and deeper to the east, 2.40m in width by 0.88m in depth. The sides were steep and concave and the base was concave.

At the extreme east end of the linear ditch, a total of four layers of fill were recorded. The primary fill (C066) lay at the base of the ditch to a depth of between 0.08m and 0.25m (Section C-C1, Fig. 15). It was composed of sterile silty sand with a greyish hue, possibly caused by leaching. A layer of light, sandy silt (C042) overlay this. C096, which superimposed C042, was a thin layer, 0.11m in depth, of sandy silt containing frequent charcoal flecks. This layer occurred in the east half of the trench (Fig. 15). Thin lenses of charcoal were contained within, and overlaid, the fill.

Layer C096 was overlain on the east end of the ditch fill by C045, a greyish mid brown silty sand of moderate compaction, which contained occasional charcoal flecks, frequent small sub-rounded stones and large sub angular and sub-rounded stones.

Charcoal from C045 produced a radiocarbon date of 910±40 BP, calibrated to AD 1030 to 1230 (Beta-229057). The ditch fill survived better on the east end of the site, becoming gradually more truncated the further west the ditch extended. It is likely that it was disturbed by later agricultural activity. The upper layers visible on the east end of the ditch did not survive on the west end. It is difficult to establish how much disturbance of the upper layers took place.

Corn drying kilns

Two probable corn drying kilns of medieval date were found in the vicinity of the ditch.

C112 (Kiln)

Approximately 40m from the east side of the development site and approximately 25m from the visible east end of the ditch C041, on its north side, was a kiln, C112 (Figs. 13, 15; Plate 12). C112 was orientated north-east/south-west along the line of ditch, C041 which it cut and was partly overlain by.

Though the ditch (C041) was cut by the kiln, C112, a layer of the ditch fill, C045, overlay Kiln C112. The kiln was keyhole shaped with an elongated north-east end, and was bowl shaped at the south-west end. It was 3.1m in length north-east/south-west by 1.2m wide at the south-west end, 0.8m wide in the centre, tapering to 0.5m at the north-east end. Its maximum depth was 0.29m in the centre. A thin, charcoal-rich lens, C116, at the base of the kiln, extended throughout its full length above its oxidised base. Above C116 was a silty, ashy, charcoal rich layer (C115) which was very similar to C096 in the main ditch (C041). A total of eight large, angular stones, up to 0.65m in length, were found in this layer. The brown clay fill (C114), overlying it, was up to 0.3m in depth. This was overlain by C113, a localised silty sand layer which underlay C045, a stony, silty sand, which was the upper fill of the ditch.

It is probable that Kiln C112 was roughly contemporary with upper ditch layer C045 which produced the C14 date of 1030-1230 AD (above). The ditch itself may belong to the same period of occupation.

C039 (Kiln)

Cut by an east/west orientated post-medieval drain/ditch, C052 (Plate 3), at a distance of 10m to the south west of C112, was a crescent shaped, shallow, trench. The cut (C039) was curved, extending about 1.2m north-south, then curving sharply to the north-east for a further 4.2m. It was 0.24m in depth (Figs. 13 and 15).

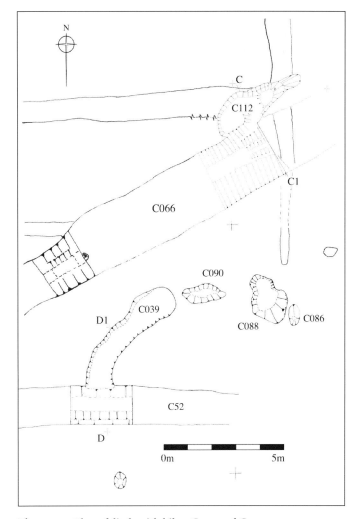

Figure 13: Plan of ditch with kilns, C039 and C112

No evidence of C039 appeared on the south side of C052. Three smaller cuts, C090, C088, C086 extended eastward from the north end of C039 and were interpreted as part of the latter feature.

C039 was very shallow with irregular edges and a flat base. The upper fill, C049, which was 0.09m in depth, comprised a stony, sandy silt with occasional charcoal flecks. This overlay a charcoal-rich, sandy silt, 0.18m in thickness, containing oxidised soil throughout and moderate inclusions of fire cracked stones (C107) which extended for 2m along the bottom of the trench. The fill composition was compatible with *in-situ* burning. Evidence for *in-situ* burning was provided by the underlying layer C040, which comprised loose, black silt with frequent charcoal and evidence of oxidisation, at the east end of the fill. The depth of the fill was 0.02m. C040 produced a radiocarbon date of 930±50 BP, calibrated to AD 1020 to 1220 (Beta-229056).

The evidence suggested that two phases of activity took place within the ditch fill, the earliest of which was reflected in Co40 and the more recent by C107 on the north end of the trench.

Three related features extended from 0.5m to 5m east of Co39. Co90, 0.35m to the east of Co39, comprised an elongated irregular shallow pit, 1.85m east-west by 0.7m and 0.2m in depth. It contained a light, greyish-brown medium sand of moderate compaction with medium and large angular stones (Co91). The second feature (Co88), approximately one metre to the east of Co90, was similarly of irregular shape, 2.15m north-west/south-east. Its south-east end was wider than its north-west end which was approximately 0.5m. It contained sterile fill, a mid brown-yellow silty sand of moderate compaction (Co89). The third feature (Co86) was located immediately east of Co88 (about 0.11m from it) and was oval in shape, 0.8m north/south by 0.45m, and 0.05m in depth. Its fill, Co87, was of light brown, silty sand containing charcoal. The curvilinear feature, Co39, is interpreted as a truncated kiln flue containing burnt material, the adjoining features, which contain no burnt material, as very truncated kiln 'bowls'. Co86, is suggested to be possibly a post-hole relating to a structure around the feature.

The hut structure of Bronze Age date and related features Co11/Co61

Nine post-holes surrounded Co11/Co61, a pit of irregular shape, 1.5m east/west, curving slightly to the south, with a maximum width north/south of 1.45m (Plate 2a). Co61 contained Co62, a sterile, mid orange-brown, medium sand of moderate compaction containing moderate sub-rounded stones. Co11 truncated the west side of Co62 (Fig. 14). It was a roughly pear-shaped cut, and was 1.5m in length east/west, 1.2m in width at the east end and 0.2m at the west. The maximum depth of the pit was 0.43m on the east side. It contained six layers of fill, the upper layers of which, Co35, Co34 and Co32, were cut by a post-hole, Co46, which was 0.27m in diameter at the rim

The primary fill of Co11, Co38, was sandy and occupied the base of the pit to a depth of 0.07m. This was superimposed by a dark brown, medium sand, Co37, containing frequent inclusions of charred grain with a moderate amount of charcoal fragments and seeds. This layer was concentrated on the south side of the pit and extended from the top of the pit, overlying Co38. The deposit was up to 0.08m thick. Overlying Co37 was a sandy, stony layer, Co36, which contained a small number of charred grain fragments which extended the full width of the pit. This layer was up to 0.15m thick and contained 1 rim sherd of Bronze Age pottery. This was superimposed

by a 0.16m thick sandy layer, Co35, containing frequent charred grain inclusions. Co35 was itself superimposed by a 0.13m thick layer of compact sand, Co34, which contained a moderate amount of charred grains. Sherds of Bronze Age pottery were found in the fill, including two rim sherds and one body sherd.

A post was subsequently inserted in the pit, cutting the upper fills (Co32, Co34, Co35) of the pit. The cut of the post-hole (Co46) was steep sided and the base concave. It was 0.29m in diameter by 0.35m in depth. Its sandy fill (Co12) contained moderate amounts of charred grain. The pottery was identified as Early to Mid Bronze Age by Rose Cleary (pers. comm.) A C14 date of 3450±40 BP calibrated to BC 1880 to 1650 at 2 sigma range (Beta 240939) was obtained from charcoal from Co35. The grains from the pit were examined by Meriel McClatchie. These were found to represent a large amount of barley and one grain of wheat (Appendix VI)

Surrounding the pits were nine post-holes forming a structure. Combined with the Co46, (the post-hole cut through the pit Co11), eight of these post-holes could form a circular structure, approximately 4.5m in diameter. The fact that the post-hole, Co46, cut through Co11 might suggest that the structure post-dated the pit, though it was probably related to it.

Post-hole 1, Co09, the most southern post, was oval with a concave base. It was 0.29m north-south by 0.34m east-west by 0.1 m in depth. The fill (Co10) contained charcoal-rich, sandy silt, loosely compacted and containing a moderate amount of small stones.

Post-hole 2 was located 2.8m north-west of Post-hole 1. Its cut, Co25, was oval and was 0.4m by 0.3m by 0.3m in depth. Its upper fill (Co26) comprised mid brown, silty sand with moderate charcoal flecks and occasional small stones to a depth of 0.15m. This overlay a 0.15m depth of charcoal-rich clay, indicating that the post may have been burnt *in-situ*.

Post-hole 3 was located 1.5m north-west of Post-hole 2. The cut (Co54) was 0.3m in diameter and 0.22m in depth. It contained a single fill (Co55) which comprised loose, dark brown, silty sand with moderate charcoal and occasional small stones.

Post-hole 4 was located 1.6m north of Post-hole 3. Its cut (Co23) was oval and was 0.3m by 0.27m by 0.33m in depth, with gradual sloping sides and concave base. It contained a similar fill (Co24) to that of Post-hole 3.

Post-hole 5 was located 1.8m north-east of Post-hole 4. Its cut (Co29) was 0.3m in diameter and 0.18m in depth, with gradual sloping sides and concave base. It contained a charcoal-rich, loose, sandy fill (C030).

Post-hole 6 was located 1.8m east-south-east of Post-hole 5. C013 was circular, 0.47m in diameter, becoming wider at the rim to 0.55m The sides tapered to 0.3m diameter. The depth of the cut was 0.6m

The upper fill (C014) comprised a charcoal rich soil, containing frequent fragments of carbonised grain throughout, and heat-shattered stones, to a depth of 0.49m. C014 overlay silty sand (C050), 0.11m in depth. The west side of the upper fill contained a possible stake-hole, 0.18m in diameter by 0.2m in depth. The fill (C047), which comprised carbonised grain within silty sand, contained a worked flat stone (04E680:047:1).

Post-hole 7 was located 1.8m south-east of post-hole 6. Its cut (C019) was oval and was 0.27m by 0.24m by 0.2m in depth, with vertical sides and a flat base. A charcoal-rich soil (C031), with carbonized seed, comprised the main sandy fill of the post-hole. This was overlaid by (C020) a sandy deposit.

Post-hole 8 was located 0.9m south of Post-hole 7. Its cut (C063) was 0.2m in diameter by 0.25m in depth. The charcoal-rich stony fill (C064) contained frequent bone.

Post-hole 9 was located 1.8m south-south-east of Post-hole 8. The cut, C067was 0.28m in diameter by 0.28m in maximum depth. The south half was truncated by a furrow. Vertical sides gave way to a flat

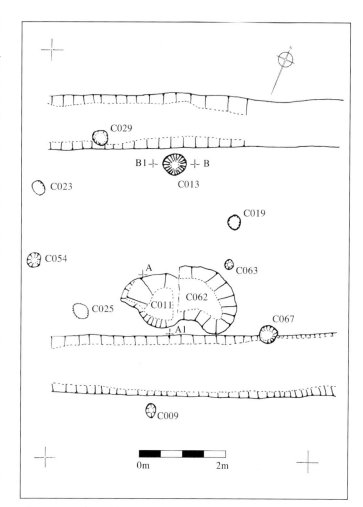

Figure 14: Plan of hut structure with postholes and pit, C011

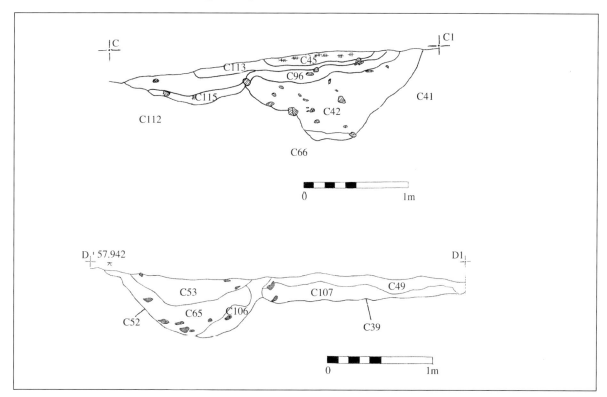

Figure 15: Sections of kilns, C112 and C039

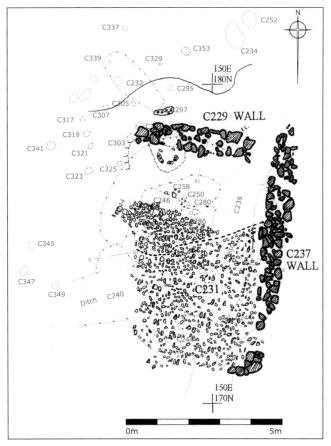

Figure 16: Plan of walls (C229 & C237) and cobbled area (C231) superimposing Ring ditch 2 (shown in grey).

base. The fill, C068, contained red to dark brown silty sand, indicating *in-situ* burning.

DISCUSSION

At Glebe south, monitoring uncovered a group of burial features set very close to the edge of the townland boundary between Glebe South and Darcystown.

The most significant feature of the excavation is the clear association of two Iron Age ring ditch burial sites (Ring ditches 1 and 2) with a group of 17 stone cist inhumations of Late Iron Age or early medieval date and the association of these with Late Bronze Age and Iron Age cremation pit burials.

The earliest find on the site was pottery from a pit in the burial area (C234), 3m north of Ring ditch 2. The pottery was identified as Late Neolithic/Early Bronze Age Beaker (Appendix II). The same pit also included Late Bronze Age pottery (Appendix II).

Immediately to the north of it, was C252, a pit containing cremated bone. The proximity to each other of these two pits would suggest they were related.

The only other dateable Bronze Age burial was a cremation pit, C278, which was cut into the area enclosed by Ring ditch 2. Charcoal from its fill produced a radiocarbon date of 2820±40 BP, calibrated to 1040-840 BC (Beta-229061), indicating a Late Bronze Age date.

The ring ditches were recognised by two circular cuts in the subsoil which revealed darker soil and charcoal. There were no surface indications of the sites and no traces of mounds or external banks. The ring ditches add to a growing *corpus* of such sites, many of which have been found in recent years. Both the ring ditches yielded cremation burials which were spread within the ditches. These were unaccompanied by pottery. Ring ditch 1 yielded a cremation deposit in a wide cut in the south-east of the ditch (C178). The cremation, C178, was placed in a section of the ditch which seemed to have been an initial cut of semi circular shape (C135). Through this cut, C135, a penannular ring (C109) was subsequently cut (Fig. 4). The reason for the cut C109, the penannular ring through the burial, is unknown as the fills of the cut do not appear to contain cremated remains. It is possible that the cremation was buried first, then a narrow penannular ring was cut to create a 'ring ditch'. The cremation in the south-east area of the ditch appears to be the only burial within the ditch.

The cremation in Ring ditch 1 was associated with three very fragmentary portions of what appears to be a fibula, possibly of Navan type, dated to *c.* the late 1st century BC to the 2nd century AD (Hawkes 1982, 62-3) and a glass bead (Plate 16). A date calibrated to 200 BC to AD 10 (Beta-229060) was yielded by charcoal from the cremation.

In Ring ditch 2 were probably four cremation burial deposits, spread in a manner resembling the laying lengthways of corpses. Fourteen small, annular, blue glass beads and an unidentified iron object was found with one of the cremations and three small blue glass beads with another. Another small miscellaneous iron object was found with one of the cremations. An amber toggle bead was found in one of the upper layers of the ditch (Plate 14). Charcoal from the cremation, C272, provided a C14 date of 360-90 BC at 2 sigma calibration (Beta 239118) for Ring ditch 2.

The laying lengthways of cremations within the ring ditch has been observed at a ring ditch at Ferns, Co. Wexford, where material very similar to that Balrothery, including strings of glass beads, iron objects and amber toggle beads were found. The site at Ferns is dated by radiocarbon to the latter centuries BC to the 1st century AD (Ryan 2000).

It is interesting that most of our evidence for prehistoric glass beads from Ireland comes from the evidence of Iron Age cremation burials. Grannagh, Co. Galway (Hawkes 1982, 60); Ballydavis, Portlaoise (Keeley 1995); Oran Beg, Co. Galway (Rynne 1970); Ferns, Co. Wexford (Ryan 2000); Raheenagurren, Co. Wexford (Breen 2006) Ask, Co. Wexford (Martin 2006; Stevens 2006); Loughey, Co. Down (Jope 1957). At these sites, the glass beads were all from Iron Age cremation burials in pits or ring ditches. The small annular beads of blue glass from Glebe South can be closely compared to those from Ferns and Ask. In most cases, the beads from each of the sites above appear to belong to the latter centuries BC to the first century AD. A ring ditch at Kilmahuddrick, Co. Dublin produced a cremation associated with a bead similar to a type commonly dated to the latter centuries three centuries BC. This was associated with cremated bone which produced a radiocarbon date which calibrated to 992-822 BC (Doyle 2005, 56, 73). However, in the same trench, stratigraphically later cremated bone produced a date of 373-111 BC. It is possible that a bead from this context may have found its way down to earlier, Late Bronze Age, layers.

The Iron Age ring ditch cemetery at Glebe South clearly continued to be recognised as a burial site into the early centuries AD. A cremation pit, C143, cut into the enclosure of Ring ditch 1, produced a C14 date (from the fill of the pit, C144), calibrated to AD 240 to 430 (Beta-229059).

Another pit, C080, a 3m long, irregularly shaped, figure-of-eight pit was located approximately 3.5-4m west of Ring ditch 2. Charcoal from the pit produced a radiocarbon date calibrated to AD 330 to 550 (Beta-229058). The nature of this pit is not known, though some cremated bone (unidentified), as well as heavily oxidised clay at its base, was found in its fill.

Cut into Ring ditch 1 in the south part of its enclosure, was a cist, Grave 6, containing an inhumation and a glass bead. The cist was rectilinear in shape, with straight edges, 0.49m in depth, and a stone-lined base. It differed from the other inhumations which were interred in shallower cists with side slabs. There was no evidence of stone walls or covering stones. All that survived of the burial was a fragment of cranium and a fragment of long bone. No parallel was found for glass bead in the fill of the cist.

This grave, Grave 6, was the deepest of all the grave cuts at 0.49 m and was characterised by its vertical sides. The burial was suggested to be wood-lined by Dr. Elizabeth O'Brien (pers. comm) who visited the site. In Britain, burials in wooden coffins were common between the 2nd-4th century AD (O'Brien 1990, 39). In the Arras cemetery at Rudstone, wooden coffins without nails or metal brackets have been recognised in 19 graves (O'Brien 1999, 13).

During the recent excavations carried out in advance of the M3 Clonee-North of Kells PPP scheme, Co. Meath at Collierstown (Clarke 2004), burials, in wood lined as well as stone-lined graves, were found in a burial site which developed from an Iron Age ring ditch.

At the cemetery site at Cabinteely, Co. Dublin which produced material from the 5th to the 12th century AD, the first phase of burial at this site featured burials in wooden cists (Conway 2000).

A total of sixteen further inhumations were found. These were located within 10m of Ring ditch 1 while a group of six of these (excluding the earlier straight-sided one, Grave 6 (which was cut within the enclosure), were concentrated along the south and south-east sides of Ring ditch 1. Four of these were actually cut into the cremation burial of the ring ditch which was located in that spot. The position of the six cist burials would suggest some sort of relationship with the ring ditch cremation burial A calibrated C14 date of AD 430-640 was obtained from 5grams of material from skeleton (C153:1) from Grave 7.

The cist burials, though in various stages of preservation, appeared to be of a single type. The human remains were placed supine with the head to the west in graves with stone lining of the sides, generally consisting of single upright slabs. The depth of the graves was quite shallow, on average, 0.2m- 0.3m, though Grave 14 was 0.45m in depth, as was Grave 17. However this grave was much disturbed by a secondary inhumation.

Capstones, placed lengthways across the width of the cists, covered the inhumations, though only eight of these survived. In general, the inhumations survived badly and in most cases they were partial. In at least two cases, cists had their contents re-interred in a recut or renovated part of the same grave, probably to make way for a new burial.

The dating of the group is of interest. Cists with lintel stones arranged in a very similar fashion and size to Glebe South were found in a large cemetery at Reask, Co. Kerry which produced a large amount of B ware. A hearth, probably associated with the primary levels, produced a date of BP 1565 ±90 (395±90, Fanning 1981, 155) while the excavator stated that 'a broad 4th to 7th century bracket could be assigned to the primary phase of occupation (Fanning 1981, 15).

An inhumation burial in a long stone cist, with the head to the west, feet to the east and no grave goods, was found at Ballykeel South, Co. Clare (Cahill, 1988). It was covered with six limestone lintel slabs, placed horizontally along the length of the cist. A sample of bone from the skeleton at

Ballykeel produced a date of circa 400 AD. It is stated by the author that the burial type may be influenced by Roman and Christian cultures in Britain and may not therefore necessarily relate to a Christian context when found in Ireland.

The burial site at Glebe South is similar to a growing number of sites at which burial was continuous from prehistory into the medieval period. In her work on Iron Age burial practices in Ireland, O'Brien refers to Carbury Hill (Site B), Co. Kildare, where the large ring barrow site was superimmposed by 15 extended inhumations, some of which disturbed cremations. One of the cremations contained iron fragments. (O'Brien, 1990, 39).

At Ballymaceward, Ballyshannon, Co. Donegal, a mound which produced Bronze Age and Iron Age cremation burials was disturbed by a number of east-west inhumations producing dates of 411-537 AD and 562-649 AD (O'Brien 1999 52-58).

At Ardsallagh, on the M3 Clonee-North of Kells scheme, Co. Meath (Linnane 2004; Clarke and Carlin 2006, 16-18), ring ditches continued as burial sites from the Early to Middle Bronze Age to the Iron Age. Ardsallagh 1 contained extended inhumation burial of Late Iron Age/early medieval date.

At Greenhills in Co. Kildare two extended inhumations were found enclosed within a penannular ring ditch (Keeley 1991, 180-201).

Relating to Ring ditch 2 at Glebe South, two rectilinear pits, C232 and C246, were very similar in shape to the group of long stone cists and they were orientated roughly north-west/ south-east. One was cut into Ring ditch 2. Though they did not contain any bone, or stone lining, it is very possible that these were inhumations similar to the group by Ring ditch 1.

The cemetery at Glebe South also contained burials dated to the Bronze Age, probably the early Bronze Age to judge from the Beaker pottery found in a pit between the two ring ditches. Pottery of Late Bronze Age date was found in the pit (C234) along with the Beaker pottery. A Late Bronze Age date of BC 1040-840 BC was yielded by charcoal from pit C278 cut within Ring ditch 2. The cemetery is therefore likely to have been in use over thousands of years with about the same length of use as Ardsallagh (Clarke and Carlin 2005 16-18).

Running north-east/south-west across the site, to the south of the burial site, on the slope of the hill, was a ditch, fairly similar to the ditches of Rosepark, on the hill to the north, associated with cereal drying kilns.

The ditch extended 60m east-west across the site at a rise of the ground level and may have been defensive. Not a great deal of material was found in the ditch. The upper ditch fill contained soil layers directly associated with a Kiln, C112, which cut it. Charcoal from the upper layers of the ditch produced a radiocarbon date of 910±40 BP, calibrated to AD 1030 to 1230 (Beta-229057). The primary ditch fill layers did not produce much evidence of activity. There were few distinctive layers and no features, finds or burning events related to the fill deposits, though it was possible that the ditch was used during an earlier phase of occupation.

Relating to the same phase of activity was another probable corn-drying kiln, C039, which was cut by a post-medieval drain C052. Three smaller cuts, C090, C088, C086 extended eastward from the north end of C039 and are interpreted as part of this feature. Most likely, they are very truncated 'bowls' of a cereal drying kiln, while C039 represents a flue C039 produced a radiocarbon date of 930±50 BP, calibrated to AD 1020 to 1220 (Beta-229056) from its fill layer, C040.

The radiocarbon determinations would suggest cereal drying activity on the hill facing that of the enclosure at Rosepark not too long before, but probably predating, the Anglo-Norman occupation of Balrothery. The kilns may have been contemporary with the secondary use of two souterrains, Souterrains 2 and 3 at Rosepark as Kilns 5 and 9 which were being used as cereal drying kilns in and around the enclosure itself (Carroll, 2002b).

Though we have medieval dates for the upper layers of the ditch, it is not unlikely that it formed part of an earlier enclosure. The ditch can be seen to potentially link with the fragment of ditch in Area 2 of the Darcystown 1 excavation (03E0067). As can be seen in Fig. 1, it appears to form a curvilinear line around the base of the hill, possibly enclosing a settlement. It is of interest that the Early to Middle Bronze Age hut site, C011, is found within this possible boundary line.

At the west end of the ditch, to the south of it, was a hut structure. A number of post-holes surrounded a pit of irregular shape, C011/C061, which contained several layers of grain (Appendix VI).

Pottery found within the fill was identified as Early to Mid Bronze Age and a C14 date of 3440±40 BP or 1880-1650 cal. BC (Beta 240939) was obtained for C035, a layer within the fill of the pit. This a most important find as it points very clearly to habitation and processing of cereals in the Early to Middle Bronze Age in Balrothery. It links the inhabitants of the area who farmed the land in the Bronze Age with the early use of the burial sites at Darcystown 1 and Glebe South.

Plate 2a: Post-holes around Bronze Age cereal-drying kiln (Co11/Co61), viewed from the west

Plate 2b: Linear ditch (Co41) with excavated Sections 1-6 and adjacent features

Plate 3: Ditch C052, east-facing section

Plate 4: Ring ditch 1 prior to excavation

Plate 5: Section I of Ring ditch 1, C166, facing east

Plate 6: Grave 6, C151, inhumation burial in Ring ditch 1,
of possible 2nd – 4th century AD type

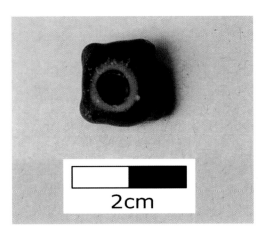

Plate 7: Blue and red bead from C152, fill of Grave 6
(cut C151)

Plate 8: Cist burial, Grave 7, C153

Plate 9: Ring ditch 2, view from the west

Plate 10: Walls and cobbled area superimposing Ring ditch 2

Plate 11: Ring ditch 2, with adjacent post/stake-holes, facing east

Plate 12: Kiln C112, south-east facing

Plate 13: Pit C080, which produced burnt material, to the west of Ring ditch 2, facing west

Plate 14: Amber toggle bead from C242, fill of Ring ditch 2

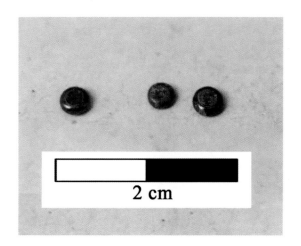

Plate 15: Blue beads from C274, fill of Ring ditch 2

Plate 16: Blue bead from C178, fill of Ring ditch 1

Plate 17: Blue beads from C290, fill of Ring ditch 2

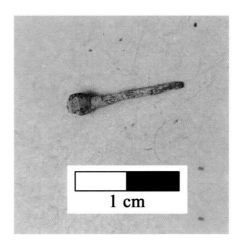

Plate 18: Copper alloy object from C109, Ring ditch 1

Plate 19: Copper alloy object from C199, Ring ditch 1

Plate 20: Iron object from C274, Ring ditch 2

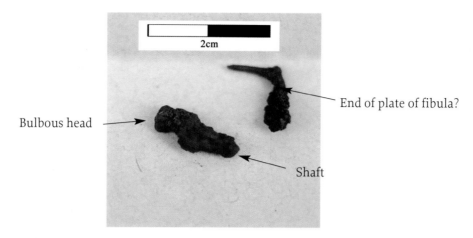

Bulbous head

End of plate of fibula?

Shaft

Plate 21: Copper alloy objects from C178, Ring ditch 1, possibly parts of a fibula

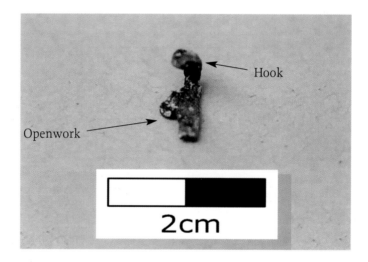

Hook

Openwork

Plate 22: Copper alloy object from C178, Ring ditch 1, possible fibula

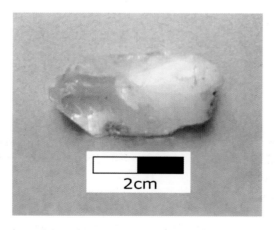

Plate 23: Quartz crystal from Ring ditch 1

References

Baker, C. 2001. Glebe South Balrothery. In I. Bennett (ed.), *Excavations: summary acccounts of archaeological excavations in Ireland 2000*. Wordwell, Bray, Wicklow.

Breen, T. 2006. Preliminary report on archaeological excavation at Raheenagurreen, Co. Wexford, Site 27 (A003/019). Valerie J. Keeley Ltd. Report on glass beads by J. Carroll. Unpublished report. National Monuments Service, DOEHLG.

Cahill, M. 1989. Ballykeel South. In I. Bennett (ed.), *Excavations: summary acccounts of archaeological excavations in Ireland 1988*. Wordwell, Bray, Wicklow.

Carroll, J. 2002a. Report on trial testing at Glebe South/Darcystown, Lusk Road, Balrothery, Co. Dublin. Licence no. 02E0043. Unpublished report. National Monuments Service, DOEHLG.

Carroll, J. 2002b. Report on archaeological excavations at Rosepark, Balrothery, Co. Dublin, 2000-2001. Licence no. 99E0155. Two volumes. Unpublished report. National Monuments Service, DOEHLG.

Clarke, L. 2007. Collierstown, Co. Meath - excavation licence no. 04E0422. In I. Bennett (ed.), *Excavations: summary acccounts of archaeological excavations in Ireland 2004*. Wordwell, Bray, Wicklow.

Clarke, L. and Carlin, N. 2006. Life and death in Ardsallagh. *Seanda – the NRA Archaeological magazine.*

Conway, M 2000. *Directors first findings from excavations in Cabinteely*. Margaret Gowen and Company. Dublin.

Doyle, I. 2005. Excavation of a prehistoric ringbarrow at Kilmahuddrick, Clondalkin, Dublin. *The Journal of Irish Archaeology* XIV, 43-76.

Fegan, G. 2000. Ballydavis, Site 2, Co. Kildare (03E0151). Valerie J. Keeley Ltd. Unpublished report. National Monuments Service, DOEHLG. Report on glass beads by J. Carroll.

Fanning, T. 1981. Excavation of an Early Christian cemetery and settlement at Reask Co. Kerry.

Proceedings of the Royal Irish Academy 81C, 67-172.

Hawkes, C. F.C 1982. The wearing of the brooch: Early Iron Age dress among the Irish. In B. Scott (ed.), *Studies in Early Ireland: essays in honour of Michael V. Duignan*. Belfast.

Hencken, H. O'Neill 1950. Lagore crannog: An Irish royal residence of the 7th to the 10th century AD. *Proceedings of the Royal Irish Academy*, 53C, 1-247.

Jope, E.M. and Wilson, B.C.S. 1957. A burial group of the first century AD near Donaghadee, Co. Down. *Ulster Journal of Archaeology* 20, 73-95.

Keeley, V.J 1991. Archaeological excavations of a burial ground at Greenhills, Co.Kildare. *Journal of the Kildare Archaeological Society* 17, 180-201.

Keeley, V.J. 1995. Ballydavis-Early Iron Age complex. In I. Bennett (ed.), *Excavations: summary acccounts of archaeological excavations in Ireland*. Wordwell, Bray, Wicklow.

Linnane, S. J. 2007. Ardsallagh, Co. Meath. In I. Bennett (ed.), *Excavations: summary acccounts of archaeological excavations in Ireland 2004*. Wordwell, Bray, Wicklow.

Martin, K. 2006. Preliminary report on archaeological excavation at Ask, Co. Wexford, Site 37 (A003/028). Valerie J. Keeley Ltd. Report on glass beads by J. Carroll. Unpublished report. National Monuments Service, DOEHLG.

O'Brien, E. 1985. Ballyman. In S. M. Youngs et al (eds.) Medieval Britain and Ireland in 1984, in *Med. Arch*. 29, 214.

O'Brien, E. 1990. Iron Age burial practices in Leinster: continuity and change. *Emania*, 7, 37-42.

O'Brien, E. 1992. Pagan and Christian burial in Ireland during the first millennium AD: continuity and change. In Edwards, N. and Lane, A. (eds.) *The early church in Wales and the west*, 130-7. Oxbow monograph 16. Oxford.

O' Brien, E. 1999. *Post Roman to Anglo-Saxon England: burial practices reviewed*. BAR British series 289, 52-58.

O'Brien, E. 2003. Burial practices in Ireland: first to 7th century AD. In J. Downes and A. Ritchie (eds.), *Sea Change: Orkney and Northern Europe in the later Iron Age AD 300-800*. Angus, Scotland.

Ryan, F. 2000. Excavation of a ring ditch at Ferns, Co. Wexford. Report on glass beads by J. Carroll. Unpublished report. National Monuments Service, DEHLG.

Rynne, E. 1970. Oran Beg ring barrow. In Delaney, T.G. (ed.), *Excavations* 1970, 10. Belfast.

Stevens, P. 2006. Preliminary report on archaeological excavation at Ask, Co. Wexford, Site 42-44 (A003/020). Valerie J. Keeley Ltd. Report on glass beads by J. Carroll. Unpublished report. National Monuments Service, DEHLG.

APPENDIX I

RADIOCARBON DATING RESULTS FROM GLEBE SOUTH, BALROTHERY, CO. DUBLIN (04E0680)
Beta analytic Inc.

Context	Sample	Description	Material	Lab code	Results	2 sigma calcibration
C272	100	Fill of Ring ditch 2	Charcoal	239118	2160 ± 40 BP	360-90 cal. BC
C040	019	Fill of linear feature C039	Charcoal	229056	930 ± 50 BP	1020-1220 cal. AD
C045	040	Fill of ditch C041	Charcoal	229057	910 ± 40 BP	1030-1230 cal. AD
C080	031	Fill of pit C80	Charcoal	229058	1640 ± 50 BP	330-550 cal. AD
C144	044	Fill of post-hole/pit cut C143	Charcoal	229059	1690 ± 50 BP	240-430 cal. AD
C178	106	Fill of Ring ditch 1	Charcoal	229060	2060 ± 40 BP	200 cal. BC-10 cal. AD
C279	101	Fill of pit cut C278	Charcoal	229061	2820 ± 40 BP	1040-840 cal. BC
C035	012	Fill of pit cut C011	Charcoal	240939	3450 ± 40 BP	1880-1650 cal. BC
C153	000	tooth from skeleton	Collagen extraction	243093	1440 ± 40 BP	430-640 cal. AD

APPENDIX II

THE PREHISTORIC POTTERY FROM GLEBE SOUTH, BALROTHERY, CO. DUBLIN (04E0680)

Eoin Grogan and Helen Roche

Summary
The site produced a small assemblage of nine sherds representing a fine late Neolithic / early Bronze Age Beaker (Vessel 1) and a Late Bronze Age domestic vessel (No. 2). Part of the Beaker was damaged by intense heat after breakage.

The final Neolithic/Early Bronze Age
Although only a portion of the base of a vessel is preserved at Glebe South, the fabric and manufacture indicate a fine vessel typical of the material from the north Leinster region. In addition to the major settlement concentrations in the Boyne Valley, Co. Meath, and Dalkey Island, Co. Dublin (Eogan 1984; Cleary 1983; Liversage 1968) several important assemblages have been identified recently including Mell and Newtownbalregan Sites 2 and 6 (McQuade 2005; Roche and Grogan 2005c; Bayley 2004; Grogan and Roche 2005a; 2005b), Co. Louth, and Kilgobbin and Newtown Little, Co. Dublin (Hagen 2004a; Ward 2005; Grogan 2004b; Grogan and Roche 2006a) (Fig. 1).

Vessels of this type have generally been assigned to Clarke's European Bell Beaker, or his Wessex/Middle Rhine types (1970). More recently, following reviews by, for example, Lanting and van der Waals (1972), there has been a greater recognition of the regional development of Beaker. Case's (1993) simpler

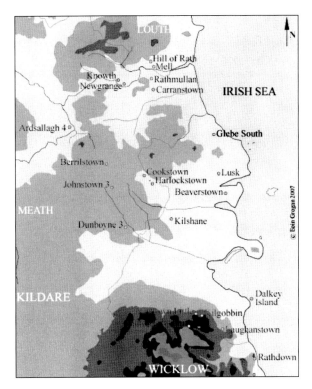

Figure 1: Distribution of Beaker pottery in north Leinster.

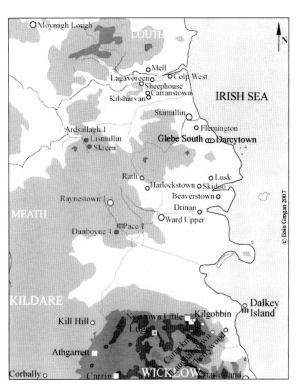

Figure 2: Distribution of Late Bronze Age pottery in north Leinster.

threefold scheme, and its specific application to the Irish material, provides a straightforward medium for insular comparison (Case 1995): the Glebe South material very probably belongs to his style 2. This material is generally dated to *c.* 2450-2300 BC.

The Late Bronze Age

Vessels similar to that from Glebe South come from Knockaholet, Co. Antrim (Fig. 3A; Henry 1934, Pl. 28. 1, 2), Circle P, Lough Gur, and Kilbane, Co. Limerick (Fig. 3B; Grogan and Eogan 1987; Grogan and Roche 2004a), Kilgobbin and Drinan (Nevinstown), Co. Dublin (Dennehy 2004; Grogan 2004b; Grogan and Roche 2006b), Ward Upper, Co. Meath (Roche and Grogan 2005b), and Priestsnewtown, Co. Wicklow (Fig. 3C; Tobin *et al.* 2004; Grogan and Roche 2004b). More recently good comparisons for the Glebe South material came from the ring ditch at Darcystown 2 and the flat cremation pit cemetery at Darcystown 1, Balrothery, Co. Dublin (Carroll 2004; Wiggins 2005; 2006; Grogan and Roche 2007a; 2007b).

Late Bronze Age coarse domestic pottery has a very wide distribution in Ireland but has only recently been recovered from domestic sites in the north Leinster region. In the past few years small assemblages have been identified at several sites in County Dublin including three at Kilgobbin

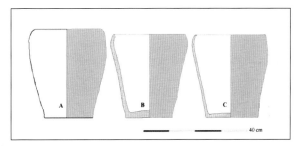

Figure 3: Late Bronze Age vessels from: **A**. Knockaholet, Co. Antrim (Henry 1934, Pl.28.2), **B**. Circle P, Lough Gur, Co. Limerick (Grogan and Eogan 1987, Pl.23), and **C**. Priestsnewtown, Co. Wicklow (Grogan and Roche 2004b, Fig. 1.1).

(Dennehy 2004; Hagen 2004a; 2004b; Grogan 2004a; 2004b), Newtown Little (Ward 2005; Grogan and Roche 2006a), Beaverstown (Hagen 2003; Grogan 2004c), Cherrywood/ Laughanstown (O'Donovan 1998; Seaver 2005), Flemington (Byrnes 2004), Skidoo (Dehaene 2004; Roche 2004a), and Lusk (Roche 2004b) to add to the important occupation site on Dalkey Island (Liversage 1968) (Fig. 2). There is important evidence of high status settlement at Moynagh Lough, Co. Meath (Bradley 2004), while the enclosed sites at Lagavooren, Carranstown, Kilsharvan and Raynestown, Co. Meath, (Clark and Murphy 2002; Russell and Corcoran 2002; Grogan and Roche 2004c) have many similar features. Pottery of this type has also come from funerary sites including Priestsnewtown, Co. Wicklow, and ritual sites such as the ceremonial enclosure at Lugg, Co. Dublin (Kilbride-Jones 1950; Roche and Eogan forthcoming). This type of pottery is firmly dated at Haughey's Fort, Co. Antrim (Mallory 1995), and Mooghaun South, Co. Clare (Grogan 2005), to between 1150 BC and 800 BC.

References

Bayley, D. 2004. M1 Dundalk Western Bypass. Newtownbalregan Excavations: Sites 111, 112 and 113: Post-excavation Assessment and Project Design. Unpublished Report for Irish Archaeological Consultancy Ltd. National Monuments Service, Department of the Environment, Heritage and Local Government.

Bradley J. 2004. Moynagh Lough, Co. Meath, in the Late Bronze Age. In H. Roche, E. Grogan, J. Bradley, J. Coles and B. Raftery (eds), *From Megaliths to Metals. Essays in Honour of George Eogan*, 91–8. Oxbow, Oxford.

Byrnes, E. 2004. Flemington, Co. Dublin. Curvilinear ditch. In I. Bennett (ed.), *Excavations 2002*, 160. Wordwell, Bray, Wicklow.

Carroll, J. 2004. Excavation of a ring ditch at Darcystown, Balrothery, Co. Dublin (04E0741). Unpublished report by Judith Carroll and Company for Fingal County Council. National Monuments Service, Department of the Environment, Heritage and Local Government

Case, H. 1993. Beakers: Deconstruction and After. *Proceedings of the Prehistoric Society* 59, 241–68.

Case, H. 1995 Irish Beakers in their European Context. In J. Waddell and E. Shee Twohig (eds), *Ireland in the Bronze Age*, 14–29. Stationery Office, Dublin.

Clarke, D.L. 1970. *Beaker Pottery of Great Britain and Ireland.* Gulbenkian Archaeological Series, Cambridge University Press, Cambridge.

Clarke, L. and Murphy, D. 2002. Excavation of a Bronze Age enclosure (Site 17) at Lagavooren Townland, Co. Meath. *Ríocht na Midhe* 13, 18–22.

O'Kelly, M. J., Cleary, R. M. and Lehane, D. 1983. *Newgrange, Co. Meath, Ireland: The Late Neolithic/Beaker Period Settlement*, C. O'Kelly (ed.), 58–117. British Archaeological Reports International Series 190, Oxford.

Dehaene, G. 2004. Skidoo, Co. Dublin. In I. Bennett (ed.), *Excavations 2002*, 187–8. Wordwell, Bray, Wicklow.

Dennehy, E. 2004. Excavations at 'Belarmine', Kilgobbin, Co. Dublin. Unpublished Report for Margaret Gowen and Co. Ltd. National Monuments Service, Department of the Environment, Heritage and Local Government.

Eogan, G. 1984. *Excavations at Knowth* 1. Royal Irish Academy Monographs in Archaeology, Dublin.

Grogan, E. 2004a. The prehistoric pottery assemblage from Kilgobbin, Co. Dublin. Unpublished Report for Margaret Gowen and Co. Ltd.

Grogan, E. 2004b. The prehistoric pottery assemblage from 'Belarmine', Kilgobbin, Co. Dublin. Unpublished Report for Margaret Gowen and Co. Ltd.

Grogan, E. 2004c. The prehistoric pottery assemblage from Beaverstown, Co. Dublin (02E1708 and 03E1634). Unpublished Report for Margaret Gowen and Co. Ltd.

Grogan, E. 2005. *The North Munster Project. Volume 1: The later prehistoric landscape of south-east Clare.* Discovery Programme Monograph 6. Wordwell, Bray, Wicklow.

Grogan, E. and Eogan, G. 1987. Lough Gur excavations by Seán P. Ó Ríordáin: further Neolithic and Beaker habitations on Knockadoon. *Proceedings of the Royal Irish Academy* 87C, 299–506.

Grogan, E. and Roche, H. 2004a. The prehistoric pottery from Kilbane, Castletroy, Co. Limerick. Unpublished Report for Eachtra Archaeology.

Grogan, E. and Roche, H. 2004b. The prehistoric pottery from Site 6B, Priestsnewtown, Greystones, Co. Wicklow. Unpublished report for Judith Carroll and Company. National Monuments Service, Department of the Environment, Heritage and Local Government

Grogan, E. and Roche, H. 2004c. The ceramic assemblage from Carranstown, Duleek, Co. Dublin. Unpublished Report for The Archaeological Company.

Grogan, E. and Roche, H. 2005a. The prehistoric pottery from Newtownbalregan 2, Co. Louth. Unpublished Report, Irish Archaeological Consultancy Ltd.

Grogan, E. and Roche, H. 2005b. The prehistoric pottery from Newtownbalregan 6, Co. Louth. Unpublished Report, Irish Archaeological Consultancy Ltd.

Grogan, E. and Roche, H. 2006a. The prehistoric pottery assemblage from Newtown Little ('Belarmine'), Kilgobbin, Co. Dublin (05E0333). Unpublished report for Margaret Gowen and Co. Ltd.

Grogan, E. and Roche, H. 2006b. The prehistoric pottery assemblage from Drinan/Nevinstown, Swords, Co. Dublin.(03E1362). Unpublished Report for Margaret Gowen and Co. Ltd.

Grogan, E. and Roche, H. 2007a. The prehistoric pottery assemblage from Darcystown 2, Balrothery, Co. Dublin (04E0741). Unpublished report for Judith Carroll and Company. National Monuments Service, Department of the Environment, Heritage and Local Government.

Grogan, E. and Roche, H. 2007b. The prehistoric pottery assemblage from Darcystown 1, Balrothery, Co. Dublin (03E0067/ 03E0067 extension). Unpublished report for Judith Carroll and Company. National Monuments Service, Department of the Environment, Heritage and Local Government

Hagen, I. 2003. Excavations at Beaverstown, Co. Dublin. Unpublished report for Margaret Gowen and Co. Ltd. National Monuments Service, Department of the Environment, Heritage and Local Government

Hagen, I. 2004a. Archaeological Excavations Interim Report. Phase 3 Development, Kilgobbin, Co. Dublin. Unpublished report for Margaret Gowen and Co. Ltd. National Monuments Service, Department of the Environment, Heritage and Local Government

Hagen, I. 2004b. Kilgobbin, Co. Dublin. Bronze Age cremation burials. In I. Bennett (ed.), Excavations 2002, 166. Wordwell, Bray, Wicklow.

Henry, S. 1934. A find of prehistoric pottery at Knockaholet, parish of Loughguile, Co. Antrim. Journal of the Royal Society of Antiquaries of Ireland 64, 264–5.

Kilbride-Jones, H.E. 1950. The Excavation of a Composite Early Iron Age Monument with "Henge" Features at Lugg, Co. Dublin. Proceedings of the Royal Irish Academy 53C, 311–32.

Lanting, J. and van der Waals, D. 1972. British Beakers as seen from the Continent. Helenium 12, 20–46.

Liversage, G.D. 1968. Excavations at Dalkey Island, Co. Dublin, 1956-1959. Proceedings of the Royal Irish Academy 66C, 53–233.

McQuade, M. 2005. Archaeological excavation of a multi-period prehistoric settlement at Waterunder, Mell, Co. Louth. County Louth Archaeological and Historical Journal 26, 31–66.

Mallory, J. 1995. Haughey's Fort and the Navan Complex in the Late Bronze Age. In J. Waddell and E. Shee Twohig (eds.). Ireland in the Bronze Age, 73–89. Stationery Office, Dublin.

O'Donovan, E. 1998. Cherrywood/Laughanstown, Co. Dublin. Prehistoric/post-medieval. In I. Bennett (ed.), Excavations 1997, 128. Wordwell, Bray, Wicklow.

Roche, H. 2004a. The prehistoric pottery assemblage from Skidoo, Co. Dublin. Unpublished report for Arch-Tech Ltd.

Roche, H. 2004b. The prehistoric pottery assemblage from Lusk, Co. Dublin. Unpublished report for Arch-Tech Ltd.

Roche, H. and Grogan, E. 2005a. Appendix A. The prehistoric pottery from Mell, County Louth. In M. McQuade, Archaeological excavation of a multi-period prehistoric settlement at Waterunder, Mell, Co. Louth. County Louth Archaeological and Historical Journal 26, 54–63.

Roche, H. and Grogan, E, 2005b. N2 Finglas – Ashbourne. Ward Upper, Co. Meath (Site 6, 03E1358). Unpublished Report for CRDS Ltd.

Roche, H. and Eogan, G. forthcoming. A re-assessment of the enclosure at Lugg, Co. Dublin, Ireland. In C. Gosden *et al.* (eds), *Communities and Connections: Essays in Honour of Barry Cunliffe*. Oxford University Press, Oxford.

Russell, I.R. and Corcoran, E. 2002. Excavation of a possible Bronze Age enclosure at Kilsharvan Townland, Co. Meath. *Ríocht na Midhe* 13, 32–4.

Seaver, M. 2005. From mountain to sea – excavations in the townlands of Glebe and Laughanstown, County Dublin. In O'Sullivan, J. and Stanley, M. (eds.), *Recent Archaeological Discoveries on National Road Schemes 2004*, 51–63. Archaeology and the National Roads Authority Monograph Series 2, Dublin.

Tobin, S., Swift, D. and Wiggins, K. 2004. Greystones Southern Access Route (GSAR), Co. Wicklow. Sites 6/6a-g, Priestsnewtown. Excavation report. Licence no. 04E0401. Unpublished report by Judith Carroll and Company for Wicklow County Council. National Monuments Service, Department of the Environment, Heritage and Local Government.

Ward, K. 2005. Archaeological monitoring and excavation (preliminary report), Newtown Little, Stepaside, Co. Dublin. Unpublished Report for Margaret Gowen and Co. Ltd. National Monuments Service, Department of the Environment, Heritage and Local Government.

Wiggins, K. 2005 Darcystown, Skerries Road, Balrothery. Licence no. 03E0067. Unpublished report by Judith Carroll and Company for Fingal County Council. National Monuments Service, Department of the Environment, Heritage and Local Government.

Wiggins, K. 2006. Skerries Road, Balrothery. In I. Bennett (ed.), *Excavations 2003*, 107. Wordwell, Bray, Wicklow.

CATALOGUE

The excavation number 04E0680 is omitted throughout; only the context number followed by the find number is included.

Where the pottery is listed in the catalogue the context numbers are in bold: *e.g.* rimsherd: **235**.1. Numbers in square brackets (*e.g.* **235**.[1–3]) indicate that the sherds are conjoined. The thickness refers to an average dimension; where relevant a thickness range is indicated. Vessel numbers have been allocated to pottery where some estimation of the form of the pot is possible.

Beaker
Vessel 1. There are 7 sherds (3 base-/lower bodysherds: **235**.[1–3]; 5 bodysherds: **235**.4, 5, 7–9) from a vessel with a low pinched-up cordon and a flat, unfooted base that expands gently into the body. The smooth buff fabric has a grey core and a medium content of sandstone inclusions (up to 6 x 6mm) and occasional tiny uncrushed quartzite pebbles (≤ 1.5mm). Burning on the base and outer body surface of **235**.1 appears to have occurred prior to breakage. During manufacture, and apparently before firing, damage to part of the body (**235**.7) was repaired with 2 small clay plugs. Body thickness: 8mm; lower body: 8.5–9mm. Base diameter: 6.8mm. Total weight of sherds: 140g.

An unusual feature of this pottery is the evidence for intense heat damage to sherds **235**.2–5: this clearly occurred after the vessel was broken as it is very marked on sherds **235**.[2–3] that join with the unaffected sherd **235**.1. The heat was sufficiently intense to cause buckling and distortion leaving smooth rounded faces along the original edge breaks. There are very distinct tiny gas pockets, similar to those that occur on the lips of crucibles, within the affected areas. It is probable that, in the prehistoric period, temperatures high enough to occasion this damage could only have been created in a metalworking context.

Late Bronze Age
Vessel 2. This is represented by a single in-turned and flat topped rim (**235**.6) from a coarse domestic vessel with a bulbous upper profile. There us a distinct narrowing to the upper neck (12.2mm thick) where the rim has been pinched and turned inward. There is a burnt accretion on the inner surface that extends to within 8mm of the rim, and on the outer where it extends onto the outer rim edge. The compact hard fabric is grey to grey-buff with a darker grey core and has a medium content of crushed dolerite inclusions (≤ 4 x 3mm, up to 10 x 6mm). Neck thickness: 15.6mm. Weight: 50g.

APPENDIX III

HUMAN OSTEOLOGICAL REPORT, GLEBE SOUTH, BALROTHERY, CO. DUBLIN (04E0680)

Patricia Lynch

The material in this report was recovered from an excavation at Glebe South, Balrothery, Co. Dublin. The data in this report is recorded as an inventory of the skeletal remains recovered and, where necessary, various morphological measurements are included. These measurements were used to estimate the age-at-death, sex estimation, and stature, where possible.

For the sex determination, a study of the pelvic region, cranium and long bones was used. A wide range of methods has been used in the age-at-death estimation. These include dental development and wear, epiphyseal union, and age-related bone changes. The long bones were measured according to the specifications of Bass (1971, 1987) using an osteometric board and a sliding calipers. Also included in this report are, where present, non-metric traits and pathologies. The pathologies are recorded according to their aetiology. The initials A.I. refers to Acquired Infection. D.J.D. refers to Degenerative Joint Disease.

The dentition is referred to, by using the initials of the relevant teeth: I - incisor, C - canine, PM – premolar and M – molar. The letters 'y.o.' are used to refer the years old of an individual.

Discussion

The human remains in this report were recovered from an excavation at Glebe South, Balrothery, Co. Dublin. The bones were in a fragmentary condition and as a result 75% of the bones were identifiable. The remains were recovered from Contexts 124, 126, 137, 139, 142, 151, 153, 172, 177, 192, 193, 214, 218 and 256.

The M.N.I. of the remains are summarized as follows;

C124-	Female,	17-25yrs
C126-	Male,	35-45yrs
C137-	Adult	
C139-	Adult	
C142?-	Adult	
C151-	Adult	
C153-	Adult	25-35yrs 156.29cms ± 3.94cms

C172-	Male	
C177-	Adult	
C192-	Male	
C193-	1) Male	172.25cms ± 3.94 / 172.71cms ± 3.94cms
	2) Female	36yrs 161.06cms ± 3.53cms
C214-	1) Male	
	2) Female	25-35yrs
C218	Female	35-45yrs 154.90cms ± 3.53cms
C256	1) Adult	17-25yrs
	2) Child	5yrs ± 16mos

The identification and analysis of diseases recorded from archaeological assemblages can help and reflect the lifestyle, diet, health and relationship with other groups and environment within which the population lived.

Acquired disease (non specific) can be identified as pitting or in the form of periostitis. This is an inflammatory process, which is identified as fine pitting, longitudinal striation and/or plaque like formations on the original surface of the bone. It can occur as a break in the surface skin or a spread of infection from some other infected area and the palate of the skull from C155 contained pitting. This could have been related to a specific infection e.g. leprosy, although there was insufficient bone to further identify it as such. The congenital absence of a tooth (Hypodontia) is present from the mandible fragment from C193 where 3rd molar was absent. The 3rd molar is the most common tooth to be affected although it is relatively rare for all of a type of tooth to be absent. The aetiology for hypodontia is unknown although heredity is certainly the most important determinant.

Dental wear and disease provide evidence of diet adequacy, method of acquiring the diet, dentistry, stress and oral hygiene. Dental disease is the commonest form of pathology recorded in skeletal populations. The dental pathologies were consistent with a society where there was poor oral hygiene causing inflammation of the soft tissues of the mouth resulting in periodontal disease.

CONTEXT NO.	INVENTORY	DISCUSSION
124 (Grave 1)	39 skull fragments including frontal, parietal, temporal and maxilla fragments including RM3-1, PM2-1, C, L M1, PM2-1, C, I2 *in situ*, loose I1, 1 mandible, all teeth present, 1R clavicle fragment, 2R scapula fragments including coracoid and acromion, 1R proximal humerus fragment, greater tubercle absent, 1L proximal humerus fragment, head absent, 1R metacarpal fragment, 2R hand phalanges, 35 rib shaft fragments, 1 sternum fragment, 6 cervical vertebra fragments, 3R pelvis fragments, 1 sacrum fragment, 1R femur, greater and lesser trochanter and distal articular surface absent, 1L femur shaft and distal articular surface, medial epicondyle and lateral condyle absent, 3R tibia fragments including medial condyle, shaft and distal medial malleolus, 2L tibia fragments including proximal articular surface, both condyles absent and 1 shaft fragment, 1R calcaneus fragment.	**Age at death estimation.** The wear of the teeth of the maxilla and mandible indicates an age of 17-25yrs (Brothwell, 1965) **Sex estimation;** Skull: The supraorbital ridge was smooth indicating *female*. Pelvis: The sciatic notch was middle. This characteristic indicated a *?female*. **Pathologies;** Dental: 3 upper molars contained enamel pearls. The incisors of the mandible are protruding suggesting an under-bite. **Non-metric traits;** A lamboid ossicle (wormian bone) is present at the suture of the occipital and parietal, Plate 1. Remains representing one Adult female, 17-25yrs.
126 (Grave 2)	6 skull fragments including frontal, L zygomatic, 1R & L parietal, occipital, maxilla with Right M3-1, Pm2-1, C, I2, Left M2-1, PM2-1, C, I1 *in situ*, 1 mandible, R ascending ramus absent, R M3-1, PM2-1, C, I2-1, L M3-1 *in situ*, 1 1st cervical (atlas) vertebra fragment, 1 distal L humerus fragment, 1 proximal ulna fragment, 1L pelvis fragment, 4 femur fragments including 2R shaft and medial epicondyle, 2L head and distal shaft.	**Age at death estimation.** The wear of the teeth of the maxilla and mandible indicates an age of 35-45yrs (Brothwell, 1965) **Sex estimation;** Pelvis: The sciatic notch was narrow. This characteristic indicated a *male*. Remains representing one Adult male, 35-45yrs.
137 (Grave 3)	32 bone fragments including 9 skull and 23 long bone fragments.	No pathologies visible. No non-metric traits present. Remains representing one adult.
139 (Grave 4)	1 petrous portion of temporal bone fragment.	No pathologies visible. No non-metric traits present. Remains representing one adult.
141 (Grave 5)	10 femur fragments.	No pathologies visible. No non-metric traits present. Remains representing one adult.
151 (Grave 6)	2 bone fragments including 1 skull fragment and one long bone fragment. t.	No pathologies visible. No non-metric traits present. Remains representing one adult.
153 (Grave 7)	1 skull, nasal area damaged, Upper R M3-1, PM2-1, C, I2, L M3-1, PM2-1, C *in situ*, 17 mandible fragments, Left ascending ramus absent, all teeth present, 11R humerus fragments including lateral head, shaft and olecranon fossa, 2L humerus fragments including head and capitulum fragment, 2L proximal ulna fragments including olecranon, 2L radius fragments including proximal head and distal shaft and distal articular surface, 2L carpal bones including scaphoid and pisiform fragments, 8 rib shaft fragments, 19 vertebra fragments representing 1st -7th cervical (including atlas and axis), 2nd - 4th lumbar, 2 sacrum fragments, 13 pelvis fragments including L auricular surface, acetabulum and body fragment, R acetabulum and auricular surface fragments, 2R femur fragment	**Age at death estimation.** The wear of the teeth of the maxilla and mandible indicates an age of 25-35yrs (Brothwell, 1965) The analysis of the auricular surface indicated an age of 35yrs (Lovejoy *et al* 1985) **Sex estimation;** Skull: The mastoid process is moderate in size. This characteristic indicated a *?male*. The nuchal crest of the occipital is slight. The posterior of the zygomatic process does not extend beyond the external auditory meatus. These characteristics indicated a *female* (Meindl *et al*, 1985). Pelvis: The sciatic notch was narrow. This characteristic indicated a *male*

CONTEXT NO.	INVENTORY	DISCUSSION
	including 1 head fragment and distal shaft and distal articular surface, medial condyle absent, 1L femur, medial epicondyle and lateral condyle absent, great trochanter damaged, 1R & 1L patella fragment, 1R tibia, fibular articular surface absent, 5L tibia fragments, proximal and distal articular surfaces present but incomplete, 2R distal fibula fragments, articular surface incomplete, 4R talus bones including 1st & 2nd cuneiform, calcaneus and talus, 2L talus bones including calcaneus and talus fragment, 5th - 2nd metatarsal fragments,	Femur: The vertical diameter of the head is 46.94mm. These characteristics *?male* (Stewart, 1979). The trochanter oblique length is 410.5mm. This characteristics indicate *?sex* (Pearson, 1919). The oblique length is 430mm. This characteristics indicate *?sex* (Thieme, 1957). Tibia: Proximal breadth - 67.74mm. This characteristic indicated a *female* (Stymes and Janz, 1983). **Pathologies;** **D.J.D.** The Left superior articular surface contains a small pit on the surface. **Infection (non-specific).** The palate of the skull contains extensive pitting. **Non-metric traits.** The Skull contains a condylar canal on the Left side of the occipital condyles. **Stature.** 1) Right Femur length 43cms. — 2.32(43) + 65.53 — 156.29cms ± 3.94 (Trotter and Gleser, 1977). Remains representing one adult, 25-35yrs.
167 (Grave 8)	1 maxilla fragment, 1 loose molar crown, 1 distal L radius, lower articular surface present, 5 carpal bones including hamate, lunate, scaphoid, capitate and pisiform, 27 metacarpal fragments including L 1-5, 3 proximal, 2 mid and 1 distal phalanges, 14 L rib shaft fragments, 7 vertebra fragments, 1L pelvis, auricular surface absent, 5 L femur fragments, 1L patella fragment, 5 proximal R & L tibia fragments.	**Sex estimation;** Femur: The L head diameter was 46.66mm. This characteristic indicate *male* (Thieme, 1957). No pathologies visible. No non-metric traits present. Remains representing one adult male.
176 (Grave 9)	11 L phalanx fragments including 4 proximal and 3 mid, 1 fragment L acetabulum of pelvis, 52 femur fragments including 37R fragments including distal articular surface, 15L fragments including shaft and distal articular surface, 1 R & L patella, 35 tibia fragments including 23 R fragments including 22 proximal articular surface and 1 distal and 12L fragments including proximal articular surface and shaft fragments, 1 distal R fibula, 7 tarsal bones including 1R calcaneus, talus, navicular, 1R & L 1st cuneiform, 1R 2nd - 3rd cuneiform, 7 metatarsals including 1R & L 1st 1R & L 2nd, 1L 3rd 1L 4th, 1R 5th, 1 1st proximal phalanx fragment.	**Sex estimation;** Femur: The bicondylar width - 77.56mm. This indicated a *?male* (Pearson 1919). Tibia: the proximal breadth - 73.25mm. This indicated an *?female* (Stymes & Jantz 1983). **Pathologies.** **D.J.D.** Three proximal metatarsal articular fragments contained osteophytic lipping on the articular facets. Remains representing one Adult of undetermined sex.
192 (Grave 11)	1L pelvis fragment, acetabulum present, 1R femoral head, R & L patella, 28 proximal tibia fragments, R & L	**Sex estimation;** Pelvis: The sciatic notch was narrow. This characteristic indicated a *male*. No pathologies visible. No non-metric traits present. Remains representing one adult male.
193 (Grave 12)	1 mandible fragment left side absent, 11 skull fragments including R & L orbit, occipital, 2R & 1L parietal, R temporal, 1 scapula fragment, 3 humerus fragments including 2R humerus, 1) proximal articular surface absent 2) distal fragment	**Age at death estimation.** The analysis of the auricular surface indicated an age of 36yrs (Lovejoy *et al* 1985) **Sex estimation;** Skull: The nuchal crest of the occipital is heavy.

CONTEXT NO.	INVENTORY	DISCUSSION
	olecranon fossa present, 4 ulna fragments representing 2R and 1L, 2 & 3 metacarpals, 1R hamate, 1 hand phalanx fragment, 12 rib shaft fragments, 1R & L pelvis fragment, 5 femur fragments including 2R & 2L, 1 shaft fragment, 1R & L tibia, L - medial malleolus absent, 1R fibula, 5 tarsal bones including R & L calcaneus, R & L talus 2nd cuneiform, R & L1-5 metatarsal, 1 phalanx fragment,	This indicated a *Male* (Meindl *et al*, 1985). Humerus: The epicondylar width was 60.94mm. This indicated an *indeterminate* (Thieme 1957). Pelvis: The sciatic notch was wide. This characteristic indicated a *female* Femur: The R head diameter was 48.23mm. The length of the R was 460mm, L was 462mm. These characteristics indicate *male* (Thieme, 1957). Tibia - 365mm length **Pathologies.** **Congenital** The 3rd molar from the mandible is absent (hypodontia). **D.J.D.** The area of attachment of the ligament of head of femur, of the R & L femur is ossified. Eburnation is present on the acetabulum at the on the L pelvis fragment. **Stress.** The area of attachment of the pectoralis major, subscapularis and supraspinatus muscles of the humerus is enlarged. The area of attachment of the popliteus and soleus muscles of the tibiae is enlarged. **Misc.** The mandible fragment contained a bone growth at PM1 socket **Stature** 1) Male right femur length 46cms. − 2.32(46) + 65.53 − 172.25cms ± 3.94 (Trotter and Gleser, 1977). 1) Male left femur length 46.2cms. − 2.32(46.2) + 65.53 − 172.71cms ± 3.94 (Trotter and Gleser, 1977). 2) Female left tibia length 36.5cms. − 2.72(36.5) + 63.781 − 163.061cms ± 3.531 (Trotter and Gleser, 1977). Remains representing two individuals, 1) Male, 2) Female 36yrs
213 (Grave 13)	1) 45 skull fragments including frontal, L orbit absent, 1R & L temporal fragments including petrous portion, R & L parietal, occipital, 25 loose teeth fragments including Upper M3-1 Lower M1-2, PM2, 15 cervical vertebra fragments including atlas and axis, 1L pelvis fragment including fragment sciatic notch and acetabulum, 1R patella, 2 femur fragments including 1 head and 9L femur shaft, nutrient foramen present, 1 intercondylar fossa, 2R tibia fragments, proximal articular surface and distal medial malleolus absent, 11L tibia shaft fragments, 4R fibula fragments, head and lateral malleolus absent, 2 tarsal fragments including R talus, 2 metatarsal fragments, 2) 19 pelvis fragments including sciatic notch and acetabulum fragment, 3R femur fragments, neck, greater & lesser trochanter and lateral epicondyle absent, 11L distal articular fragments, 2 fragments distal R tibia, 1 distal fibula fragment, 10 calcaneus fragments,	**Age at death estimation.** 1) The wear of the loose teeth indicates an age of 25-35yrs (Brothwell, 1965). **Sex estimation;** 1) Skull: The supraorbital ridge was smooth indicating *female*. The mastoid process is small in size. This characteristic indicated a *female*. The nuchal crest of the occipital is moderate. This indicated a *?female* (Meindl *et al*, 1985). Pelvis: The sciatic notch was wide. This characteristic indicated a *female* 2) Pelvis: The sciatic notch was narrow. This characteristic indicated a *male* Remains representing 1) Female 25-35yrs, 2) Adult male

CONTEXT NO.	INVENTORY	DISCUSSION
218 (Grave 14)	Skull fragments including maxilla LM1, PM1, C, I2, R M2-1, C *in situ*, frontal, L absent, R & L parietal, occipital, R & L zygomatic, facial bones, 1 mandible, LM3-1, PM2-1, C, I2-1, R M2-1, PM2-1, C, I2-1 *in situ*, 6 metacarpal fragments including 4L, 2 scapula fragments including 1R with glenoid cavity and coracoid process present, 1L scapula fragment including body and acromion fragment, 1R & L clavicle, 4 humerus fragments including 1R greater tubercle and lateral condyle, 2L fragments, head and shaft, 4 radius fragments including 3R & 1L proximal fragments, 1R & L ulna shaft fragment, 1 manibrium of sternum fragment, 14 rib fragments including 9R with 1st, 5L including 1st, 29 vertebra fragments including 7 cervical including atlas and axis and 12 thoracic and 2 lumbar, 1R & L pelvis fragment, sciatic notch and acetabulum present, 3 femur fragments including 2R and 1 almost complete L, 1L patella, 7 tibia fragments including 6R fragments, medial condyle and medial malleolus absent, 1 complete L, 1L distal fibula fragment, 10 talus bone fragments including R & L calcaneus, R & L talus, R & L navicular, R & L cuboid, R & L 1st cuneiform and L 3rd cuneiform, 8 metatarsal fragments including R 2-4, L 1-5, 5 phalanges including 1st proximal, 4 mid.	**Age at death estimation.** The wear of the teeth of the maxilla and mandible indicates an age of 35 - 45yrs (Brothwell, 1965) **Sex estimation.** Pelvis: The sciatic notches were wide. This characteristic indicated a *female*. Femur: L head diameter - 36.84mm. This indicated a *female* Tibia: The distal breadth measured 42.22. This indicated a *female* (Stymes and Jantz 1983). The size and development of the tarsal bones indicate a petite *female*. **Pathologies.** **Dental.** Maxilla: R M3 was lost ante-mortem, M1 contained a large caries on the crown and an abscess on the lingual surface of the root, exposing it, L M1 a small caries was present on the crown and an abscess exposed both roots. M2 & 3 were lost ante-mortem. Moderate alveolar resorption was present on the alveolus margin Mandible: Moderate alveolar resorption was present. Moderate-mild calculus was present on the buccal surface of the I & C. A caries was located at the junction of crown and root of the L M3. An abscess was located at the buccal surface and affected the roots of L M1 The R M3 was lost ante mortem. **Stature.** 1) Female left tibia length 33.5cms. − 2.72(33.5) + 63.781 − 154.901cms ± 3.531 (Trotter and Gleser, 1977). Remains representing one Female 25-35yrs, Mandible: Moderate alveolar resorption was present. Moderate-mild calculus was present on the buccal surface of the I & C. An abscess was located at the buccal surface and affected the roots of L M1. The R M3 was lost ante mortem
256 (Grave 17)	28 skull fragments including frontal, R & L temporal, L zygomatic, sphenoid, maxilla, all teeth present, loose developing PM2-1, M1-2, 1 L mandible fragment with M3-1, PM2-1, C *in situ*, loose I1-2, 2 distal humerus fragments, R & L7 vertebra fragments, 1R scapula fragment including glenoid cavity and axillary border, 1L clavicle, 3 ulna fragments including 2R and 1L shaft fragments, 8 rib shaft fragments, 3 femur fragment including proximal R,	**Age at death estimation.** The wear of the teeth of the maxilla and mandible indicates an age of 17-25yrs (Brothwell, 1965) The development of the loose developing PM 2, M1, M2 indicated an age of 5yrs ± 16mos (Ubelaker 1978). No pathologies visible. No non-metric traits present. Remains representing one adult 17-25yrs and one child 5yrs ±16mos

Calculus, which is an infectious dental disease, consists of plaque (microorganisms which accumulate in the mouth) that had mineralized in the mouth as a result of poor oral hygiene. Calculus was visible on many of the teeth from the almost complete mandible from C218. Calculus can irritate the gingival tissues that can cause inflammation resulting in alveolar resorption and therefore periodontal disease.

Alveolar resorption is caused by inflammation of the gingival tissue or periodontal disease and results in the resorption of the bone along the alveolar margins, porosity and / or periostitis. Alveolar resorption was also recorded on the mandible fragment from C218.

Dental caries are also very common and can be identified as opaque areas on the enamel or cavities. These occur as a result of the fermentation of food sugars (commonly found in carbohydrate rich food) by bacteria that occur on the tooth surface. A large one was present on the crown of the Upper RM1 and a small one on the neck of Lower Left M3 also from C218.

Abscesses can be caused if an individual develops periodontal disease and a periodontal pocket. This is initiated by the accumulation of plaque between the soft tissue of the gum and teeth. Micro-organisms accumulate in the pulp cavity, inflammation begins and a body of pus (dead cells) forms. As the pus accumulates, pressure builds up and eventually a sinus (hole) is formed on the surface of the jawbone in order to allow the pus to escape. One abscess was present at the socket of Upper Right M1 exposing the root and Left M1 exposing both roots. An abscess was also present on the lower Left M1.

The Lower Right M3, and Upper Right M3, Left M3 & 2 from C218 were absent. These had been lost ante-mortem, and the alveolar bone had closed. This could indicate a form of dental practice.

Two molars, RM3, LM1 from C124 contained enamel pearls. These occur as a result of an extension of the crown enamel, if it is clustered it is referred to as a pearl. These are not visible if the teeth are embedded in the alveolus. Little is known of their distribution or significance. The incisors of the mandible of C124 are protruding possibly as a result of an under-bite. Degenerative joint disease is recognised as remodelling (formation or destruction) of a bone/bones and is the most common disease to appear in the skeletal record after dental disease. Osteoarthritis most frequently occurs as a result of the destruction of weight bearing joints (vertebrae, hip, knee). The cause of osteoarthritis is unknown although it is thought to be caused by wear and tear related to hard work and/or ageing. Osteoarthritis can also develop as a result of a trauma to a joint, and may occur at any age.

A vertebra from C153 contained a small pit on the articular surface indicating mild arthritis of the spine. Three proximal metatarsal articular fragments from C177 contained osteophytic lipping on the articular facets indicating mild arthritis of the foot. The acetabulum from C193 contains eburnation of the surface. This occurs as a result of the cartilage of the joint being destroyed. As a result, the underlying bone becomes very hard and polished (eburnation). The area of attachment of the ligament of head of femur, also from C193, of the R & L femur is ossified. This is also as a result of an increase use of the joint, coupled with the degenerative joint disease of the acetabulum.

The stress related trauma pathologies suggest important information about the lifestyle (economy, culture and occupation) of a population. From C193, the area of attachment of the pectoralis major, subscapularis and supraspinatus muscles of the humerus is enlarged, the area of attachment of the popliteus and soleus muscles of the tibiae is enlarged, this is as a result of the increase of the usage and therefore, increase, in size of the attaching muscles.

Two non - metric traits/variations were recorded. These are morphological variations in the skeleton, which cause no discomfort and are thought to be genetic (Sjøvold 1984, 1987).

A lamboid ossicle (wormian bone) was present on the skull from C124. These are extra or supernumerary bones that occur within the skull sutures. It has been suggested that the high frequencies of sutural ossification at locations of the skull correlates with high price of wheat possibly implying an adverse affect on nutrition (Bocquet-Appel 1984). On the skull from C155, there is a condylar canal to the left occipital canal (Finnegan, 1978).

One miscellaneous pathology was identified. This was a bone growth on the mandible from C193, located at the PM1 socket.

It was possible to estimate the stature of four individuals:

C153, 156.29cms ± 3.94,
C193, Male, 172.25cms ± 3.94 & 172.71cms ± 3.94cms,
        Female, 161.06cms ± 3.53cms
C218, Female, 154.90cms ± 3.53.

Therefore in conclusion, the remains recovered were analysed and identified as sixteen adults and one child. Of the adult remains, because of the fragmentary condition of the bones it was only possible to identify the sex of five males and four females. A full range of ages was recorded from 45 (the eldest individual) to 5yrs±16mos (the youngest). The stature of four individuals was estimated, one of which was male and two of which were females.

The identification of diseases indicates to us the health of the assemblage.

Dental problems were the most common with calculus, alveolar resorption, dental caries and an abscess. Enamel pearls and a possible overbite were also identified.

Degenerative joint disease was also present on one vertebra fragment and one hip fragment and this is thought to be related to hard work /old age.

Acquired infection was also present one instance.

The presence of stress related trauma indicated a society where much physical work was carried out.

One miscellaneous pathology was also identified as a bone growth on a mandible.

References

Bass W.M. 1987. *Human Osteology: a laboratory and field manual.* Colombia.

Bocquet-Appel 1984. Biological Evolution and history the 19th Century Portugal. In G. N. van Vark and W. W. Howells (eds.) *Multivariate Statistical Techniques in Physical Anthropology*, 289-321. Reidle Groningenn.

Brothwell D.R. 1981. *Digging up bones.* Oxford University Press (3rd edition).

Lovejoy, C.O., Meindl, R.S, Pryzbeck, T.R. and Mensforth, R.P. 1985. Chronological metamorphosis of the auricular surface of the ilium: A new method of determining adult age at death, *American Journal of Physical Anthropology*, 68, 15-28.

Meindl, R.S., Lovejoy, C.O., Mensforth, R.P. and Carlos, L.D. 1985. Accuracy and direction of error in the sexing of the skeleton: Implications for palaeodemography. *American Journal of Physical Anthropology*, 68: 79-85.

Pearson, K. 1919. A Study of The Long Bones of The English Skeleton 1: The Femur. *Company Research Memoirs, Biometric Series X*. Dept. Applied Sciences, University of London.

Sjøvold, T. 1984. A report on the heritability of some cranial measurements and non-metric traits. In G.N. van Vark and W.W. Howells (eds.). *Multivariate Statistical Techniques in Physical Anthropology*, 223-246. Reidle, Groningen.

Stewart, T.D. 1979. *Essentials of Forensic Anthropology.* Springfield, Illinois.

Symes, S.A. and Janz, R.L. 1983. Discriminant function sexing of the tibia. Paper presented at the 35th Annual Meeting of the American Academy of Forensic Sciences, Cincinnati.

Thieme, F.P. 1957. Sex in Negro Skeletons. *Journal of Forensic Medicine* 4:72-81.

Ubelaker, D. 1978. *Human skeletal remains: Excavation, analysis, Interpretation.* Adline Publishing Company, Chicago, Illinois.

APPENDIX IV

ANALYSIS OF CREMATED BONE, GLEBE SOUTH, BALROTHERY, CO. DUBLIN (04E0680)

Patricia Lynch

Introduction

The cremated human bone in this report was recovered from Glebe South, Balrothery, Co. Dublin. The preservation of the bone was very poor with all of the material in a very fragmentary condition. As a result of this only *c.* 10% of the recovered bone was identifiable.

The data in this report is recorded as an inventory of the identifiable bone.

The presence of any pathology and non-metric trait are recorded, described and where necessary, photographed.

Where possible, age-at-death and species estimation are also recorded.

CONTEXT NO.	INVENTORY	COMMENTS
80, Sample # 89.	5g of cremated human bone 3.7mm – 22.56mm including: 1 rib shaft fragment Insufficient bone to estimate sex or age at death. Remains representing one adult.	No pathologies present. No post-mortem trauma present.
115, Sample # 51.	75g of cremated bone fragments 3.3mm - 40mm with soil inclusions, 73g after cleaning including: 9 skull fragments including 1R petrous portion of temporal bone, 3 ulna shaft fragments, 1 vertebral spinous process and articular process fragment, 3 femur shaft fragments, 2 tibia shaft fragments.	No pathologies present. No post-mortem trauma present. Insufficient bone to estimate sex. Remains representing one adult.
178, Sample # 49	530g of cremated bone fragments 3.3mm - 40mm with soil inclusions, 472g after cleaning including: 18 skull fragments, 1 molar tooth fragment, 5 humerus shaft fragments, 3 ulna shaft fragments, 1 mid hand phalanx, 2 distal hand phalanges, 1 vertebral spinous process fragment, 2 rib shaft fragments, 4 femur shaft fragments, 7 tibia shaft fragments, 29 articular surface fragments.	No pathologies present. No post-mortem trauma present. Insufficient bone to estimate sex. Remains representing one adult.
239, Sample # 86	20g of cremated bone fragments 2.22mm - 27.72mm including: 1 rib shaft fragment, 1 spinous process fragment, 1 tibia inferior fibular articular surface Remains representing one adult.	No pathologies present. No post-mortem trauma present. Insufficient bone to estimate sex.
242, Sample # 85	4g of cremated bone fragments 2.11mm - 14.09mm including: 1 skull fragment. Insufficient bone to estimate sex. Remains representing one adult.	No pathologies present. No post-mortem trauma present.
266, Sample # 107.	65g of cremated bone fragments 4.34mm - 32.14mm in soil, 57g after cleaning including 1 skull fragment, 4 articular surface fragments. Remains representing one adult	No pathologies present. No post-mortem trauma present. Insufficient bone to estimate sex.

CONTEXT NO.	INVENTORY	COMMENTS
272, Sample # 55.	44g of cremated bone fragments 4.55mm - 25.65mm in soil, 34g after cleaning including: 15 skull fragments, 1 rib shaft fragment, 2 articular surface fragments. Remains representing one adult.	No pathologies present. No post-mortem trauma present. Insufficient bone to estimate sex.
273, Sample # 111.	28g of cremated bone fragments 4.87mm - 24.78mm in soil, 22g after cleaning including: 6 skull fragments, 1 distal hand phalanx. Remains representing one adult	No pathologies present. No post-mortem trauma present. Insufficient bone to estimate sex.
274, Sample # 110.	83g of cremated bone fragments 2.82mm - 23.64mm in soil, 71g after cleaning including: 12 skull fragments, 1 tooth root fragment, 3 rib shaft fragments, 1 vertebral spinous process fragment.	No pathologies present. No post-mortem trauma present. Insufficient bone to estimate sex. Remains representing one adult.
289, Sample # 102.	8g cremated unidentifiable bone fragments 3.81mm - 24.55mm in soil, 3g after cleaning. Insufficient bone to estimate sex. Remains representing one adult.	No pathologies present. No post-mortem trauma present.
290, Sample # 114	46g cremated bone fragments 2.50mm - 20.10mm in soil, 37g after cleaning including: 5 skull fragments, 1 capitulum fragment of the humerus, 1 distal hand phalanx, 2 rib shaft fragments.	No pathologies present. No post-mortem trauma present. Insufficient bone to estimate sex. Remains representing one adult.
293, Sample # 84.	62g cremated bone fragments in soil 5.75mm - 28.55mm, 56g after cleaning including; 36 skull fragments, 2 tooth roots, 1 olecranon fragment of ulna, 2 mid hand phalanges, 2 rib shaft fragments.	No pathologies present. No post-mortem trauma present. Insufficient bone to estimate sex. Remains representing one adult.

Discussion and Conclusion

These cremated bone fragments were recovered from the excavation at Glebe South, Balrothery, Co. Dublin. The bones were in a very fragmentary condition and as a result of this it was only possible to identify 10% of the bone. It was not possible to identify the bones from C289.

The bone samples were recovered from C80, C115, C178, C239, C242, C266, C272, C273, C274, C289, C290, C293. In all 970g of cremated human bone in a soil matrix was recovered, 852g after cleaning.

The minimum number of individuals of the analysis is further summarized as follows:

C80   1 Adult
C115   1 Adult
C178   1 Adult
C239   1 Adult
C242   1 Adult
C266   1 Adult
C272   1 Adult
C273   1 Adult
C274   1 Adult
C289   1 Adult
C290   1 Adult
C293   1 Adult

While some individual bones and tooth roots were identified, the cremated bone was too fragmentary to further identify sex estimation or age at death. The density of the bones from each context suggests remains of adults.

There was no evidence of pathologies and non-metric traits in the assemblage, but this probably was as a result of the fragmentary condition of the bone fragments.

In summary, the remains of twelve skeletons were identified. The bone was too fragmentary to identify sex estimation or age at death.

APPENDIX V

ANALYSIS OF CHARCOAL FROM GLEBE SOUTH, BALROTHERY, CO. DUBLIN (04E0680)

Ellen O'Carroll

Introduction

Seven charcoal samples from an excavation at Glebe South, Co. Dublin were submitted for analysis. The site comprised a number of archaeological features including two ring ditch burial sites (Ring ditches 1 and 2); some pits containing prehistoric pottery and cremated bone; cremation burials of the early centuries AD; at least one inhumation burial probably sub-Roman in date; associated inhumation burials of probable Iron Age to early medieval date; a medieval ditch 60m in length and activity related to cereal drying

The charcoal was sent for species identification primarily for analysis prior to 14C dating. A general analysis was also undertaken on the range of tree species which grew in the area, as well as the utilization of these species for various functions.

Wood used for fuel at prehistoric sites would generally have been sourced at locations close to the site. Therefore charcoal identifications may, but do not necessarily, reflect the composition of the local woodlands. Larger pieces of charcoal, when identified, can provide information regarding the use of a species.

The charcoal sampled and analysed from Glebe South was excavated from a cremation pit, C279 dated to the Later Bronze Age (1040-840BC), a second cremation pit, C144, dated to Early Iron Age AD 240 – 430, the fill of two kilns (C040), a Late Iron age / early medieval pit, C080, a pit, C012, and the fill of a ring ditch C178 (200BC-AD10).

Methods

The process for identifying wood, whether it is charred, dried or waterlogged, is carried out by comparing the anatomical structure of wood samples with known comparative material or keys (Schweingruber 1990). The identification of charcoal material involves breaking the charcoal piece so as a clean section of the wood can be obtained. This charcoal is then identified to species under an Olympus SZ3060 x 80-zoom stereomicroscope. By close examination of the microanatomical features of the samples the species were determined. The diagnostic features used for the identification of charcoal are micro-structural characteristics such as the vessels and their arrangement, the size and arrangement of rays, vessel pit arrangement and also the type of perforation plates. All samples were suitable for species identification.

Results

TABLE 1 Results from charcoal identifications at Glebe South, Co. Dublin

Feature no.	Sample no.	Species	Feature type and date
279	101	* Pomoideae (3g) and blackthorn (2g)	Cremation pit 1040-840BC
80	31	Hazel (20g) and blackthorn (4g)	pit AD330-550
45	40	Hazel brushwood (178g)	Linear ditch AD 1030-1230
12	15	Hazel (10g), Alder (7g) and ash (10g)	Fill of pit/post-hole
40	19	All ash (16g)	Fill of kiln. Medieval. AD 1020 to 1220
144	44	Hazel (4g) and birch (1g)	Cremation pit AD240-430
178	106	Mainly ash (3g), hazel (1g) and birch (1g)	Fill of ring ditch. 200 BC to AD 10

* Pomoideae includes apple, pear, hawthorn and mountain ash. It is impossible to distinguish these wood species anatomically.

TABLE 2 TAXA REPRESENTED IN THE IDENTIFIED SAMPLES

Botanical name	Species
Corylus avellana	Hazel
Prunus spinosa	Blackthorn
Fraxinus excelsior.	Ash
Pomoideae	Apple type
Betula sp	Birc

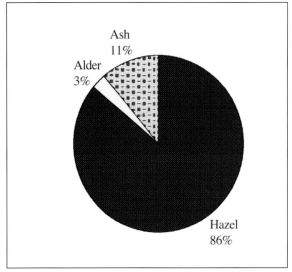

FIGURE 3: TAXA IDENTIFIED FROM THE MEDIEVAL FEATURES

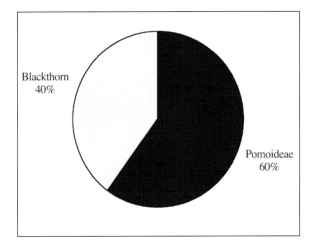

FIGURE 1: TAXA IDENTIFIED FROM THE PREHISTORIC EXCAVATED FEATURES

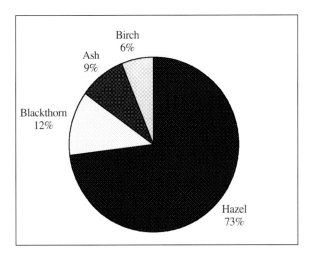

FIGURE 2: TAXA IDENTIFIED FROM THE IRON AGE FEATURES

Discussion

Six taxa were present in the charcoal remains. As the samples were mainly identified for dating purposes the full quantity of each sample was not analysed and therefore the range of taxa may be non-exhaustive.

The range of species identified from the features analysed includes large (ash), medium sized trees (alder and birch) and smaller scrub or hedgerow trees like blackthorn, hazel and pomoideae.

The majority of the charcoal identified was derived from wood which was gathered fresh with few insect channels present in the remains. There were some insect channels noted on the blackthorn charcoal from the fill of the pit C080 which is indicative of wood selected from forest floors or fallen branches.

The charcoal samples analysed are most likely to represent firewood used in Glebe South during all periods of habitation. The pomoideae and blackthorn identified from the cremation pit C279 and the hazel and birch identified from the later dated cremation pit is not in keeping with results from other analysed sites in Ireland where oak is generally the dominant species used at cremation sites. These cremation pits may be associated with a different ritual practice associated with these cremated bodies or may indicate that oak was not accessible in large quantities to the inhabitants at the time of the cremations.

Ash and hazel may have been used either as firewood or as a structure associated with pit, C012 and kiln, C040. Ash charcoal is an excellent fuel and hazel charcoal has been identified from kilns excavated in the vicinity of Glebe South in Rosepark (99E0155) and Balrothery (04E0741).

There are inherent problems in re-constructing the environment at the time of use of the site due to the low quantity of samples and charcoal fragments identified from the assemblages. It is generally accepted that between 50 and 100 samples are required to fully re-construct the environment of the catchment area of a site. However some conclusions and further discussions can be drawn from the work above.

The local environment of the sites is mainly indicative of a dryland environment in all periods. However there were some wetland species identified both from the Iron Age (birch) and the later medieval periods (alder) which suggests access to a wetter environment in the area at the time of the Iron Age and the medieval periods.

The large quantities of ash and hazel in the Iron Age and later medieval period is interesting and agrees well with pollen records as Hall and Pilcher point out from the pollen records that 'the ash population expanded late in Irish woodland history....it is possibly one of the most common hedgerow trees in Ireland' (Hall & Pilcher, 2001, 35). The hazel identified from the Iron Age/ medieval features also fits in well with other identified assemblages in Ireland. O' Donnell has identified charcoal from a series structures along the gas pipe line and hazel and ash appear to dominate in the Iron Age periods (Grogan, O'Donnell and Johnston 2007, 51).

The ash and hazel would have grown in drier conditions preferring free-draining soils and nutrient-rich clays. Local hedgerows or low woodlands comprising hawthorn / wild apple / mountain ash, blackthorn and cherry may have also been growing in the area in the prehistoric period after the land was cleared by the early farmers. The ash and hazel also identified from the Iron Age/later medieval periods may also have been growing in the nearby hedgerows. Taxa that are more likely to be located in wetter areas include alder and birch.

Summary and Conclusions

Six taxa were present from the features investigated. The species identified are more indicative of a dryland terrain where scrub material prevailed in the early historic periods and hazel and ash woods were more evident in the later periods. Birch was identified from the Iron Age ring ditch C178 and also the Iron Age cremation pit C144. This may suggest a relationship between the features or at least a similar woodland environment at the time of use of the two sites. Birch is a coloniser and will colonise land that has been cleared.

The absence of oak charcoal in the cremation samples may be indicative of a different ritual associated with the cremations as oak is generally the main taxon identified from other analysed cremation deposits in Ireland.

Ash and hazel may have been used either as firewood or as a structure associated within the pit, C012 and kiln, C040. Ash charcoal is an excellent fuel and hazel charcoal has been identified from kilns excavated in the vicinity of Glebe South in Rosepark (99E0115) and Balrothery (04E0741).

The blackthorn, mountain ash/hawthorn/apple may have grown locally in a hedgerow type of environment. The ash and hazel may also be associated with a hedgerow although these trees can also grow in a coppice woodland or understorey in a larger wooded area.

A wetland area or open land was also present as alder and birch was also identified from the Iron Age and later medieval assemblage.

References

Beckett, J.K. 1979. *Planting Native Trees and Shrubs*. Jarrold & Sons Ltd, Norwich.

Grogan, E, O'Donnell L and Johnston, P. 2007. *The Bronze Age Landscapes of the pipeline to the west*. Wordwell, Bray, Wicklow.

Nelson, E.C. 1993. *Trees of Ireland*. The Lilliput Press, Dublin.

Warner, R.B. 1987. A proposed adjustment for the 'Old-Wood Effect'. In Mook, W. & Waterbolk, H. (eds.). *Proc. 2nd Symp of 14C & Archaeology, Groningen 1987*, 29, 159-172.

Webb, D.A. 1977. *An Irish Flora*. Dundalgan Press Ltd, Dundalk.

Schweingruber, F.H. 1990. *Microscopic Wood Anatomy*. 3rd edition. Birmensdorf: Swiss Federal Institute for Forest, Snow and Landscape Research.

Stuijts, I, 2001. Charcoal identification from Rosepark, Balrothery, Co. Dublin (99E0155), unpublished post excavation report. In J. Carroll, 2002. The Excavation of a multi-ditched enclosure at Rosepark, Co. Dublin (Licence no. 99E0155). Unpublished report. National Monuments Service, Department of the Environment, Heritage and Local Government.

APPENDIX VI

ANALYSIS OF NON-WOOD PLANT MACRO-REMAINS

Meriel McClatchie

A soil sample from one deposit (C035) at Glebe South, Balrothery was presented for analysis. The sample contained a large quantity of charred naked barley grains, representing a cereal type that is often associated with Bronze Age sites in Ireland. A possible wheat grain and a weed seed were also present. Cereal chaff was absent from this deposit. The cereal grains are likely to represent residues from crop-processing or cooking activities at Glebe South, which could have been deposited in a range of circumstances.

Introduction

Archaeological excavations were carried out at Glebe South, Balrothery, Co. Dublin during 2004 under the direction of Frank Ryan of Judith Carroll & Co. Ltd. It appears that Glebe South was the location for human activity over several millennia, with a number of different activity areas being recorded. One soil sample (C035) from an Early-Middle Bronze Age corn-drying kiln (C011) at Glebe South was presented for archaeobotanical analysis. This report will detail the types of plant remains recorded in C035, in addition to interpreting the remains in their wider context.

Methodology

The soil sample was processed using conventional flotation methods, with the smallest sieve mesh-aperture measuring 250^2m. The identification of the archaeobotanical material was carried out using a stereo-microscope, with magnifications ranging from x6.3 to x50. The sample was scanned in order to confirm the presence of archaeobotanical material, which was then extracted and sorted into general groupings on the basis of visual comparison of morphological features. The archaeobotanical material was identified by comparison to reference material in McClatchie's collection of modern diaspores, as well as the drawings and photographs from various seed keys (Anderberg 1994; Beijerinck 1947; Berggren 1969; 1981; Katz *et al.* 1965). Cereal grains were recorded as 'whole' if the embryo was present. Some of the material was distorted or fragmented, and was identified to genus or family level only. The identified taxa are listed in Table 1. Common names follow those provided in *New flora of the British Isles* (Stace 1991) and *Domestication of plants in the Old World* (Zohary and Hopf 2000).

Non-wood plant macro-remains recorded

Introduction

C035 was a fill of C011, which was interpreted as a possible corn-drying kiln. C011 was a pear-shaped pit – the 'bowl' of the kiln – containing several layers in which cereal remains and sherds of Early-Middle Bronze Age pottery were recorded. Radiocarbon dating of charcoal from C035 produced an Early-Middle Bronze Age date (2‰ calibration: 1880-1650 BC; Beta-240939). A number of post-holes surrounding C011 may either post-date the possible kiln or may be contemporary, perhaps representing the remains of a shelter. Evidence for *in-situ* burning was recorded in a number of the post-hole deposits.

Plant remains

Due to the very large quantity of plant macro-remains present in C035, a representative sub-sample of *c.* 13.5% was analysed. Analysis of the whole sample would therefore have produced more than seven times the quantity of identified remains listed in Table 1.

Analysis of the C035 sub-sample produced evidence for a large quantity of charred grains of (*Hordeum vulgare* var. *nudum*) naked barley, including examples of six-row naked barley. A substantial quantity of poorly preserved charred grain fragments of Cerealia (indeterminate cereal) was also recorded. One possible charred grain of *Triticum* sp. (wheat) was present, as well as a small charred seed fragment that could only be identified to the Caryophyllaceae (pink) family.

TABLE 1 NON-WOOD PLANT MACRO-REMAINS RECORDED IN C035

Botanical name	Plant part	Common name Sample 013	Context 035
CARYOPHYLLACEAE			
Caryophyllaceae	Seed fragment	pink	1
GRAMINEAE			
cf. *Triticum* sp.	grain	possible wheat	1
Hordeum vulgare subsp. *vulgare* var. *nudum*	grains	6-row naked barley	418
Hordeum vulgare var. *nudum*	grains	naked barley	1165
Hordeum vulgare var. *nudum*	grain fragments	naked barley	386
Hordeum vulgare L.	grains	6-row barley	12
Hordeum vulgare L.	grains	barley	39
Hordeum vulgare L.	grain fragments	barley	23
Cerealia	grain fragments	indeterminate cereal	484
	Total	**2529**	

Note that the above represents a c.13.5% sub-sample of the total deposit

Discussion

Types of plant macro-remains

The cereals present at Glebe South are predominantly of naked barley, with a single grain of possible wheat also recorded. Barley, particularly the naked variety, has traditionally been viewed as the predominant cereal type of Bronze Age Ireland (Jessen and Helbaek 1944; Monk 1986). Recent research has clearly demonstrated that cereal economies of earlier Bronze Age Ireland are, however, often rather mixed, with regular evidence for wheat and hulled barley being recorded at more recently excavated sites (Fuller *et al.* in press).

Section 3.2 above notes that only a sub-sample of C035 was examined due to the large quantity of plant macro-remains present – it is estimated that the whole deposit contained *c.* 12,000 whole barley grains, mainly of naked barley. The recovery of such a large quantity of naked barley grains is relatively unusual in an Irish Bronze Age context, although a small number of other sites – such as the Late Bronze Age hillfort at Haughey's Fort, Co. Armagh (Mallory 1995) – have also produced similarly large assemblages of naked barley (with few other plant remains present).

One possible wheat grain was recorded at Glebe South. The identification of wheat species by grain alone is generally unreliable (Hillman *et al.* 1996), and well-preserved chaff (such as spikelet forks and glume bases) is instead a more reliable indicator of

wheat varieties. Such chaff remains were, however, absent from the examined deposit at Glebe South.

C035 was a remarkably 'pure' grain deposit, in that almost all 'contaminants' had been removed – no chaff was recorded and only one weed seed fragment (of the pink family) was observed. The pink family contains a large number of genera and species that can be found growing in a wide variety of environments. It is possible that this weed seed represents a plant that was growing in the background environment of the site, becoming charred accidentally. The seed fragment may alternatively represent a weed that was growing alongside and was inadvertently harvested with the cereal crop.

Context of plant macro-remains

C035 was the fill of C011, which was interpreted as a corn-drying kiln, due to the irregular shape of the pit, and the presence of *in-situ* burning and cereal grains. The drying of cereals may have been required prior to the storage of grain (in order to reduce the moisture content), or in the preparation of foodstuffs and ales. Current archaeological evidence indicates that the construction of a formal corn-drying kiln would have been somewhat unusual during the Bronze Age – corn-drying kilns are more often associated with the historic period in Ireland (Monk and Kelleher 2005). Other uses for this pit should therefore also be considered. It is possible that this feature instead represents a cooking/roasting pit, which would

TABLE 2 RADIOCARBON DATING RECOMMENDATIONS (∗ = suitable for dating)

Material	Weight	AMS	Conventional
cf. Wheat grain	<0.5g	∗	...
Barley grains	c.15g	∗	∗
Indeterminate cereal grains	0.5g	∗	...
Weed seed	<0.5g	...	...

explain the presence of food remains and *in-situ* burning. The presence of a substantial quantity of poorly preserved cereal grain fragments in Co35 indicates that this deposit may have been subject to considerable movement before its final deposition. It is possible that the pit was originally constructed for uses unconnected with food preparation – when the pit went out of use, it may have been designated a location for the deposition of 'waste', with cereal remains and broken ceramic sherds being amongst the debris eventually placed into the pit.

The presence of food remains in Co35 should not, however, be automatically interpreted as representing 'domestic' activity. Foods can be an important element of ceremonial activities, with even the waste from such activities being accorded special treatment (Brück 2000). It is therefore possible that the placing of food remains into the pit, along with other materials such as broken pottery vessels, may represent ceremonial activity that was taking place at Glebe South. Brück (1999) and Cleary (2006) have highlighted the placing of 'domestic' materials, such as quern stones and food remains, in symbolic depositions on a range of settlement sites in Middle Bronze Age Ireland and Britain. The evidence for food remains within a pit at Glebe South can, therefore, be interpreted in a number of ways.

Radiocarbon dating recommendations
Charcoal from this deposit has already been radiocarbon dated to the Early-Middle Bronze Age. If further dating is required, only the barley grains will provide sufficient weight for a conventional radiocarbon date. Alternatively, the barley grains, possible wheat grain and/or indeterminate cereal grains can be used in AMS dating (where a single grain may provide sufficient weight). It is recommended that the cereal grains are used in dating, rather than the weed seed – only one small fragment of a weed seed was recorded, and there is a possibility that it may be residual.

Conclusions
Analysis of archaeobotanical material from a deposit (Co35) at Glebe South produced evidence for a large cereal grain assemblage – more than 12,000 whole grains in total – dating to the Early-Middle Bronze Age. The cereal grains mainly consisted of naked barley, with a possible wheat grain also recorded. Cereal chaff was absent from the examined deposit, while only one weed seed fragment was recorded.

The cereal grains were located in an irregularly shaped pit, which was interpreted as a corn-drying kiln. It is suggested that this pit may also/instead have functioned as a cooking pit. Alternatively, the pit may have been used in activities not associated with food preparation – the cereal remains may represent a secondary deposit, placed into the pit when it had gone out of use.

While the function of the pit and the nature of activities at this location can be debated, it should be noted that cereal assemblages of this size are not often found in Irish Bronze Age deposits. It should also be remembered that preservation by charring is biased in favour of plants that are more likely to come into contact with fire, such as cereals. It is therefore probable that the people taking part in activities at Glebe South would have made use of a far wider range of plants than those represented in the examined deposit.

References

Anderberg, A.-L. 1994. *Atlas of seeds part 4: Resedaceae-Umbelliferae.* Stockholm: Swedish Museum of Natural History.

Beijerinck, W. 1947. *Zadenatlas der Nederlandsche Flora.* Wageningen: H. Veenman & Zonen.

Berggren, G. 1969. *Atlas of seeds part 2: Cyperaceae.* Stockholm: Swedish Museum of Natural History.

Berggren, G. 1981. *Atlas of seeds part 3: Salicaceae-Cruciferae.* Stockholm: Swedish Museum of Natural History.

Brück, J, 1999. Houses, lifecycles and depositions on Middle Bronze Age settlements in southern England. *Proceedings of the Prehistoric Society* 65, 145-166.

Brück, J. 2000. Settlement, landscape and social identity: the Early-Middle Bronze Age transition in Wessex, Sussex and the Thames Valley. *Oxford Journal of Archaeology* 19(3), 273-300.

Cleary, K. 2006. Irish Bronze Age settlements: more than meets the eye? *Archaeology Ireland* 20(2), 18-21.

Fuller, D.Q, Stevens, C. and McClatchie, M. (in press). Routine activities, tertiary refuse and labor organization: social inferences from everyday archaeobotany. In M. Madella and M. Savard (eds), *Ancient plants and people – contemporary trends in archaeobotany.* Tucson: University of Arizona Press.

Hillman, G.C., Mason, S., de Moulins, D. and Nesbitt, M. 1996. Identification of archaeological remains of wheat: the 1992 London workshop. *Circaea* 12, 195-209.

Jessen, K. and Helbaek, H. 1944. Cereals in Great Britain and Ireland in prehistoric and early historic times. *Det Kongelige Danske Videnskabernes Selskab Biol. Skrifter,* 3(2).

Katz, N.J., Katz, S.V. and Kipiani, M.G. 1965. *Atlas and keys of fruits and seeds occurring in the quaternary deposits of the USSR.* Moscow: Nauka.

Mallory, J.P. 1995. Haughey's Fort and the Navan Complex in the Late Bronze Age. In J. Waddell and E. Shee Twohig (eds), *Ireland in the Bronze Age: proceedings of the Dublin conference, April 1995,* 73-86. Dublin: Stationery Office.

Monk, M.A. 1986. Evidence from macroscopic plant remains for crop husbandry in prehistoric and early historic Ireland: a review. *Journal of Irish Archaeology* 3, 31-6.

Monk, M.A. and Kelleher, E. 2005. An assessment of the archaeological evidence for Irish corn-drying kilns in the light of the results of archaeological experiments and archaeobotanical studies. *Journal of Irish Archaeology* 14, 77-114.

Stace, C. 1991. *New flora of the British Isles.* Cambridge: Cambridge University Press.

Zohary, D. and Hopf, M. 2000. *Domestication of plants in the Old World.* Oxford: Oxford University Press.

CHAPTER 5

Discussion

Judith Carroll

The three prehistoric to early medieval burial sites are discussed in relation to development of burial and habitation in Balrothery, including information from the adjacent enclosure site of Rosepark

A series of excavations was concentrated in an area to the east, south and south-east of the village of Balrothery, yielding evidence of occupation from the Neolithic, and of farming, habitation and burial from the Early-Middle Bronze Age. There was extensive burial in these townlands from the Late Bronze Age to the Iron Age with evidence of habitation, particularly in the Late Iron Age. The prehistoric burial site at Glebe South continued in use into the early medieval period when there was substantial evidence of habitation in the adjacent sites of Darcystown 3 (licence no. 02E0043) and Rosepark (99E0155) in particular. Occupation and burial in the townlands of Glebe South, Darcystown and Rosepark, are clearly contemporary.

The Neolithic
A single pit containing Middle Neolithic hemispherical vessels with grooved decoration was found in Darcystown 1. Related charcoal provided a calibrated C14 date of the late 4th millennium BC. It is possible that the pit was a burial in which the bone had completely decayed. It was found only 5m from a group of Late Bronze Age burials and may possibly have formed the earliest burial feature.

The pit may also have been domestic. As indicated by Wiggins in Chapter 3, the recently found Neolithic enclosure site at Magheraboy, Co. Sligo produced 55 pits containing dark deposits and domestic rubbish, including pottery.

The east coast of Ireland was of particular interest to the earliest Neolithic farming communities to judge by the distribution of Passage tombs. Though there were Passage tombs cemeteries as far west as Sligo, there were particular concentrations in the eastern counties, including the Meath/ Dublin area. The Boyne Valley cemetery, the Bremore and Gormanstown cemeteries including the nearby Passage tomb of Hampton Demesne attest to substantial Neolithic settlement of the area. The

pottery from the Darcystown 1 has been closely compared by Grogan and Roche to similar types from Knowth as well as several other eastern sites.

The Early-Middle Bronze Age
A pit containing Beaker pottery at Glebe South suggests that the burial site in the townland originates as early as the Late Neolithic/Early Bronze Age. Evidence of a structure interpreted as a round house of Early/Middle Bronze Age date was also found close to the south-west of the burial site. Analysis of cereal remains associated with the structure by McClatchie (Appendix VI) indicated the cultivation of barley in the area.

The Bord Gáis Éireann Pipeline to the West has revealed Bronze Age activity of comparable date in the vicinity of the Balrothery sites as shown in Chapter 1 above. Approximately 2.5m north-west of Glebe South, at Clonard or Folkstown Great, a round house yielded a C14 date of Middle Bronze Age date. A concentration of stake-holes outside it yielded a C14 date of Early Bronze Age date (Grogan, O'Donnell and Johnston 2007, 218). At Flemingtown, approximately 4km north-west of Glebe South, a cereal-drying kiln producing barley was found and can be compared to a similar example at Doonmoon, Co. Limerick which was dated to the Early Bronze Age (ibid., 219).

A habitation site consisting of a hearth, pits and post-holes, producing domestic Food Vessel pottery, as well as a possible rubbing stone and dates suggesting activity in the period 2050-1880 BC, was found at Gormanstown (ibid., 234) approximately 5km from Glebe South and Darcystown. These sites indicate contemporary Early to Middle Bronze Age habitation in nearby townlands.

The Late Bronze Age
In his 1981 article on Iron Age burial in Ireland, Raftery commented that the paucity of information

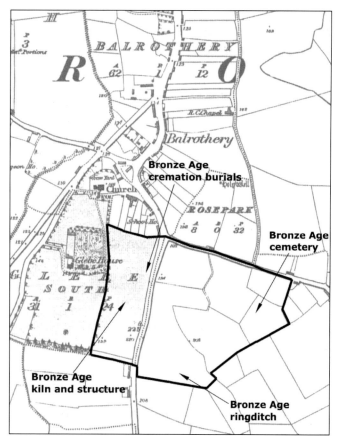

Figure 1a: First edition OS map (1837-41) showing location of areas of Bronze Age activity

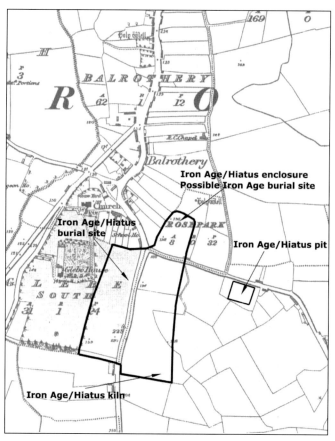

Figure 1b: First edition OS map (1837-41) showing location of areas of Iron Age (very approximately 500BC - 400AD) activity

on Late Bronze Age and Iron Age burials made it impossible to reflect on innovation or continuity between the two traditions (Raftery 1981, 177). Only two confidently dated Late Bronze Age burials were listed in his article – Rathgall, Co. Wicklow and Mullaghmore, Co. Down. Since 1981, due mainly to development related archaeology, the data has multiplied several times.

One negative aspect to the record of recent development-related burials is the lack of survival of associated above-ground features such as banks and mounds. Sites invisible from the ground form the bulk of prehistoric burial excavations carried out in the present day. Normally found as a result of geophysical survey, testing or monitoring for development schemes, the sites are generally revealed in a damaged state.

Most ring ditches found in their truncated states, without banks and ditches, would probably originally have fitted into categories of barrow discussed by Newman (1997, 157-168). However, the lack of mound, cairn or even ditch evidence for sites disallows full categorisation of burial types. Very often the only features which may survive for discussion are the cuts of burial pits, enclosing ring

ditches or other negative features.

The analysis of the Darcystown/Glebe South burials should be viewed with reference to similar Late Bronze Age burial excavations. This has been done in detail in the preceding chapters where the authors have discussed recent comparable evidence in detail

At Darcystown 1, as shown by Wiggins, a cemetery of Late Bronze Age coarse ware pots containing cremations was found. The burials were seemingly unenclosed by features, such as ring ditches, but comparisons have been made to other excavated Late Bronze Age burials which may have been enclosed by less durable structures than ring ditches or may have been covered by unenclosed cairns of stone.

It is suggested in Chapter 3 that that the ring ditch of Darcystown 2 may originally have been cut around a burial cairn of stone which, like Carrig, Co. Wicklow (Grogan 1990, 12-14), contained cremation burial associated with coarse ware pots. It is proposed that the ditch was cut around the ring ditch into which the stone of the cairn was deposited to form a causeway. This would explain the presence of the very large amount of stone spread over one section of the ditch, forming a causeway. The stone was mixed with clearly associated cremated bone and coarse ware pottery, which appeared to have been tipped into the ditch from above its inner side.

In Chapter 4, Ryan discusses Bronze Age burial pits associated with the Iron Age ring ditch and early medieval long stone cist cemetery of Glebe South. In the enclosed area of Ring ditch 2, a Late Bronze Age burial pit, producing a C14 date of the 9th to 11th century BC, was found. Between the two ring ditches were two pits, one containing both Late Neolithic/Early Bronze Age Beaker pottery and Late Bronze Age coarse ware, another containing cremated bone. The origin of the burial site is thus likely to have been in the Late Neolithic or Early Bronze Age. The Late Bronze Age cremation pits here may have been of similar origin to thosae of Darcystown 1.

Is it possible that Iron Age Ring ditch 2 of Glebe South, which encircled one of the Late Bronze Age cremation pits, was cut around an earlier burial monument? The excavated Iron Age ring ditches of Glebe South did not yield any evidence, within the ditch cuts, of Late Bronze Age use, but it is possible that they were cut around earlier monuments.

The Balrothery sites have added substantial information to the record of Late Bronze Age burial in Ireland which has grown so much since the 1990's. Can we yet begin to identify trends and patterns which might allow us to make deductions on continuity or development between the Late Bronze Age and the Iron Age?

Habitation coeval with the Late Bronze Age burials is indicated by the burnt mounds at Darcystown 1 which produced calibrated C14 dates ranging from the beginning of the 14th century BC to the beginning of the 10th century BC. One of the mounds produced evidence of a structure which may be added to the small list of structures existing for such mounds compiled by O'Neill (O'Neill 2003-4, 83), as discussed by Wiggins in Chapter 2, who also refers to the possible use of the sites for steam bathing.

The other burnt mound at Darcystown 1 produced evidence to suggest a wattle lined trough. It is of great interest that a burnt mound trough lined with wattle was found only a kilometre west of the site in Knock during the Bord Gáis Éireann excavations (Grogan, O'Donnell and Johnson 2007, 225). A similar wattle-lined trough has also been found in Ballygawley, Co. Tyrone (pers. comm. Paul Masser, Headland Archaeology Ltd.), as discussed in Chapter 2.

The Iron Age

The two Iron Age ring ditches found in Glebe South were of a different burial form to the ring ditch burial of Darcystown 2, which was Late Bronze Age. Within the two ring ditches were found spreads of charcoal and cremated bone. Glass beads, including a large number of small blue glass beads, parts of strings of beads, iron objects, and an amber toggle bead were found in Ring ditch 2. A glass bead, iron fragments and three very small fragments of a fibula of possible Navan type were found in Ring ditch 1. There was no pottery in either ring ditch. A date of 200 BC to the very early 1st century AD was obtained from the cremation in Ring ditch 1. A date of the 4th century BC to the late 1st century AD was obtained from one of the cremations in Ring ditch 2.

The cremation burials appeared to have been spread lengthways in Ring ditch 2 (there were at least four). There may only have been one cremation in Ring ditch 1 as there was only one large deposit of cremated bone.

The deposition of cremated bone in ring ditches of Iron Age date has been noted by Eogan in his description of a ring ditch at Ballybronogue South, Co. Limerick, which contained artefacts dated to the years around the birth of Christ. Eogan lists a number of Iron Age ring ditch sites such as Grannagh and Oranbeg, Co. Galway, Tumulus 8 at Carrowjames, Co. Mayo, as well as the Ballydavis, Co. Laois sites, which contain cremation deposits seemingly placed deliberately in the cut of the ring ditch (Eogan 2000, 9-10). The corpus of Irish Iron Age ring ditches excavated to date is discussed by Ryan in Chapter 4. Deliberate deposition of cremated remains in the ditch is also noted by Ryan in relation to his excavation at Ferns, Co. Wexford (Ryan 2000). The Glebe South evidence adds to the number of Iron Age cremations deposited in ring ditches in this manner.

There is not a great deal of evidence for habitation contemporary with the cremation burials in ring ditches at Glebe South. In Darcystown 1, two features, C078 and C086 in Area 2 which contained neither pottery nor cremated bone were found side by side. C077, fill of C078, produced heat shattered stone and charcoal which yielded an early Iron Age date of Cal. BC 410-370. Whether the features were related to habitation or burial is not known.

The earliest find from Rosepark, 100m north of the Glebe South cemetery is a bead of Guido Class 8, found in a linear trench, indicating a date of the latter centuries BC to the 1st century AD for the trench, which predates the later ditches on the top of the Rosepark hill.

The Late Iron-Age/early medieval hiatus: burial

One of the most interesting aspects of this series of excavations was the combined evidence of the sites at Darcystown and Glebe South with Rosepark for occupation and burial dating from the obscure phase of Irish history and archaeology between the Late Iron Age and the mid-first millennium AD.

This period has been referred to as the 'hiatus' in which the archaeological record is unclear and there is a lack of identified site types and artefact assemblages. It has been suggested that the lack of diagnostic artefact types may be due to a general use of perishable materials for domestic activities and decoration, artefacts indistinguishable from those a few centuries later (Raftery 1972, 53).

Certainly, very few artefacts of this period were found at Balrothery and the only evidence that we have of habitation around this time is from C14 dates from a number of features. These point to fairly extensive activity in the area between the 3rd and 5th century AD.

At Glebe South, as shown by Ryan in Chapter 4, Iron Age ring ditches of the latter centuries BC to the 1st century AD clearly continued to be recognised as burial sites into the mid first millennium AD. A cremation pit, cut into the enclosure of Ring ditch 1 in Glebe South, indicated that prehistoric burial traditions may have continued into the 'hiatus' period. This cremation pit produced a date from charcoal in its fill, calibrated at 2 sigma range to the early/mid 3rd century AD and the early/mid 5th century AD.

An enigmatic feature, C080, a 'figure-of-eight' shaped pit, produced evidence of intensive burning and small fragments of cremated human bone. It is possible that it was a cremation pyre. It was sited 3m to the west of Ring ditch 2 and produced a C14 date of the early 4th to mid 6th century AD.

One of the most remarkable discoveries of the excavations as a whole was a possible wood lined grave. Cut into Ring ditch 1 was Grave 6, which contained an unburnt inhumation and a glass bead. This grave was rectilinear in shape, with straight edges 0.49m in depth and a stone-lined base. It was orientated north-west/south-east in contrast to the other inhumation graves which were orientated east-west. There was no evidence of stone lining or covering stones. The burial was suggested to be wood-lined by Dr. Elizabeth O'Brien who visited the site. As stated by Ryan in Chapter 4, burials in wooden coffins were common in Britain between the 2nd-4th centuries AD (O'Brien 1990, 39). In the Arras cemetery at Rudstone, wooden coffins without nails or metal brackets have been recognised in 19 graves

(O'Brien 1999, 13). Ryan also quotes comparisons in Ireland from Cabinteely, Co. Dublin (Conway 2000). and Collierstown, Co. Meath where wood-lined, as well as stone-lined graves, were found on a site which developed from an Iron Age ring ditch (Clarke 2004).

The inner enclosure at the top of the hill at Rosepark produced a date of cal AD 255-411 (Carroll 2002; ibid. 2008) from charcoal from a context also producing bone from domestic animals. Very similar dates were obtained for two of the large group of cereal-drying kilns at the base of the hill, which were part of the complex of features at Rosepark. It is reasonable therefore to suggest that for some period between the early 3rd and the early 5th century AD, a defensive ditched enclosure was occupied on top of the hill and that cultivation and farming of the area took place from this centre. This centre was coeval with the burial site of Glebe South.

In the fields south of the Rosepark enclosure, at Darcystown, a number of similar cereal-drying kilns, mainly of keyhole shape, were found. At Darcystown 2, as described in Chapter 3, a keyhole-shaped kiln of the same date as the Rosepark kilns above (early 3rd to early 5th century) was found and would suggest related contemporary activity. During monitoring in Darcystown 3 under licence 02E0043 (Carroll 2004), a large number of kilns and pits were found spread over the field (see Fig. 1, Chapter 1). Most of these were keyhole-shaped and similar to those found at Rosepark and Darcystown 2. Two of these kilns yielded dates to between the early 5th and mid 7th centuries AD (ibid.).

During the excavation of Darcystown 1, as described by Wiggins in Chapter 2, a pit producing charcoal was found in Area 1 of the excavation. It yielded a C14 date of the 3rd to the 5th century AD indicating activity of similar date to Rosepark in the area. The nature of the pit is unknown.

The C14 dates from isolated features such as the pit in Darcystown 1, the evidence from Rosepark and the corn-drying kilns in Darcystown 2 and Darcystown 3 as well as the burial evidence in Glebe South suggest occupation of the three townlands simultaneously during the early-mid first millennium AD. Analysis of animal bone in the layer producing the 3rd to 5th century date at Rosepark indicates that cattle were the chief domesticates at that time (McCarthy in Carroll 2002; ibid. 2008).

Analysis of the plant remains in the two kilns dated at Rosepark indicates that cereals, chiefly barley, were being cultivated and that barley was being malted for beer (Johnson in Carroll 2002; ibid. 2008) around the 3rd to 5th century AD.

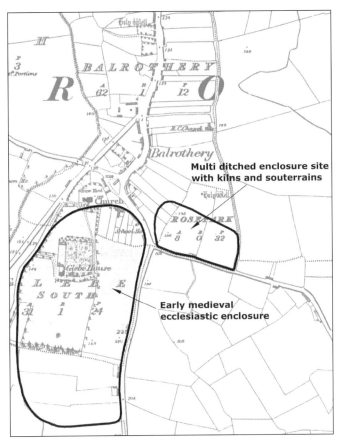

Figure 2a: First edition OS map (1837-41) showing location of areas of early medieval activity

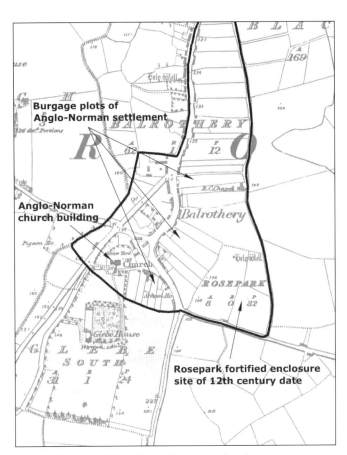

Figure 2b: First edition OS map (1837-41) showing location of areas of Anglo-Norman activity

The early medieval period

A total of sixteen further inhumations in long stone cists were found at Glebe South indicating clear continuity into the early medieval period of the Iron Age ring ditch burial site. These inhumations were located within 10m of Ring ditch 1. Six of them were concentrated along the south and south-east sides of Ring ditch 1. Four of these, including the burial (C153), which yielded a C14 date of cal. AD 430-640, were actually cut into the cremation burial contained by the ring ditch.

The long stone cist burials contained human remains without grave goods, placed supine, head to the west, in a grave with stone-lined sides, generally consisting of single upright slabs. Capstones, placed lengthways across the width of the cists, covered the inhumations, though only eight graves with capstones survived.

Ryan, in Chapter 4, references a number of sites yielding evidence of capstone-covered long stone cists, including Reask, Co. Kerry, Ballykeel South, Co. Clare and Ballymaceward, Co. Donegal. The evidence suggests that such stone cists, constructed from slabs placed on edge to form a box and covered with flat slabs placed across the width of the box, date from the late 4th to early 7th century AD. O'Brien suggests

that these may date as far as the 8th century AD (O'Brien 2003, 67).

Ryan has also shown that the site at Glebe South, with its continuity from the early prehistoric into the early medieval period as a burial site, is not unique. Several other sites have produced evidence of such continuity, though Glebe South, along with Ardsallagh, Co. Meath, is probably one of the longest in continuous use known. Other sites such as Ballymacaward in Co. Donegal, Carbury Hill (Site B), Co. Kildare, and Greenhills, Co. Kildare, as well as Collierstown, Co. Meath, have produced evidence of later inhumation burials superimposing ring ditch burials.

From so much rapidly accumulating evidence, we may find that burial traditions of the Bronze Age and the Iron Age extended into the first half of the first millennium AD, perhaps only gradually changing. During the early centuries AD, we may have examples of new types of burial introduced from Britain and native burial traditions co-existing.

Rosepark, so close to the burial site at Glebe South, was occupied, as stated above, as a defensive habitation site from probably the 3rd or 4th century AD throughout the early medieval period. It yielded several C14 dates ranging from the 3rd/4th to 7th/8th century. Several sherds of E ware from different parts of its branching ditches suggested much activity around the enclosure during the 6th/7th centuries. An iron escutcheon of possible early medieval date was found in a ditch associated with an entranceway. It has been suggested (Carroll 2008) that c. the 7th century, the nuclar enclosure at Rosepark within the ditched defences was also used for burial, while the site may have partly become an open settlement by the time the large number of souterrains were built around the early 9th century AD.

It appears, so far, from the excavations of St. Peter's Church in the centre of the village of Balrothery, that the church belongs to the Anglo-Norman period. Though Souterrain ware was found during the trial testing at St. Peter's church by Murphy, this may date as late as the 12th century (Murphy 2002, 10). Otherwise, archaeological investigations in and around the area by Baker (Baker 2005, 319-331) and Murphy, have revealed only remains post-dating the 12th century (see Chapter 1). It is strange that there is no identified burial site other than that at Glebe South, where the remains are scant and seem to be no later than the 7th century in date.

It is possible that a pre-Norman church may have been situated south of the Anglo-Norman village church, bounded by the curve of the road in Glebe South (see Fig. 2, Chapter 1). The distinct curve of the road southwards around the north end of Glebe South, from the centre of the village, is clear on the first edition Ordnance Survey 6 inch map and may delineate a curvilinear enclosure at this point. A further curve westwards is indicated on William Petty's map of 1655 (Fig. 1, Chapter 1). A curve to the south is indicated by the townland boundary of Glebe South at its south end. It was within the area of this 'enclosure', to the east, that the Iron Age/early medieval burials of Glebe South were found.

The townland name of Glebe South itself denotes land belonging to the church. The church of Balrothery and its lands were granted to Tristernagh Abbey between 1200-1224 (Clarke 1941, 2) by the Anglo-Norman landowner, Geoffrey de Costedin, with the assent of the 'parson of the church', Patricio de Rosel. That there was actually a church at Balrothery pre-dating the Anglo-Norman period is indicated by a record of a suit taken by the Archbishop of Dublin in the early 13th century in relation to this grant because, as stated in Alen's Register, the church at Balrothery 'pertained as of ancient right to the church of Lusk' (McNeill 1950, 33).

An ecclesiastical enclosure extending south of the major defensive settlement site of Rosepark may therefore have existed in the early medieval period.

It is interesting that no finds or features predating the 12th century have as yet been found to the north or west of Rosepark. Even though much development during the later medieval period may have obliterated earlier remains, excavations in large open areas, such as the grounds of St. Peter's Church and the field of Old Coach Road to the north of Rosepark, tested by Bolger in 2001, yielded only remains of 13th/14th century date, as discussed in the section on 'previous excavations' in Chapter 1.

In contrast, prehistoric and early medieval activity around the village was concentrated in Rosepark, Glebe South and Darcystown townlands, to the south and east side of the village of Balrothery. The townlands are situated in the area of two natural hills: the small steep hill of Rosepark and the wide gently rolling hill of Darcystown/Glebe South.

It may be concluded that prior to the arrival of the Anglo-Normans in Balrothery, a settlement had developed from early prehistoric origins on the south and east side of the village. In particular, both burial and habitation evidence suggest that the area was intensely occupied in that cross-over period between the later Iron Age and early medieval period. The area of Darcystown and Glebe South, as well as Rosepark, continued to be occupied into the early 2nd millennium AD, and it is possible that Glebe South townland, perhaps based on its prehistoric origins as a burial site, comprised an early medieval ecclesiastical site of Balrothery.

References

Baker, C. 2005. Balrothery Co. Dublin. In T. Condit and C. Corlett (eds.). *Above and Beyond-essays in memory of Leo Swan*. Bray, Co. Wicklow, 319-331.

Bolger, T. 2001. Archaeological excavation at Old Coach Road, Balrothery, Co. Dublin. Unpublished report. National Monuments Service, Department of the Environment, Heritage and Local Government.

Carroll, J. 2002. Report on excavation at Rosepark, Balrothery, Co. Dublin. Licence no. 99E0155. Unpublished report. National Monuments Service, Department of the Environment, Heritage and Local Government.

Carroll, J. 2004. Archaeological excavation at Darcystown 3, Balrothery, Co. Dublin. Licence no.

02E0043. Unpublished report by Judith Carroll and Co. Ltd. National Monuments Service, Dept. of the Environment, Heritage and Local Government.

Carroll, J. 2008. *Archaeological excavations at Rosepark, Balrothery, Co. Dublin.* Dublin.

Clarke, L. 2007. Collierstown, Co. Meath - excavation licence no. 04E0422. In I. Bennett (ed.), *Excavations: summary acccounts of archaeological excavations in Ireland 2004.* Wordwell, Bray, Wicklow.

Clarke, M. V. 1941. *Register of the priory of the Blessed Virgin Mary of Tristernagh.* Transcribed and edited from the manuscript in the Cathedral library, Armagh. The Stationary Office. Dublin.

Conway, M 2000. *Directors first findings from excavations in Cabinteely.* Margaret Gwoen and Company. Dublin.

Eogan, J 2000. New light on late prehistoric ritual and burial in County Limerick. *Archaeology Ireland* 14, 8-10.

Grogan, E. 1990. Bronze Age cemetery at Carrig, Co. Wicklow. *Archaeology Ireland* 4 (no. 4), 12-14.

Grogan, E., O'Donnell, L. and Johnston, P. 2007. *The Bronze Age landscapes of the pipeline to the west – an integrated archaeological and environmental assessment.* Wordwell, Bray, Wicklow.

Johnston, P. 2002. Report on plant remains from Rosepark. In Carroll, J., Report on excavation at Rosepark, Balrothery, Co. Dublin. Licence no. 99E0155. Unpublished report. National Monuments Service, Department of the Environment, Heritage and Local Government.

McCarthy, M. 2002. Report on faunal remains from Rosepark, Balrothery, Co. Dublin. In Carroll, J. 2002. Report on excavation at Rosepark, Balrothery, Co. Dublin. Licence no. 99E0155. Unpublished report. National Monuments Service, Department of the Environment, Heritage and Local Government.

McNeill, C. 1950. *Calender of Archbishop Alen's Register c. 1172-1534.* Prepared and edited from the original in the registry of the United Diocese of Dublin, Glendalough and Kildare. Dublin.

Newman, C. 1997. *Tara: an archaeological survey.* Discovery programme monograph 2. Dublin.

O'Brien, E. 1990. Iron Age burial practices in Leinster: continuity and change. *Emania,* 7, 37-42.

O' Brien, E. 1999. *Post Roman to Anglo-Saxon England: burial practices reviewed.* British Archaeological Reports (British series) 289, 52-58.

O'Brien, E. 2003. Burial practices in Ireland: first to 7th century AD. In J. Downes and A. Ritchie (eds.), *Sea Change: Orkney and Northern Europe in the later Iron Age AD 300-800.* Angus, Scotland.

O' Neill, J. 2003-4. Lapidibus in igne calefactis coquebatur: The historical burnt mound tradition. *Journal of Irish Archaeology* XII and XIII, 79-86.

Raftery, B. 1972. Irish hillforts. In C. Thomas (ed.) *The Iron Age and the Irish sea province,* 37-58. London.

Raftery, B. 1981. Iron Age Burials in Ireland, in D. Ó Corráin (ed.), *Irish Anitquity. Essays and Studies presented to Professor M. J. O'Kelly,* 173-204. Cork.

INDEX